How To Partner *with* Managed Care

A "Do-It-Yourself Kit"
for Building Working Relationships
& Getting Steady Referrals

"*T*his is an outstanding book!...a "Do-It-Yourself Kit" for surviving and thriving in the managed care marketplace. It delivers very practical information on how therapists can get onto managed care panels, market to managed care to receive referrals once on the panel, and communicate in cooperative ways with utilization reviewers...It is all here!...The book is direct, practical and readable."

—Anne Thureson, C.S.W.
Washington State Chapter,
National Assn. of Social Workers

"The upbeat style and terrific detailed organization of this book made the necessary chore of learning more about managed care surprisingly pleasant and manageable...it made it easy for me to find the answers to my questions."

—Marti Baerg, M.A., M.F.C.C.
President, Santa Clara County Chapter,
Calif. Assn. of Marriage & Family Therapy

"The text is quite readable and extremely clear...The clinical information in the sections on Brief Therapy is particularly helpful."

—Robert Zussman, Ph.D.
President, New Mexico Psychological Assn.

"If you are willing to accept the idea that managed care is here to stay, this book will be a big help. This is a good book for those in practice, and...should be mandatory for those just starting a private practice."

—Simon J. Epstein, M.D.
Connecticut Psychiatric Society

"I appreciated the informal style and wit of your book, but most important, it is a realistic and practical guide for providers about how to deal with the ever increasing influence of managed behavioral health care. It also provides simple, but not simplistic, approaches to defining client problems. This will be invaluable to providers, but it will also be helpful to our own case management staff in clarifying poorly focused case formulations. We will be ordering additional copies so that key members of our staff will have the book for their own reference."

—William E. Ford, Ph.D.
Vice President and Director,
Mutual of Omaha Integrated Behavioral Services

"Prior to owning this book, I had some treatment reports returned. With the help of your book—I rewrote these reports and they were fine! You have a gem of a book—I have been praising your book to others therapists...it is indispensable!"

—Ellen R. Adams, M.S.W., A.C.S.W., B.C.D.
Clinical Social Worker, Murray Hill, N.J.

"Now I know who those flies on the wall were: the Brownings! You *really* got into the mind of a case manager. The 12 Do's and 12 Don'ts were perfect! . . . the book is a MUST for all clinicians."

— Carol Kryder, M.A., M.F.C.C., C.M.F.T.
Case Manager, Value Behavioral Health, Bellevue, WA

"This is one of the best-written, most helpful books I've read thus far on managed care. It's comprehensive, direct and readable!"

— Judith Gringorten, M.S.W.
Clinical Social Work, New York, N.Y.

"This text offers a wealth of helpful, concise information that is encouraging to those who are overwhelmed by the changing world of

— William H. Balch, Ed.D., L.M.F.T.
President, Tenn. Assn. of Marriage & Family Therapy

"Excellent, comprehensive, and thorough."

— Robert H. Small, M.D.
Psychiatry, Kirkland, WA

"Excellent! I read it cover to cover. You have convinced me to 'get on board' and stop resisting."

— Mary Wegmann, Ph.D.
Port Angeles, WA

"I found the text wonderfully *easy to read.* It's totally practical, with clear examples of hands-on approaches for dealing with managed care, and the people who manage it. A substantial survival kit for private practitioners facing managed care in the 90's."

— Venus S. Masselam, Ph.D.
President, Middle Atlantic Division,
American Assn. of Marriage & Family Therapy

"This book focuses on helping the mental health provider find their way through a broad variety of potential pitfalls. They present concrete and specific guidelines for wooing managed care referrals..."

— Barbara F. Herman, Ph.D.
Director of Mental Health and Substance Abuse,
MetroHealth, Indianapolis, IN

"Although this is a new publication, this resource is a classic!...It incorporates timeless business strategies and principles that have been tested and proven effective all over the country. It is a tool that should be on every therapist's bookshelf. If you are only going to buy one book on managed care, this is the one to buy!"

— Rose Piper LaCroix
Senior Director of Professional Relations,
Charter Medical Corporation

How To Partner *with* Managed Care

A "Do-It-Yourself Kit"
for Building Working Relationships
& Getting Steady Referrals

CHARLES H. BROWNING, Ph.D.
BEVERLEY J. BROWNING, Ph.D.

duncliff's *international*

3662 Katella Avenue
Los Alamitos, CA 90720

Published by:
DUNCLIFF'S INTERNATIONAL
Professional Publications Division
3662 Katella Avenue
Los Alamitos, California 90720
Phone   (800) 410-7766
Fax   (310) 799-6657

FIRST EDITION — THIRD PRINTING

Library of Congress Cataloging in Publication Data

Browning, Charles H.
      How to partner with managed care : a "do-it-yourself-kit" for
building working relationships & getting steady referrals / Charles
H. Browning, Beverley J. Browning. -- 1st ed.
          p.   cm.
      Includes bibliographical references and index.
      ISBN 0-911663-84-3 (softbd.) : $29.95
      1. Psychiatric consultation.   2.   Medical referral.
    I. Browning, Beverley J.   II. Title.
      RC455.2.C65876   1994
      616.89--dc20   93-23447
                                                                 CIP

Quantity-order discounts and multiple copies of the Browning Outcomes Survey Scale (BOSS)
are available from the publisher. For information, call 1-800-410-7766.

Dedication

To our Adam — who was given, and was taken from us
in June, 1980. He is in far better hands, in a far better place
as he rests from all his labors.
Indeed, his works in our lives
do follow him. (Rev. 14:13)

TABLE OF CONTENTS

Acknowledgements with Sincere Gratitude

The book you hold in your hand is much, much more than the work of two individuals. Many special people influenced our lives in ways that made it possible for us to bring this text to you. We'd like to introduce you to them and thank them openly here.

First, we are thankful for our wonderful children: Jennifer, Faith, David and Seth — during the past 10 months (which seemed like years) they probably have seen more of our backs than our faces as we consulted, wrote, edited, re-wrote, and re-wrote again. We thank them for their understanding, patience and love.

Next, we are deeply grateful to a staff of people who are more to be called "gifts" than employees. Marion Nixon, office manager par excellence — how many times she came into our offices with her usual joyful optimism during those early adjustment days of "Managed Care Miseries" and said, "Well Dr. Browning, we have another challenge before us!" Note the word "challenge" — while we were thinking "catastrophe." Without you, Marion, we may have abandoned ship in the midst of those turbulent "baptism of fire" days of sailing the sea of Managed Care. Would that every therapist reading this text could find the spirit, the intellect and the personality of a Marion Nixon.

And Peggy Oquist — Marion's "right-hand-copilot" and a source of sunshine in our administrative office. Peg's skilled and perceptive interactions with case managers has probably saved our clinical necks more than a few times, as we struggled to avoid many of the blunders and errors we'll warn you about in this book. And without you, Peg, our documentation and voice-mail updates would doubtless be hopelessly behind. Thank you for helping to preserve our reputation for excellence. That reputation is, in great part, due to your diligent work and marvelous outlook on life.

Thanks also to Stephanie Smith — whose smiles and caring attitude brings encouragement to the many patients she greets in our waiting rooms. Steph's always-reliable attention to the "little things" in the daily operation of the therapy and consulting practice, and publishing company helped ease the heavy load on us as we worked on this text month after month. Steph is another gift for whom we are so thankful.

And what would we do without Linda Wong, C.P.A. — Her wise and skillful navigation through the sea of Managed Care forms, numbers, discounts, co-payments, insurance claim forms, end-dates, certified sessions, *ad infinitum, ad nauseum* — how could any of our staff therapists have survived it all without you? Besides all her expertise with the details, she always radiates joy, gentleness, endless patience, integrity and unswerving loyalty. What a special human being God created when He made Linda Wong.

And Margie Gahan — although she has moved on to new challenges, we remember her with fond appreciation for her help in making the adjustment to all the billing, co-payments, no-co-payments, discounted fees, and collections involved in the Managed Care metamorphosis. She was a great blessing to us all.

And special thanks to Kerri Briggs — without whose patient instruction this book would never have found its way into the Macintosh. We are grateful to Kerri for curing our "computer phobia" as well as our "computer illiteracy."

And we are grateful for her successor, Uyen Le, without whose skilled computer talents none of us would receive those much-needed fruits of our labors — reimbursement checks from the many insurance companies.

We want to express our appreciation as well to our part-time support staff, Jennifer Browning and Stacy Alyea. They, too, have helped bring smiles and encouragement to our staff and our patients. We thank them for taking time to step off of their university "treadmill" to pitch in to help us grow.

We have truly been blessed with a gifted clinical staff: Gail Carr, M.A., Robert Dienstag, Ph.D., Tom Hammond, M.S., Don Ingle, B.D., Peggy Luttrell, M.A., Janine Lee, M.A., Rafik Sidrak, M.D., Phil Templeton, M.A., and Jesse Trice, M.A. Their creativity, compassion for people, and their friendship are incomparable gifts for which we are thankful. We thank them, each one, for bearing with us and making their own "sail adjustments" to the changing winds of Managed Care. What an incredible group of people — how truly blessed our patients are to have them as therapists, and we, to have them as our friends and colleagues.

And to Susan Calisher-Foote — who brought her unique expertise to us from her hospital experiences "taming" the Managed-Care giants. How thankful we are that she made the decision to join us, and for all she has taught us. May many of you reading this text find someone who is as adept at marketing and program coordination, and just as lovely a person.

Special gratitude to Mary DeGiacomo — the resident and gifted "psychologist of Huntley Avenue", and a beloved mother. Our thanks for her varied contributions to self-esteem, stubborn and persevering independence, without which a book of this type would not exist (and for putting up with C.B. through half a century).

To Dorothy Pilone, our other beloved mother, whose eagle-eye kept you from reading countless glitches and errors and just-plain-dumb mistakes made in the manuscript. She is an editor most New York publishers would kill for. And to Fred Pilone, for putting up with us borrowing her for hour upon hour from his "keeping company" with her, and for his wisdom and savvy about life, which has guided us in many of our business decisions. A man of deep insights and great kindness, for whom we are thankful.

And to Mark Kelly — our very best friend, who has taught us to laugh at ourselves, laugh at life, and how to "lighten up" from the seriousness of the early days of the "Managed Care Wars." How we thank him for making us take needed breaks from our work on this book to "kick back," take vacations, and celebrate life. A dear and precious friend.

Thanks to all those case managers who had patience and mercy upon us as we struggled, often stumbling and falling, to learn our way around Managed Care. Although they are all too often seen as adversaries, in reality they have done much to help teach us and train us. We thank them all for their tutorial talents and valuable contribution to this work.

We want also to thank the many patients who tolerated our absence during all those Monday's as we were away from the office working on the manuscript. They graciously adjusted their schedules to accommodate ours. One of the happy, good things about Managed Care is that it allows the opportunity to be a part of seeing those many lives changed, healed, and restored. They truly are the reason we all must work diligently together to make Managed Care work in this country. What wonderful people they are!

Finally, to One who should have been thanked first ... we are deeply grateful to God for granting us the privilege of serving those we see in therapy, and for sharing with you the material in this book, and most of all, for the honor of knowing Him.

May He see fit to help you "adjust your sails" as you sail pleasant seas, and "may the wind be always at your back, may the sun shine warm on your face, may the rain fall soft upon you, and may God hold you softly in the palm of His hand." *

---

* Adapted from an Irish blessing: Copyright, Bollind, Inc., Boulder, CO

We are permitted, thanks to Charles Schulz, to listen in on a dialogue between two familiar friends:

Lucy: "Do you think anybody ever really changes?"
Linus: "I've changed a lot in the last year."
Lucy: "I mean for the better!"

Mental health practitioners have also witnessed a rising flood of changes in the last few years — but they, like Lucy, question whether these changes have been "for the better."

Many of the clinicians we talk to day by day informally, and those we see in practice development consultation, are in one accord in their assessment of the changes brought about by Managed Care. And that assessment is hardly favorable.

An article in the *American Journal of Psychiatry* provides a powerful metaphor illustrating how a majority of therapists feel about their encounters with Managed Care. The article's subtitle[*] reads:

"Bambi Meets Godzilla!"

Does that image ring true for you as well? If so, that is why this book exists.

Recently we were talking with a colleague who asked what we planned to do over the upcoming holiday weekend. We indicated that we planned to work on the final touches on the manuscript of this book. She asked, "What is the book about?" We responded, "How to partner with Managed Care." Her response confirmed again to us the need for this text. She rolled her eyes, waved her hands in animated frustration, and groaned, "Oh God! You mean *the*

---

[*]   Parloff, M.B. (1982). Psychotherapy research evidence and reimbursement decisions: Bambi meets Godzilla. *American Journal of Psychiatry*, 139, 718-727.

nightmare of managed care, don't you? ... Or is it *Managed Care Nightmare!"* She was quite serious.

One psychologist who called us for help in adapting her private practice to Managed Care in one eastern city said this: "Even though I know I have to accept it and work with it, I absolutely despise and detest Managed Care!"

One of her colleagues from a different New England state echoes her sentiments, complaining, "I resent someone looking over my shoulder, making me justify what I do, telling me how to do it, telling me how much I can charge, and to top it off, paying me less for the 'privilege'!"

A social worker in her own California practice put it like this: "I'm going to change the whole way I run my practice ... if I have to reduce my fees to $25 an hour to avoid the Managed Care inquisition, I'll do it!"

Frustration. Confusion. Disorientation. And outright hostility — all characterize the reactions of healthcare professionals in these days of rein-tightening, cost-controlling, gate-keeping, watch-dogging, session-limiting, external constraints we call *Managed Care.*

We see the same kind of mood and climate in letters we receive from clinicians requesting consultations for building practices that can survive in the real world of Managed Care. Many therapists discover, the hard way, that Managed Care is here to stay, and that it is growing ever stronger and more influential.

Here are some of the verbatim questions from therapists who have finally accepted the realities of Managed Care, and are ready to learn how to *work with it.* Their concerns are typical:

"How can I work effectively with managed care with the minimal amount of problems?"

"What does it take to be successful working with managed care?"
"What are the best, and what are the worst Managed Care companies to work with?"
"We are interested in more effectively approaching managed care and employee assistance programs. How would we go about forming an association or group practice to get accepted on more panels?"
"How do you even become a provider with Managed Care firms?"
"We are on many Managed Care network panels, but we don't get referrals from them. What are we doing wrong? What should we do differently?"
"We are referring away many Managed Care clients to other therapists. Is there any way these prospective new clients can help us get on these panels and be approved as preferred providers?"

Three years ago we didn't receive inquiries like this. As recently as two years ago it was unusual for clinicians to even mention Managed Healthcare. But in almost all our consultation work, and in discussions with colleagues, the common theme is the same — What to do about managing to survive the onslaught of Managed Care controls?

Managed Care is as much about *managing change* as it is about a new form of healthcare constraint system. As Ronni Sandroff points out in her insightful article, "The Psychology of Change" (*Working Woman,* July, 1993), in order to qualify, and requalify for a place in the workplace team,

"many of us require an overhaul of our psyches. We need to unlearn basic assumptions...The goal: To transform ourselves into quick-change artists who can turn on a dime, shrug off past successes and failures, and frequently reinvent ourselves to fulfill the new roles that suddenly replace the old."

What an accurate picture of what those of us in mental healthcare are experiencing during these transition days into a whole new form of practice. Change isn't easy!

Over the last few years we have learned (the hard way) how to "reinvent ourselves", how to "shrug off" the way we used to manage and market our practice, and how to fulfill the new roles, and rules, that have suddenly replaced the old. The fruits of those labors are what you are about to encounter in this text.

It is our sincere hope that what you learn, and what you thereafter implement, as a direct result of this material, will help you not only cope with, but cooperatively *partner with* Managed Healthcare systems.

Bambi meeting Godzilla is no pleasant encounter. Unless, of course, Bambi learns the tools, tactics and the strategies to tame the beast and live happily-ever-after in the forest together.

We trust, therefore, that this textbook will be as much a "taming manual" as a "training manual." May you enjoy the excitement of the adventure as you give Managed Care case managers what they want — i.e., time-sensitive, solution-focused, cost-effective services; and Managed Care case managers give you what you want — new client referrals, and many of them.

"Partnering" with Managed Care means, in essence, that the most important person in the equation, *the patient,* gets what he or she wants — results. A triple-win arrangement.

While all change involves some measure of loss, it also opens up new opportunities for gain for those who know where and how to find them. We have written this book so that all parties actively participating in the healthcare game can survive, thrive and prosper. Patients get less symptoms and more peace of mind. Managed Care and insurance companies spend less on healthcare and get more early discharges. And you get more referrals and have fewer blank spaces in your appointment book!

Finally, a word to those students who find themselves about to enter the real world of practicing what they've learned all those years in graduate school. We hope that when you complete your study of this text, you will be equipped to understand and effectively present yourself to many Managed Care organizations. It is unfortunate that at this writing very few graduate programs of counseling or psychology prepare their students for the "Godzillas" they are about to encounter out there after graduation and licensure. If you are part of a graduate program enlightened enough to offer Managed Care preparatory training, count yourself fortunate. Most students, without this training, will find themselves, like Bambi, face-to-face with "giants" in the "promised land."

For the newcomer, and for the seasoned therapist alike, we invite you now to enter the land of the Managed Care giants. With this manual in hand, you should be able to tame even the scariest of them, as you prosper in peaceful and cooperative coexistence, together serving the most important one of all — the client or patient.

CHB/BJB

Chapter One

The Land of the Managed Care Giants

Personal Notes

Chapter One

The Land of the Managed Care Giants

While working on the manuscript for this text we received something in the mail that helped us cope with the stresses and strains of researching and writing. In the mail was a small sample of Extra Strength Tylenol with an accompanying flyer listing many of the common maladies that cause us to need this medicine for symptoms like "stress headaches, stomach upset and other pains" (and occasional writer's block). Here's a sample of the items on that nasty list:

copier out of paper	auto accident	no air-conditioning
waiting in line	didn't get raise	highway construction
short on cash	April 15th	in-laws
out of order sign	letter from IRS	computer virus
ripped slacks	lost job	bad haircut
luggage damaged	lost contact lens	expired driver's license
bad investment	broken tooth	out of deodorant
overdue bills	dental appointment	airport fogged in
lost reservations	lost phone message	bounced check
jury duty	ready teller down	inconsiderate smokers
broken heel	too many red lights	broken shoelace
speeding ticket	impossible deadlines	spilled coffee
loud neighbors	another parking ticket	weight gain
expired service contract	unreasonable co-workers	opened own business

The list goes on and on. But with all those dreaded things, there's one subject conspicuously missing. Yes, you guessed it — the dreaded two words that cause "headaches" and "stomach upsets" and "other pains" for many a health professional today. Those two words are — *Managed Healthcare!* In the minds of many psychotherapists who work in private practice, the concept "Managed Care" falls somewhere along the continuum between an IRS tax audit and a root canal.

Land of the Managed Care Giants: Not a Pleasant Place For Many Clinicians

For more than 15 years we have prescribed many remedies and techniques to assist colleagues in building successful practices in their communities all over the United States, Canada, Australia, and in Europe. During the past few years we have observed a common theme emerging. In telephone consultations as well as in workshops and seminars, therapists complain almost universally about their primary source of "pain" — Managed Care!

Certainly extra-strength pain killers can help, but they can only temporarily ease the discomfort. And as you know, symptom coverup only leads to symptoms again showing up. When the pain relievers finally begin to wear off, the therapist finds that the Managed Care Reality awaits; staring him or her again straight in their clinical face.

As we tell our colleagues: Buckle your seat belts, shift into a different gear, and maneuver yourself through some new obstacles, because the days of the pay-as-you-go patient, or the "my insurance will pay 80% of the fee" client are fast disappearing in your rear-view mirror! Up ahead? The Twilight Zone ... well, not really, but to many in private practice, it might as well be called that. The Land of The Managed Care Giants is a scary place and full of danger for many clinicians these days. But it's a territory that is probably here to stay (at least in some form). If you are serious about having a practice of your own, or a successful in-patient program, you must accept this reality, learn how to deal with those "giants," and come to believe that, yes indeed, this scary land can actually become a Land of Milk and Honey.

From Whence Cometh the Giants?

How did the American healthcare system get so complicated? What happened to the days of practitioner autonomy, patient freedom of choice, and reasonable and customary fees? And what conditions created the climate for the Managed Care "giants" to multiply and inhabit the land? Let's review some historical developments to help answer these questions. This should also help provide an understanding of the Managed Care phenomenon itself and facilitate our willingness to adjust ourselves to the future realities of peaceful coexistence with them.

It all started, it would seem, with a reckless abuse of privileges and services. Too many lawsuits. Too much paperwork. Too many hospital admissions. Too long hospital stays. Too many surgeries. Too many specialists. Too many high-tech diagnostics. Too many out-patient visits over too long a time. Too high fees for services. And too many unnecessary and/or inappropriate services. A malady of excess.

There are essentially 5 key trends in American healthcare that brought the Managed Care giants into the land:

1. Unnecessary and inappropriate utilization of services
2. Virtually unlimited access to high-tech equipment and expensive procedures
3. A lack of incentives for healthcare providers to control costs in a predominantly fee-for-service insurance system
4. An overemphasis on ongoing treatment of diseases and disorders, rather than preventative education
5. An inordinate focus on insight, awareness and exploratory factors, rather than goal-focused symptom reduction

The Federal government reports that the national consumer price index, representing the cost of goods and services in the United States, increased 63% from 1980 to 1993. By contrast, the cost of healthcare has risen 193% in the same time period. Americans are spending $733 billion a year on healthcare (including mental health), more than double the amount spent 7 years before. Spending for healthcare increases some $90 billion per year. Without some form of cost-controlling measures, it it estimated that by the year 2000 the figures will double again.

The cost of healthcare is soaring for both government and private business. The Federal and state Medicaid tab jumped over 38% in 1992 to a staggering $128 billion, and is expected to increase over 12% per year unless cost-cutting measures are taken. In the private sector, U.S. business spent in 1992 nearly $4,000 per employee for healthcare benefits; a total of $196 billion. The typical company spends approximately 45% of after-tax profits on employee healthcare benefits, "an enormous handicap in any race against international competition who have no such burden" (*Fortune,* Oct. 19, 1992, p. 89). General Motors alone, for example, spent $3.4 billion for employee healthcare in 1992, or *$929 for every car that rolled off the assembly line.*

Each year American business spends from 7% to 15% of the health benefits dollars on mental health, with a 20%+ increase year after year (Montgomery, *Personnel Journal,* 1988, 67, 86-91). According to R. Donkin in "The New Mental Health Watchdogs, Can They Deliver?" (*Business & Health,* 1989, Feb., 16-18), "Mental health benefit costs are rising twice as fast as all other medical benefits." One major Florida employer reported *an increase of 459%* in mental health benefits for employee dependents over a 3 year period (Prospero, *Business & Health,* 1987, Dec., 32-33). Ouch!

What accounts for these staggering statistics in both medical and mental healthcare costs? A recent study (in progress) by the Rand Corporation suggests that from 20% to 33% of all U.S. healthcare is "unnecessary or inappropriate." This amounts to over $150 billion spent on needless or wasteful care.

This "malady of excess" brought on the remedy we now call Managed Care.

An Operational Definition of
Managed Care (A Profile of the Giants)

In the broadest terms, Managed Care (also called Managed Healthcare or Managed Competition) is any system created to slow down or control rising healthcare costs by means of some "external review", "watchdog", or "gatekeeper" organization or group overseeing and scrutinizing the work of a professional provider or facility.

There are 5 strategic components of most Managed Care systems:

1. Screening and restricting appropriate and necessary services provided to patients
2. Reducing or limiting fees charged for professional services and procedures
3. Eliminating unnecessary, wasteful, or inappropriate care
4. Assuring quality of cost-effective services rendered
5. Providing a source of patient referrals and timely payment to providers who work cooperatively with the system

Managed Care is driven by and operates on a two-edged incentive system. These incentives motivate (a) the subscriber or employee, and (b) the healthcare provider to work cooperatively to control and reduce costs while at the same time receiving quality care.

Employers offer incentives to employees to join Managed Care plans by the employer paying a higher percentage of the healthcare cost (typically 80%) if the employee sees a Managed-Care-approved provider. The employee who chooses to receive care on a fee-for-service indemnity insurance basis from a provider who is not a "preferred provider" must pay more of the bill out-of-pocket (typically 40-50%).

Practitioners who elect to join a Managed Care panel or network are rewarded in several ways. Most importantly, of course, is the promise of ongoing, regular referrals of new patients to their practices. They are also assured of payment on a predictable basis. In turn these providers agree to reduce their fees (typically from 10-25% or more), to limit the duration of care, to use the more cost-effective lowest level of care possible to render quality service (e.g., out-patient not in-patient), and to cooperate with external screening and review by case managers. The loss of professional autonomy and reduced income — although not a happy duo — is usually worth the trade off for an enhanced referral influx to the practice, in these tough economic times.

Although the system is still evolving, there are basically 4 types of organizations that provide Managed Care "gate-keeper-watchdog" plans: (1) HMOs — *health maintenance organizations*, (2) PPOs — *preferred provider organizations,* (3) EAPs — *employee assistance programs,* and (4) UR — *utilization review.*

1. *HMOs* are closed-group ("staff-model") systems in which patients covered by this plan can receive reimbursable care *only* from providers employed by the HMO organization. The HMO is paid on a per-capita basis (a pre-determined amount per subscriber) covering most services and procedures, as opposed to itemized fee-for-services. Under this model, the dual responsibility of cost-containment and quality service delivery are tightly controlled by the HMO. Because subscribers pay a flat monthly premium for all care, HMOs can be conceived as "the healthy subsidizing the sick" (*New England Journal of Medicine,* Sept. 3. 1992, Vol. 327, No. 10, p. 743). The largest HMOs are the Kaiser-Permanente Medical Care Program in the west, and the Health Insurance Plan of New York.

2. *PPOs* are less restrictive on practitioners and patients, while at the same time containing healthcare costs by gatekeeping and external review controls. Practitioners join panels or networks as "preferred providers", providing services to patients in their own offices, operating semi-autonomously. Case managers are typically highly trained, skilled clinicians. To qualify for referrals under this arrangement, clinicians must agree to reduce their fees to negotiated contract levels, limit the length of services in a cost-effective manner, and abide by other restraints

enforced by the PPO's external reviewers (case managers). The patient may elect to see providers outside the PPO plan at a significantly higher cost to himself or herself. PPO provider panels may be "open" or "closed". When a panel is termed "closed" it is, in reality, *partially open — to those who know how to win the favor of the gatekeepers.* It is "closed" to those who don't. You'll learn in this text how to maneuver through those partially open gates by becoming "Managed Care friendly."

3. *EAPs* emerged because of the growing problem of alcohol and drug dependency and abuse in the workplace. It was believed that by matching an employee with the most appropriate source of treatment in a triage-type of screening, healthcare dollars could be saved. Savings resulted because of early problem identification and effective treatment interventions. Typically an employee consults an EAP manager voluntarily or via supervisory referral. The EAP manager may provide minimal intervention and then refers him or her to a provider known to be brief-therapy, symptom-reduction oriented. Most EAP referrals operate on a "hands-off" trust basis — the practitioner is not required to submit to ongoing review or restrictions of the EAP, as is the case with most Managed Care PPOs. However, referrals from EAPs carry with them the understanding that early, successful discharge results in more referrals from a happy EAP case manager. EAP Managed Care is handled by trained clinicians and is one of the more gentle forms of external control.

4. *Utilization Review (UR)* is commonly bemoaned by many clinicians as one of the most intimidating, frustrating, and time-consuming forms of external reviews. UR typically requires the practitioner to provide a detailed written justification for treatment, the regular submission of comprehensive treatment plans, and planned discharge goals. These are then scrutinized for medical necessity and appropriateness by a utilization reviewer, usually a psychiatric nurse or mental health clinician. A specific

number of sessions are authorized (or denied), and additional sessions must be justified. UR tends to be highly restrictive and is sometimes considered adversarial by clinicians in private practice and hospital programs. This is unfortunate, since reimbursement (and sometimes referrals) depend on favorable treatment from the reviewer. You'll also learn in this text simple techniques for "winning friends and influencing case managers," in all 4 Managed Care systems.

Evolution in the Land of Managed Care

As this material goes to press, Managed Care continues to evolve, growing ever-stronger and more influential in its efforts to control spiraling healthcare costs. For nearly a century now some form of external gate-keeping, watchdog mechanism in American healthcare has been quietly, but steadily, growing. We have identified 7 distinct stages in the development of Managed Care controls:

The first generation of Managed Care began early in the 20th century. In 1910 Dr. Abraham Flexner undertook a research project to define the quality of medical school in the United States. Thanks to such efforts, many "diploma mills" were eliminated. In 1913 the American College of Surgeons was formed to regulate standards of education and performance in the U.S. At the same time city, state, regional, and national professional associations were formed to license and monitor healthcare services.

The second generation of Managed Healthcare began in the 1920s. It focused on peer and utilization review of in-patient care within hospital settings. Although these review committees themselves had little impact on cost or quality, they gave birth to the concept of an external agent reviewing the quality, necessity and appropriateness of care.

A third generation of external healthcare review appeared in 1952 with the creation of the Joint Commission on Accreditation of Hospitals (now called the Joint Commission on Accreditation of Healthcare Organizations). The Joint Commission replaced the American College of Surgeons as the responsible body for monitoring and certifying compliance with professional standards of operation of in-patient facilities. Ask anyone who has been through a Joint Commission visit — "intimidating" is the word most often heard.

During this period of evolution a fourth generation of cost-controlling healthcare management was taking place. Employees were offered an HMO option that provided a full-range of services for a lower, fixed monthly premium. The HMO's in-house controls kept tight reins on type, duration, and cost of services, and helped wean the American public gradually away from an independent, freedom-of-choice mind set. Henry J. Kaiser was overjoyed at its success, while most American healthcare practitioners strongly opposed HMOs as an "aberration" within a free market, fee-for-service system.

A significant legislative event brought on the fifth generation. In 1982 The Peer Review Improvement Act was enacted. With this legislation the Utilization and Quality Control Peer Review Organization (now called PRO) was born. This requires providers to Medicare patients to release all pertinent patient information to a private external review organization. This was like a potent fertility drug producing multiple births. An explosion of Managed Care firms burst on the scene with the way cleared for utilization review by private organizations.

On the heels of the Peer Review Improvement Act emerged a sixth generation of healthcare controls. Systems arose that pre-negotiate how care is to be provided, agreeing in advance about criteria, quality, and cost of care. These were called preferred provider organizations (PPOs).

PPOs significantly reduced the amount of in-patient utilization, shifting to an out-patient orientation. At the same time, they demonstrated cost savings in healthcare by limiting needless services and shortening the duration of services through goal-focused outcome criteria. Although many clinicians complain about the 3 "i's" of Managed Care PPOs — *intrusion, invasion, and inquisition* — the facts nevertheless validate their cost effectiveness.

The seventh generation of healthcare controls and constraints is now in the germination phase. As Bradford Gray writes in *The Profit Motive and Patient Care* (1991), we are now living through

> "...an unplanned national experiment to see how much medical care can be managed through the use of incentives and review mechanisms."

Indeed, we are now living the "unplanned national experiment", trying to "stop the bleeding" in a healthcare system that is hemorrhaging from a loss of cost controls. Some form of external constraints and reviews will, no doubt, act as the tourniquet. From all indications, it's going to be a longitudinal "study" over several years duration. How long, no one knows. What form the ultimate external cost-containing model will take, is just as much a mystery. According to one healthcare report in *The New England Journal of Medicine,*

> "Most of the legislative proposals to reform the health care system, regardless of the ideological stripe of the sponsors, *promote expansion of managed care.* Private business...views managed care as its best current hope to control costs and preserve the dominance of the health system by private providers and payers"
>
> (Sept. 3, 1992, Vol. 327, No. 10; *emphasis added)*

Clearly, government, business, and those who pay the bills — the insurance companies — are all agreed: Managed Care, in some form or another, is here to stay. And like the behaviorist's mice, pigeons or guinea pigs in the midst of their own experiments, the sooner we respond favorably to the experimenter's proddings, the sooner we can settle in to something a whole lot more safe, stable and secure.

The Lay of the Land:
A Current Perspective

Life in the Land of the Managed Care giants is far from safe, settled, and secure these days. With the soaring cost of healthcare in the U.S., some business and insurance companies have been tempted to consider dropping mental health coverage completely. However, two factors have prevented them from doing so: (1) research shows conclusively that mental health treatment significantly cuts the cost of other medical healthcare expenses (Follette & Cummings, *Medical Care,* 1967, 5, 25-35; Jones & Vischi, *Medical Care,* 1979, 17, 12); and (2) Both state and federal legislation prohibit dropping mental health coverage from employee's benefit plans. Twenty-nine states require companies to offer minimum mental health benefits (Billet, *Compensation & Benefits Review,* 1988, Sept./Oct., 32-35). Federally-qualified HMOs are required by law to offer some component of mental healthcare (Budman, in *Linking Health & Mental Health,* p. 103-114).

In a recent national survey of employers, 95% of respondents reported that mental health benefits were included in total healthcare coverage (LaSota, *Business Insurance,* 1988, 23). Until the 1980s mental healthcare was financed primarily by traditional indemnity insurance, fee-for-service coverage, paying all or a given percentage of all services rendered by a provider of the patient's choice. Those days are fast disappearing with some form of Managed Care taking its place.

The Managed Care giants are multiplying and filling the land. Wise (*Psychotherapy,* 1988, 25, 415-419) estimates that from 5,000 to 6,000 major U.S. companies now utilize EAP Managed Care for their employees.

The business literature contains many reports of the cost savings realized by those companies which elect to use UR, utilization review, in managing mental healthcare. For example, many companies, like Bloomingdale's and Xerox, are strong promoters of UR, reporting savings of over 20% on mental healthcare (Lee, *Counseling & Clinical Psychology,* 1988, 5, 61-66; Mahoney, *National Underwriter,* 1988, 92, (46), 45, 48-49; Prospero, *Business & Health,* 1987, 32-33). Utilization review is finding its way more and more into out-patient care, but the savings reported thus far are primarily due to cuts made in hospital care.

During the past decade, enrollment in HMOs increased from 10.2 million to almost 39 million subscribers by the end of 1991 — over 300% increase! Growth in PPOs was similarly rapid: Only 1.3 million households were enrolled in PPOs at the end of 1984. Only 5 years later in 1989 the figure rose to 18 million families covered by this form of Managed Care. Data indicates that in1990, "...virtually all health insurance packages are now subject to various forms of utilization review" (Iglehart, *The New England Journal of Medicine,* 1992, 9, 744).

In 1994, 38 million people had no health insurance whatsoever. Another 30 million poor were insured by federal-state Medicaid insurance, while 35 million received federal Medicare coverage. Of those fortunate enough to have employer-sponsored health insurance, over 45% of them were covered by some form of, you guessed it — *Managed Care.*

A review of patient-tracking data from our own practice in southern California indicates the following: The impact of Managed Care on practice income due to Managed Care reduced fees was minimal prior to 1991. Until that date, more than 80% of all patient income was from indemnity insurance patients (60%), and full-fee cash patients (20%). The remaining 20% was traceable to union contracts and some form of Managed Care.

At this writing, only 4 years later, the numbers tell a dramatic and strikingly different story. Over 60% of all practice income now derives from Managed Care patients. This, as you might suppose, also represents a considerable reduction in fees-per-session-hour — our standard fee for individual psychotherapy is $110 per hour; the average fee received from Managed Care referrals is $78 per session hour. A $42 per hour reduction in fees charged and paid. And, dear colleague, this 38% reduction in our standard fee, and our willingness to accept $42 less per hour for the same expertise and care, in exchange for future referrals from case managers — this is precisely why Managed Care works. Yes, $110 beats $78 any day of the week. But, $78 also beats 0, zero dollars per hour ($0.00), wouldn't you agree?

This, dear colleague, is what they call *incentivization of the provider.* In truth, we have indeed been incentivized! It's much like the well-known little riddle, "In the forest, where does the gorilla sleep?" Answer: "Anywhere he wants to!" In the Land of the Managed Care giants, the "giants" do carry a lot of weight, have a powerful influence, and can dictate the terms.

Well, there you have it; the lay of the land. We trust that what you have encountered in this first chapter gives you a feel for, and puts a handle on the Managed Care phenomena — what we (tongue-in-cheek) have called the "giants".

To prepare you for the next chapter, we'd like to share a quote with you that warns of the absolute necessity of making the adjustment to Managed Care. In *Managing Managed Care* (Goodman, Brown, Deitz, American Psychiatric Association, 1992), we are solemnly reminded,

> "Private practice is becoming an endangered species. Unless mental healthcare practitioners can articulate what they are doing for their patients and also convincingly explain why they are doing it, purchasers and providers are going to be increasingly unwilling to pay for their services. If mental

healthcare services are too subjective to quantify, they may well be too subjective to pay for."

(Also see *The Quality Management Professional's Study Guide,*
Managed Care Consultants, 1991)

In a recent issue of *Newsweek,* we find a cartoon of a dejected, out-of-work lumberjack sitting on a tree limb, axe across his knees. Alongside him sit 3 little spotted owls on another limb, asking him pointedly, *"How does it feel being an endangered species?"*

We certainly have worked diligently in our own practice to avoid this fate, and we've been quite successful in doing so, thank God. One of our objectives in this text is to help your practice survive and stay off that dreaded "Endangered Species List" of practices and practitioners who failed to make the adjustment to those giants who now occupy the land.

Can it be done? No question about it. We did it, and we did not have the guidance of the book you now hold in your hand. With what you find in the pages ahead, you have all the tools, tactics and techniques to not only survive the Managed Care giants, but you'll learn how to "tame" them and live in a mutually rewarding land together — serving many needy people in your practice or facility.

We'll share with you what we learned "the hard way", so that you can avoid much of our trial-and-error blunders. We'll show you specific and simple ways you can articulate what you are doing for your patients and convincingly explain why you are doing it. We'll also show you how to "quantify" what you do so that any hard-nosed, watchdog gatekeeper will be delighted with you — so delighted that they enter your name at the very top of their Preferred Provider List.

Chapter Two

On Adjusting Attitudes
and Taming Giants

Personal Notes

Chapter Two

On Adjusting Attitudes
and Taming Giants

For many years we relied on our own marketing wits (and prayers) to build a growing practice, and have enjoyed sharing that knowledge with many therapists over the years. The methods worked fine, phones rang, and many patients found their way into our offices. But as time passed it became acutely obvious that those tried-and-true marketing techniques were not quite enough to sustain consistent growth. Why? Because when the phone rang the prospective patient on the other end said with increasing frequency something like this: "I belong to the Land-of-the-Scary-Giants Health Plan, are you a preferred provider?"

If we were not, we lost the opportunity to serve a needy patient and we referred them to someone who was a preferred provider. Blank spaces in our appointment book began telling the story; and the story was not pleasant.

So, like the rest of you, we became painfully aware that gear-shifting was in order. We either had to learn how to deal with this new, strange territory, *or else.* We had to find out how to win the favor and market ourselves to the Managed Care gate keepers, and how to persuade those gate-keeping case managers to continue referring new business to us. If we refused to learn these secrets of survival, we would need to buy the latest edition of *"What Color Is Your Parachute"* and find some other, safer place to earn a living. So, we got out our own Extra Strength Tylenol, buckled our seat belts, shifted attitudinal gears and began experimenting and maneuvering and testing. Our daily "New-Patient Tracking Sheets" told us how wretchedly or how wonderfully we were doing.

Yes, the early stages of dealing with the Managed Care "giants" were rough — frustrating and scary. But we kept reminding ourselves of what Edison was reported to have said when someone asked him, "Mr. Edison, how could you stand it having nearly 10,000 failures in a row before hitting on the electric light bulb?" Edison replied:

> "I didn't have 10,000 failures. I simply had 10,000 opportunities to learn how NOT to do it the next time."

So, dear reader, we'll spare you all the headaches and stomach upsets and "other pains" of our many flops, foibles, and failures — and did we have a flurry of them! We'll simply show you the tools, the tactics and the techniques that finally paid off for us. We'll show you why we now find as many Managed Care patient names in our appointment books as there are full-pay patients.

We'll show you what can make the "light go on, and stay on" for getting those Managed Care gate keepers to (1) like what you do, (2) put you on their Preferred Provider List, (3) become "satisfied customers" who trust your work and who are eager to grant additional sessions and make new referrals to you on a regular basis.

But before getting into the nuts-&-bolts of successfully marketing your services to Managed Care, let's consider your possible need for AA. No, not Alcoholics Anonymous, but *Attitude Adjustment.*

Managed Care:

Bother?

What do you see here? Are you scratching your head wondering, "What in the world is this bizarre collection of

* Graphic design by Sandor Csikesz, 1993

lines? — and what does this have to do with Managed Care or adjusting my attitude?"   Look carefully and describe what you think you see. The words "Managed Care" and "Bother" are easily defined, right? But if you use the same perceptual processes, you'll stay stuck.

And stuck isn't fun.

To get unstuck you have to let go and adjust your perceptual conditioning.   Here's a hint if you're still struggling with it: Like reading this book, all your life you've been trained to expect that words will appear in black ink on white paper.   Suppose, instead, someone reverses things on you and a word actually appears in *white* letters! Now do you see it?

After we adjust our perceptual rigidity and come at the whole thing differently, we see plainly the word "WHY" and the message is complete — "Managed Care: WHY Bother?" And now that you know what all those bizarre markings say, you can not go back to your previous state of uninformed confusion, can you?

The same holds true for many therapists when it comes to their attitudinal mind-sets regarding Managed Care. If we are going to survive in private practice in this turbulent world of economic instability, we must accept new realities, define success in different ways, and "go with the flow."

It is our opinion that *any therapist, group of therapists, or facility who rigidly refuse to adapt their thinking, their business, and their clinical practices to the constraints of today's PPO, HMO, EAP, and Managed Care "real world," that therapist, group, or facility will be unable to sustain independent practice due to financial reversals, and their story will eventually be told in the mental health obituary columns.*

These are not smooth and pleasant words, are they? But, like the physician informing his patient of a malignant lump; to withhold the truth is doing his patient no favor.

There are certain atypical exceptions to this hard reality. For some therapists dealing with EAPs, HMOs, PPOs, Utilization Reviewers, and Managed Care companies may not be necessary if that therapist: (1) desires only a very small, part-time practice to supplement other income, (2) the therapist is a skilled, aggressive expert at marketing his/her services to upper middle-class and upper-class individuals, or (3) the practice's primary source of income is from corporate consultations.

But if your objective is to build a prosperous, growing practice that will show a healthy profit and loss statement in the 21st Century, attitude adjustment is a *must.*

The "Why bother?" is something we commonly hear from clinicians these days. These are therapists who are frustrated by the impact that Managed Care has had on their work. They feel betrayed and offended. They are angry. All the work they have done preparing for their "dream" of private practice seems unfairly threatened by this new "menace" to their professional freedom. They resent the infringement on patient confidentiality, the loss of their freedom of ethical treatment of choice, loss of the right to set competitive fees for services They also resent the demand to justify their professional conduct to the gate keepers, and the mountain of paperwork required, all the while receiving lower fees for doing more work.

The why-bother-with-Managed-Care attitude is an outward expression of all these accumulated "pains" released as resistance to change. But as we oft' tell our teenage children when they complain that something isn't "fair," — Remember, Sweetheart, "L-I-F-E" can also stand for "Life Isn't Fair Ever." Sad, but true. And Managed Care realities aren't fair either.

For many therapists the words "Managed Care" trigger pain, loss and grief; i.e., the pain of the loss of personal and professional freedom, and the threatened death of a dream. Like grieving the loss of anything dear to us, after moving through the stages of denial, anger, and depression somewhere in the process we must fling ourselves with reckless abandon (mixed well with know-how)   into the phase called ACCEPTANCE!

It is our hope that the material we share here will help you to do that, and in doing so, will help you redefine and reframe the Managed Care dilemma to find freedom, success and the fulfillment of your dreams in new ways.

Dear colleague, we have compassion for and empathy with you, because on the leeward side of Acceptance, we've worked through our own wounded dreams and know that dreams can be rewoven. So hang in there, take heart, and read on.   And consider these special words from J. B. Priestley (which could have been written about the "new day" of Managed Care) —

> *I have always been delighted*
> *At the prospect of a new day,*
> *A fresh try,*
> *One more start,*
> *With perhaps a bit of magic*
> *Waiting somewhere*
> *Behind the morning.*

"What if I don't want to get involved with Managed Care in my practice?"

How often we hear this refrain in our practice development consultations. Perhaps you feel this way? If so, give thought to what follows. It may be time for a consciousness raising as we shift into the gear marked "Managed Care."

Getting back to our interactions with our children (we can learn a lot from kids, can't we?) — we sometimes find ourselves (and our bone marrow) throbbing to the tortuous beat of rap, or some other such "music", and we inquire in our middle-aged wisdom, "How can you listen to that stuff?" Their response was: "Parents, it's a new century! Wake up and smell the coffee!" We can remember our own parents saying the same kind of things when we blasted Elvis Presley "music".

The kids are right. These are different times. And the coffee's brewing and if you want to succeed and survive as a mental health provider, you must face facts. What are the facts? Glad you asked . . .

1.   The amount private business is spending for healthcare is devouring more and more of the all-important profit dollar. In the 1960s business spent about 6 to 8% of the profit dollar on employees' healthcare. Today in the 90s, would you believe, it's up to 50%! Ouch! And it's projected to be above 60% when we cross over into the 21st Century.

2.   The cost of mental health coverage has contributed in a big way to this scenario. In 1980 we spent $35 billion for mental health and chemical dependency treatment. Costs rose to $50 billion in 1983, and, brace yourself, to $80 billion in 1990! Double ouch!

3.   It is estimated that only about 3% of the population use mental health benefits. But their utilization amounted to 30% of hospital days covered in 1988.

4.   Expenditures for healthcare in the United States are the highest on planet Earth. Sometimes it's not fun being first.

5.   Costs for mental health coverage for dependents have gone through the roof. One Florida company reported an increase of 459% from 1979 to 1981 for child and

adolescent psychiatric hospital admissions.

6.   Some companies have gone belly-up, bought the farm, kicked the bucket and have otherwise checked out in bankruptcy because of the healthcare crisis on the dollar.

7. During the past 20 years there have been increasing reports of over-utilization of mental health benefits, especially for hospital and residential treatment care. The complaint leveled against some in private practice has been the tendency toward "heal 'em slow, rake in the dough" long-term treatment.

Freud may have been brilliant, but the meaning of "short-term care" was not part of his analytical model. Alfred Wellner, in his article, "Some Thoughts on the Future of the Professional Practice of Psychology," hit the nail on the Freudian head when he said,

> "...we are moving from an independent provider system to a contract system. The days of "unmanaged care" when entrepreneurs such as Sigmund Freud practiced as unregulated individuals without the need to determine medical necessity, diagnosis, criteria for care, and the end point for treatment, seem to be over."
>
> *Professional Psychology: Research & Practice, 1990, Vol. 21, No. 2, 141-143*

Well, we won't go so far as to say that those happy, good old days are "over," because there will always be some fortunate souls out there who can afford fee-for-services. There will be patients who refuse to accept PPO preferred providers, and insist on self-selected therapists.   These patients will find their names in our appointment books. But that population is "shrinking," excuse the choice of words here, and to build balanced, financially viable practices for the future, we cannot rely exclusively on them.

What can we rely on? Marketing to the Managed Care gate keepers, as well as to the pay-as-you-goers.

Establishing your practice on referrals from fee-for-service patients alone is like rowing a 30-foot boat in the ocean. Yes, you may move the thing through the water for a while, but not for long. You get pretty tired pretty fast, and then you end up dead in the water. Better and wiser to put up the sails and let the winds drive you along, wouldn't you agree? And if you lick your finger and hold it in the air, you'll find that the wind is coming from one direction — *Managed Care.*

So what if you don't want to get involved with all of the controls, hassle, and paperwork of the Managed Care "mess?" The facts just discussed should convince you of this one thing: The emphasis now with employers, insurance companies, and those external reviewers they hire is *the bottom line.* Is this an exaggeration? We don't think so. The Managed Care gate keepers will refer the patients under their "management" to therapists who are bottom-line-minded and are known to be "team players."

If you refuse to join the "team," your appointment book will have plenty of room for doodling and other leisure-time activities. Are there therapists who persist in refusing to get on board? Yes, we meet them in consultations month after month. Are they managing to survive and pay the bills? Yes, although income is down. Can they hope to remain in practice in the future? Here's the rub — Although you may get by now, if you don't become visible and known as a Managed Care team player now, getting on one of those Preferred Provider referral lists later may be almost impossible. Even now, in the fairly early days of the changeover, some therapists get this response to their requests to be PPO good-guys, "We're sorry, our panel is full and we have no need for providers in your area. Thank you anyway." Like jumpin' a train: if you don't get aboard now, while it's still movin' slow, it'll be mighty hard later as it picks up speed. It may turn out to be *now or never.*

Before you decide not to court the gate keepers and integrate Managed Care as another vital source of future practice referrals, give it serious thought, along with this —

> "Go to the ant...consider her ways, and be wise: Which having no guide, overseer, or ruler, provides her food in the summer, and gathers her food in the harvest."
>
> *Proverbs 6:6-8*

Winter cometh! Feel the chill? Better gather in now while we may, because it may be very hard to gather it in later.

Enough about attitude adjustment. We'll leave the final decision to you. We don't even know whether Managed Care as it now exists will be around in the year 2,001, but we are sure of this: Some form of external control will exist, and all we can hope is that because of our cooperation "playing the Managed Care game," we can avoid socialized national healthcare, utilization review hatchet-men (or is it hatchet-persons?), or worst of all, the elimination of all mental healthcare benefits — God forbid!

At least now we have a fighting chance to help our patients get the help they need; even if we must do it in fewer sessions while under the watchful eye of case managers. But if you cherish the idea of having your own independent practice, as we do, it sure beats the alternative! After all, in the final analysis it may be that had it not been for the advent of Managed Care, industry could have eliminated entirely the "burden" of paying for employees' mental health benefits.

So, dear colleague, since reality has chosen to take a new turn in the road, shall we follow her to see where she leads, and learn how to turn adversity into adventure?—Our adversary into our ally?

Mirror, mirror on the wall
Life just isn't fair at all!
What with all the cares we bear,
Like taxes, death, and Managed Care!
But you, Reality's face display,
Crying, "Managed Care is here to stay!"
So, for practice, pride, and self-esteem,
Guess I'll just have to join the team.

We have met the enemy, and the enemy is _____ ____

Fill in the blanks. If you wrote "Managed Care" in these spaces, you have either been dozing or brain-dead while reading what has come before. Awaken, dear colleague, and re-read, reconsider, and repent.

But if you wrote "our attitudes" or "resisting change," or something like this, you are not brain-dead, you are wide awake, and you are now ready to face the challenge of courting the gate keepers of Managed Care.

If Ralph were here today, observing what we are going through together facing the Land of the Managed Care Giants, Emerson would doubtless repeat again his words of encouragement—

> "Our strength grows out of our weakness. When we are pricked and stung and sorely shot at, then there is awakened in us the indignation that arms itself with secret force. A great man is always willing to be little. Whilst he sits on the cushion of advantages he goes to sleep. When he is pushed, tormented and defeated, he has a chance to learn something."

Pricked, stung, sorely shot at, pushed, tormented, and our comfortable *status quo* cushion jerked out from under us without our permission — yes, the revolution in healthcare has dealt thusly with us, wouldn't you agree? But with awakened indignation, and armed with secret force, we have the chance to learn something about how to flourish in adversity and how to let change open new opportunities for your practice.

The impact of Managed Care controls
on private practice: 10 important advantages

Once we are willing to lay aside our hostilities and extract our heads from the sands of denial, we should be able to see some very real advantages to Managed Care:

1. As we noted before, without this form of external fiscal control, mental health insurance benefits could become but a happy memory of the good old days.

2. For those clinicians who adjust their attitudes and join the "team," the Managed Care case managers can become a sweet source of success to a private practice; acting as a kind of "referral broker" to that clinician.

3. Managed Care may, in fact, help us manage to provide better care to our patients; getting our sights clearly fixed on objectives, goals and outcomes, rather than insights or awarenesses for their own sakes. And, after all, our patients come to us for *results,* as well as insights.

4. The ongoing interactions with our case manager colleagues can help keep us sharp clinically; linking treatment methodology tightly to diagnosed maladies.

5. Time-limited, focused treatment can help encourage us to help our patients build a support network upon which to depend, separate from reliance on the therapist alone.

6. Short-term, result-oriented counseling tends to be exciting, challenging, and fast-paced. This may keep us from getting bogged down, stuck, or having long periods when the patient seems not to progress.

7. Accountable to produce measurable results faster, we may find ourselves digging out and blowing the dust off those books we used to disdain as "simplistic"; you know, the ones about "Brief Psychotherapy." Managed Care may

manage to stretch some of our clinical skills beyond the old stuff we learned way back in grad school. And perhaps it's about time?

8. Time-limited and controlled intervention may help many patients escape the unsuspected snare of addiction to psychotrophic meds administered as an adjunct to their ongoing, long-term therapy. It has too often been the sad truth that long-term treatment results in long-term drug dependence.

9. For far too long our profession has been too fuzzy and less than precise as clinicians have prided themselves in being "eclectic"; meaning (in our opinion) "if it feels good, do it." Perhaps the external accountability for outcome will refine what we do and bring us closer to a true science of human healing.and recovery.

10. Last and perhaps least in terms of how much it holds our interest, is the economic advantages derived by our participation in helping to reduce the drain on the health dollar to American business. We are in truth members of a much larger "team" or system, and if we can build a healthier economy as well as healthier patients, then the whole system should benefit.

Chapter Three

Partnering with Managed Care:

Building the Future Referral Base for Your
Practice by Cooperating with Case Managers

Personal Notes

Chapter Three

Partnering with Managed Care:

Building the Future Referral Base for Your Practice by Cooperating with Case Managers

I ndeed, there are some good things that the healthcare metamorphosis unveils for you. Not the least of which are more new patient names in your appointment book and a busier waiting room. All that accountability and paperwork are worth the effort when you have the opportunity to sit face-to-face with new patients every week — week after week.

Formula: Cooperating With Managed Care = New Referrals.

But there's more to it than that, isn't there? "Managed Care = New Patient Referrals" ... *to whom?*   Those case managers don't get out the Yellow Pages directory to find a competent therapist to refer someone to, do they? They don't even send someone in need of counseling to just anyone on their own Preferred Provider List. As a matter of fact, we have heard many colleagues say, "I'm on the referral list of XYZ Health Care, and I've never gotten a single referral?"

What's the problem? Why no referrals? They've got all the qualifications needed to be chosen as a Preferred Provider, yet the phone doesn't ring. Why not?

It is probably for the same reasons that many therapists fail to get non-Managed-Care clients or patients. They think that simply being degreed, licensed, certified and highly skilled at their profession will attract new business to their practice. Result? All that expertise and no one to practice it on.

Why? Because this therapist (and 7 out of 10 therapists who are equally qualified and equally dormant) are unprepared to market their services effectively.

To get prepared to market to the Managed Care gate keepers, and to have the pleasure of practicing your skills on many new, needy patients, consider carefully the information that follows. Then put it into action. Then hire additional trusted staff to work with you — you'll need them!

To equip you rapidly with the marketing technology you will need to join forces with your Managed Care colleagues, we'll first present the most frequently asked questions that we are confronted with in consultations and at seminars, and then provide you with no-nonsense, no theoretical-fluff answers that you can really *use.*

Here's how to establish a positive, profitable partnership with Managed Care gate keepers:

The 12 "MUSTS" case managers want from you: Do them faithfully and they will faithfully refer

First of all, keep in mind that we are coming at this from a marketing point of view, not a political, business, insurance, or economic perspective. The experienced marketing professional begins always *from the point of view of the target audience, asking, "what are their most pressing needs?"*

If you were hired as a case manager for a large Managed Care company, you would be reminded that your job is to help cut healthcare expenditures for the hiring company who pays your salary. Yes, your responsibility is to assure clients who belong to this health plan that they will receive effective, ethical treatment to resolve their mental health problems and disorders. But you will be reminded, that if your Managed Care company doesn't manage to cut the health care dollar at the end of their existing contract, that you, and they, will be out of a job.

1. So when you, as a clinician, are interfacing with case managers, keep in mind that they are trying to serve two "masters" — their ethical commitment to assist in the best treatment available to the patient, *and* to do it in the most cost-effective way possible (to render unto Caesar the things that are Caesar's — $). Your job, then? To help him or her meet those two pressing needs and to pull off this balancing act, however delicate it may be.

2. They want focused symptom reduction. They want results that the patient will accept as satisfactorily meeting their needs and solving their problems. They want lasting relief of personal and interpersonal conflicts for the clients they represent. And they want results that are measurable within a reasonable number of sessions.

3. They similarly want a defined, time-limited course of treatment. They expect the treatment plan to be structured and goal-focused. And they want to show those who have hired them that they have carved deeply into the healthcare dollar, saving thousands for "Caesar."

4. And they want you to help them do both of these jobs in the most efficient manner possible. They don't want long, wordy reports. They don't want long, wordy telephone updates. They don't want to waste time calling you or writing to you reminding you to get your paperwork in on a particular client. They want that paperwork submitted to them on time; filled out completely, legibly, and according to *their structure, not yours.*

5. To save time, they usually prefer that you leave a short and sweet voice-mail message rather than consuming their time, and yours, playing telephone tennis. And they want you to help them interact with their "slow-moving"' computers by giving them accurate spelling of the patient's name and social security number.

6. They want you to have all session dates ready at hand before you call. Have diagnostic DSM-III-R (or DSM IV) codes prepared and ready before you call. And have a *succinct summary* ready to give them when you call. Don't ramble all over the clinical countryside. Try to summarize in short, one-sentence quickies the gist of the case. 1,2,3, period. Don't try to impress them with your clinical skills and jargon. Be professional, but be a person as well. Friendly. Courteous. Competent. And brief.

7. They want sharp, well-defined treatment plans with methodology and time requested or number of sessions, appropriate to that diagnosis.

8. They expect you to be able to briefly tell them how you arrived at a specific diagnosis and the criteria underlying this decision.

9. They expect you to have well-defined plans for the use of collateral and adjunctive outside resources to facilitate early discharge and patient support; such as physician assessment for meds, support groups, action-oriented homework, journaling, workbooks, recovery groups, and so forth. These should be part of your discharge planning right from the first intake interview.

10. If you are recommending psychiatric or CD hospitalization you are expected to have strong justification for doing so. If there is any way you can use more frequent outpatient care, day-treatment care, or mobilize outside resources to make hospitalization unnecessary, do it — as long as the patient's best interests are not compromised, that is. Keep in mind, dear colleague, that the gate keepers are sticklers about delimiting outpatient treatment, and they are even more zealous when it comes to guarding the gates of the institutions! Help them guard those gates, and enter those gates only rarely in severe cases. The days of "vacation" hospitalization, at least when Managed Care is on duty, are over, folks — and rightly so.

11. They want you to be ready to help schedule a particular client they want to be seen as early as possible, so that the client knows that the case manager is truly there to help them, not to hinder them. Treatment, after all, begins in the case manager's office and extends into yours. The smoother and more efficient the transition in, *and out,* of your care, the more case managers smile. And, *if you make 'em smile often enough, guess who they'll think of when they need to make tomorrow's referrals?*

12. They want happy, satisfied clients who will report back to the employers who referred them, that their lives are more fulfilling and more free from the problems that drove them to get help. And they want employers' reporting concrete and beneficial changes on the job as a result of what you do in therapy for them. If they get these kinds of results, you'll become known to them as one of the elite providers, and when contract renewal time rolls around, they'll keep their job. And they'll keep sending people to you!

These are some important keys for working effectively with Managed Care reviewers. Now let's take a look at the dark side — what they *don't want.*

12 things Managed Care reps DON'T WANT: Do them and you'll become *provider non grata*

Many therapists find the gates tightly locked to them because they unknowingly blunder into one or more of these "no-no's" and alienate case managers. It's easy to make a good impression, when you know the rules; but it's so very hard to reverse making a bad impression when you violate them! When the rules are violated, referrals tend to be eliminated.

So here, for your diligent consideration, is our "Managed Care *Provider-Non Grata* Dirty-Dozen Hit List." Step very carefully as you tread this mine field:

1. Psychoanalysis, dynamic, analytical, insight therapy, and even "supportive" or Rogerian counseling are unacceptable modalities of care. Case managers also raise a suspecting eyebrow if you call yourself "eclectic."

2. Similarly, long-term treatment is out.

3. Long-term hospitalization is out.

4. Supportive marital therapy is unacceptable, unless you can clearly justify a definite Axis I or II diagnosis in one of the parties concerned.

5. Unsupported diagnostic criteria or fuzzy-thinking, and "iffy"-diagnoses are out. Case managers want definitive diagnoses typically within the first 3 sessions, or sooner. They don't want you taking 10 sessions to make up your mind on the correct diagnosis.

6. They don't want floundering, wandering, drifting, no-direction treatment plans. "Well, I plan to see her in individual psychotherapy for about 12 sessions to explore co-dependency issues and to facilitate communication with her husband." Did you hear that mine go off? Better not step on it yourself!

7. They do not like certain diagnoses used without specific interventions recommended to address the accompanying symptoms; for example, a diagnosis of "generalized anxiety disorder" without a referral to a physician for anti-anxiety meds; or "major depression" without a referral for anti-depressant "med trial." The assumption may be that "the therapist is not making the appropriate medical referral which may enable this client to depend on him/her, thus lengthening treatment, and is failing to strategically plan for discharge." You never want them to think such things of YOU! Ask case managers their attitude toward such referral-linked diagnoses.

8. Certain disorders almost always dictate the prescription of support group or recovery group involvement. They know it, and you should know it. Fail to recommend such outside help for CD, eating disorders, sexual addiction, abuse and incest survivors, gambling addiction, and other obsessive-compulsive disorders and you position yourself as *provider non grata.* Again, when you prescribe outside resources from early on in the therapy, you show yourself faithful in planning for discharge, not for long-term treatment dependency.

9. Case managers turn into big, green, wild-eyed meanie monsters with fire coming out of their mouths when they don't get that paperwork returned to them on time and carefully prepared. They actually etch into their computer screens how reliable a therapist is getting the paperwork back to them. They don't like making referrals to people who cause them headaches or produce more work for them. If you hate the increased paperwork, better do some serious cognitive restructuring, my friend! It's here to stay.

10. Therapists who consistently ask for extensions beyond sessions requested do not make happy Managed Care campers. They don't like to feel as if they are being manipulated. If you ask for 8, stop at 8. This should cause you to work hard at planning for discharge support from the very outset.

11. They don't appreciate therapists who don't return calls promptly. If you use an answering machine or service, check it often and return calls *ASAP.* If you have a secretary, have her/him return calls promptly for you until you can call them back personally. And if you can't reach them personally, be sure to leave a voice-mail message in crisp, brief detail. Never, ever fail to return calls from case managers!

12. They listen carefully to client complaints about the care, or lack of it, they are receiving. Too many complaints means: (1) ineffective treatment, (2) unhappy employers, (3) more work for the case manager, and (4) more and more empty places in your appointment book due to referral interruptus.

Avoid these mines and deadly mistakes and you'll make case managers appreciate you. Those new names decorating the pages of your appointment book represent their "Thank You" notes!

How to get case managers to prefer *you* as a favorite referral source over other Providers

How do you cause them to perceive you as a favored, trusted, and frequently-chosen referral source, with a long list of qualified providers in front of them? Simple. Do, and don't do, the things in the lists we just gave you. We've learned the hard way many of these things (stepping on a few mines of our own!), and you can profit from our experience.

So we'll assume that you take seriously and abide by these things. But there's more. Like any courtship, there must be a warm-up phase of getting acquainted, building trust and respect, and then kindling the need to partner together on a regular basis. You must, therefore, know how to introduce yourself. Then prove yourself trustworthy. Then distinguish yourself as positively different from your colleagues on their provider list. It's also important not to get complacent as you continue to maintain and nurture these relationships.

You ask, "Is all this 'courtship' stuff really necessary to get referrals from the gate keepers?" As Pete Rose might say, you bet! It's smart marketing. And it's not optional. Let's talk now about the "how to's" of gate keeper courtship.

How do Managed Care companies select Preferred Providers?

Obviously, a therapist must be degreed and licensed (if the state requires it) to practice psychotherapy. He or she must have the maximum levels of malpractice insurance available for clinical practice. And in most cases, they prefer therapists who practice in professional locations as opposed to in-home offices.

All this being nailed down and in order, next comes location. The Managed Care company wants to provide referrals to therapists conveniently located near the clients' home or workplace. So location of your office(s) is key. Having more than one office location may provide an advantage.

Orientation is important. They want therapists who understand and provide short-term, results-oriented counseling that is more in line with the "mechanical" model (diagnose it and fix it now) rather than the medical model (diagnose it via analysis of underlying etiological causation and work toward longitudinal amelioration, someday...). Fix it now is what they want.

Specialization is next. They are looking for therapists with know-how and experience in specific problems and disorders. Often this is your entree. Can you work effectively with alcohol, drug, eating disorders? Can you help on a short-term basis survivors of childhood sexual abuse? Suicidal crisis interventions? Panic attacks? Stress disorders? You hurt yourself if you approach case managers and say, "I'm a marriage, family and child counselor, period." Focus. Specialize. Emphasize and position one to three clinical strengths.

They prefer therapists who offer a *One Stop Service Shop.* Translation: A *group practice* that has several specializations, therapists with ample hours open for referrals, psych med evals available, psych testing available, child and adolescent therapy, CD specialty, crisis intervention specialist, and someone focused on women's issues — these tend to be the high-demand clinical modalities they look for in a short-term-oriented group practice with both male and female clinicians.

More and more you will find Managed Care reps looking for therapists who tilt toward *group therapy* as their modality of choice. Why? More clients can be seen at one time, and groups tend to be more time and topic structured. Fees for services are also reduced to the company paying the bills. Having a symptom-focused, time-limited program of group therapy may, in fact, open "panel doors" that remain closed to your "generic" colleagues.

Do these describe your practice? If so, you are in good position to be among the most highly valued providers..

What to do if you are on the approved referral list, but you don't get referrals

Somebody's getting them, right? Why not you? Because you are leaning on yesterday's laurels. Today when a client asks for a therapist in their area, someone else's practice comes to the front burner of their mind. What to do?

1. Have you asked the big question? You can't be proud, you have to find a way to ask the big question: "What's the best way to receive referrals from you?" Or, "I sure would appreciate getting some new clients from you." Or, "Are there any specific steps I need to take to receive new client referrals from you?" Or, "Are you looking for any particular specialty area for referrals to new providers?" You have not because you ask not!

2.   Do you use every Managed Care client as an opportunity to cultivate your personal/professional relationship with the case manager? Be positive, friendly, human — not a stuffy, clinical machine. Their job is tough enough. Make them laugh occasionally. If they mention personal issues, *write them down on case manager profile cards.* Use index cards or a case file to record all your interactions with reps. If they talk about their upcoming Hawaiian vacation, cruise or trip, write it down.   Then mention it next time in passing. A loss in their family? Send a sympathy card. Out sick? Mention it. We all are more favorably disposed to someone who cares more than someone who is "strictly biz." Be a professional *person.*

3. Do you religiously follow all the two-dozen items on those lists we gave you? All of them!

4. Do you send case managers regular, succinct updates on clients under their supervision?   Not just ongoing treatment reports, but progress summaries? Simply give patient's name, SS#, number of sessions, goals reached, discharge planning update.   Keep it short, and they'll perceive you as going that all-important extra mile to distinguish you from all others on the list (who don't do things like this!). They also like quarterly updates of stats.

5. If you can discharge a patient prior to the expected date anticipated by the case manager, make sure you advertise the fact. Let them know it. They'll remember it. They'll remember *you.*

6. Do you attend meetings where you are likely to rub elbows with case managers? EAP organizations. Special workshops. Conferences. Open houses. Mixers. Forums.

7. Do you send case managers announcements of any workshops, seminars or courses you put on? Do you send them announcements or flyers on upcoming groups or support groups you sponsor? Do you send them any

articles you've had published? Your new book? Your new practice brochure? An article you've found helpful? Send any of these with a short note saying something like, "thought you might enjoy this!" How many therapists think to do any of these things? If they don't, and you do, how do you think your name compares with the other umpteen on the provider referral list? Enough said.

8. When you blow it, mess up big time, fail to send in paperwork on time, fail to return a call, or otherwise demonstrate your flaws and foibles, *don't defend yourself and make feeble excuses.* What should you do? Admit it fast. Point the finger at self and ask for mercy. Acknowledge how you screwed up, what you have learned by this mess-up, and thank them for being patient with you as "humanity strikes again!" The humble road leads to the happy ending. How often case managers must endure all kinds of defensive and empty alibis. How refreshing when a clinician knows how to say, "Well, I really dropped the ball, didn't I? I appreciate your patience; please forgive me.—Thanks."

Those are just a few things that can help to distinguish you among the other generic names on the approved provider list — and as your name comes to mind, referrals come your way!

If you're not on their approved referral list, use these 7 methods to get your name included

1. Start by doing what most clinicians do (but don't stop there). You call the Managed Care company and ask for Provider Relations. Begin by telling them who you are, mention your specialty areas and location of your practice, and ask for provider application materials to be sent to you. Ask as you do this if they are accepting new providers in your area who offer your specialties. Don't be discouraged if they say, "no." We'll handle that little challenge later.

2. Next, prepare a *Practice Profile Summary Letter.* You simply get a list of all the Managed Care, PPO, HMO, and EAP companies in your practice area and send them all provider request packages. With the letter you include (1) proof of state licensure, if applicable to your state), (2) proof of malpractice liability coverage, and (3) your vitae or resume.

The cover letter is all-important. Here's a sample of an effective letter. Pay careful attention to the confident (not pleading or begging) tone of the letter, the convenience of the practice, the credibility of the group profiled, the straightforward "short-term" or "brief" orientation that is emphasized, and the delineation of specific problem areas and specialty areas common to Managed Care reviewers:

(YOUR LETTERHEAD)

Case Manager's Name, Title
Managed Care Organization
Address

Dear Ms. Gatekeeper *(always use a specific name):*

Thank you for this opportunity to offer our services as a group practice to your clients as a part of your Preferred Provider network.

Our counseling practice is conveniently located in north Orange County, only minutes from Long Beach, Huntington Beach, and the Anaheim area; convenient to 3 freeways.

We are a group practice of licensed MFCCs, clinical psychologists, and consulting psychiatrist. Staff therapists are experienced in brief, solution-focused, cognitive/behavioral therapy and recovery services. We also provide counseling for Spanish-speaking and multi-cultural clients. In addition, we provide professional Christian counseling for clients requesting this orientation.

Both male and female therapists are available on a 24-hour, 7-day-a-week crisis basis. Evening and Saturday appointments are provided for clients' convenience. Our psychiatrist maintains Saturday hours for clients' unable to take time off from work for appointments.

You'll find that we understand the needs of managed care, enjoy working with case managers, and have worked effectively with several provider panels.

Within a solution-focused, time-sensitive orientation, our staff's areas of specialization include:

Chemical dependency	Depression & mood disorders
Child & adolescent disorders	Short-term marital therapy
Sexual addiction	Psychosomatic disorders
Crisis intervention	Grief and bereavement therapy
Childhood sexual abuse	Work-related problems
Anxiety and panic attacks	Domestic violence & women's issues

We appreciate the opportunity to offer our staff's services, and would like to receive information and application materials for becoming a group practice preferred provider. I've enclosed licensure, insurance, and curriculum vitae on each of our staff for your review. Thank you.

Yours sincerely,

Sample   Practice   Profile   Summary   Letter

This is a good example of a one-step practice-profile introductory letter. All salient data are there in one place for evaluation of your work as a potential provider.

3. Some clinicians prefer to use a two-step approach, sending a very brief overview letter that refers the reader to an accompanying *Practice Profile Sheet.* The Practice Profile Sheet should contain the following information:

(a) A brief overview description of the practice: Number of staff therapists, area(s) of specialization, how long in practice, location, and other Managed Care organizations, EAPs, or employer groups you serve. *(If you don't catch their interest in this paragraph, they may not read the rest of your profile: Remember to stress (1) the multi-specialty services offered, and (2) locations served).*

(b) Brief listing of all staff therapists, their licensure, and specializations. *(The inclusion of a psychiatric consultant on staff is an asset).*

(c). Brief but detailed statement of your orientation, describing your concept of *"brief therapy." Words like "time-limited, time-sensitive, goal-focused, outcome-directed, focused, cognitive, behavioral, and measurable" communicate quickly that you understand brief therapy.*

(d) Statement of your willingness to work cooperatively with Managed Care clients, your desire to get actively involved with quality, time-sensitive case management, and your understanding of Managed Care documentation. *(The key here is to position yourself as Managed Care "fit and friendly."*

(e) Mention your practice's strong reliance on client homework as an integral part of the treatment plan. Some items to mention might include, for example, bibliotherapy, journaling, charting, contracting, audio- and videotapes, workbooks, workshops and seminars. Point out that these innovative homework devices enable you to "stretch out" treatment for less-frequent visits, resulting in earlier discharges.

(f) Explain specifically, but briefly, how your practice utilizes and depends on outside agencies, support groups, self-help groups, the clergy, low-cost clinics, or other no-cost, supportive resources. Emphasize shifting client's dependency away from therapy to these groups.

(g) Point out that you offer evening and weekend appointments (if you do), and that your staff is available on a 24-hour basis via beeper and/or answering service for crisis situations.

(h) Show how you track client outcome from intake to discharge and through aftercare, and that you can send quarterly reports summarizing utilization statistics (with client statements). If you don't do outcome studies at present, start now. You'll find a simple system for outcome research in Chapter 9. Send examples of outcome instruments, if you have them.

(i) Provide names and phone numbers of other Managed Care reviewers or EAP reps who can be contacted for references as to the quality of work you provide. Give actual names and numbers; don't say, "references available upon request." This enhances your credibility, whether these people are contacted or not.

(j) Include a section clearly designating your location. List several of the larger cities within a 20 to 30-minute driving time to your office, and *include a map* showing these cities surrounding your office(s) location(s). This helps the provider relations gate keeper to quickly see your usefulness to their clients.

The jury is still out on which works best — the Summary Profile Letter or the Practice Profile Sheet just described. But by all means, try them, along with curriculum vitae, proof of licensure, current liability insurance status, and proof of incorporation (if applicable). Then follow it up with a telephone call to the director of Provider Relations Department about 5 days later.

4. Contact EAP managers in local companies. Ask them how you might become an approved provider for the Managed Care companies they represent. This method will work best if you can tell them you are already working with some of their employees, or if the EAP rep knows you..

5. Use your hospital staff membership as leverage. Find out who handles liaison work between the hospital and Managed Care plans. Contact this person, tell them you're on the staff, and ask if they can help get the gates open.

6. Another way to get on their list is to use your relationship with any client who is already covered by their plan as leverage to get the keeper to open the gate. If you get a call from a prospective new patient who has Managed Care coverage, call and ask for a case manager. Tell them a client is asking to see you. Ask how to get on their provider list. You can also ask for what is called *ad hoc* approval. This puts you on a special, one-time-only approval status for this particular patient. This gives you the opportunity to cultivate a relationship with this case manager to prove your worth to them. Later you can more easily get full-status provider approval as one of the team players. And be sure, as you get to know the case rep, to ask their advice and assistance on how to get your name on the official provider roster. They already know the inside politics and can help you make key contacts.

7. You can also find out who sits at the top of the company (the president, director, CEO) and send them a package introducing yourself; sending your vitae, licensure, liability insurance, and a cover letter. In this letter highlight why you believe your practice can be an asset to their company, particularly focusing on your areas of specialization and any information that separates you from most other clinicians. Then ask her/him to advise you of the next step.

You're using the top-down, trickle-down effect here. About four days after mailing this, call his/her office and ask if your materials were received. Your hope is that it will be passed down to the proper level, usually the head of Provider Relations. Why go this route? Because it is possible that because your packet trickles down, your application may be perceived as having added weight.

If the gates remain tightly closed after trying these 6 methods, you'll need to move into Phase II tactics. You'll learn how these work in the next chapter.

Chapter Four

Phase II Marketing Tactics:
The 10 Simple Things You Can Do to Get Preferred
Provider Status When the Panel is "Closed"

Personal Notes

Phase II Marketing Tactics:
The 10 Simple Things You Can Do to Get Preferred
Provider Status When the Panel is "Closed"

Two signs come to mind. One actually appears outside
a convent, and it reads:

> KEEP OUT!
> TRESPASSERS WILL BE
> PROSECUTED TO THE FULLEST
> EXTENT OF THE LAW.
>
> Signed: *The Sisters of Mercy*

The other allegedly appears outside the Aspen estate of
John Denver; remember him? — the love-peace-save-our-
planet singer of sweet love songs. Passers by are greeted
with this little message on a 10-foot-high gate:

> GO AWAY!
> YOU ARE NOT WELCOME HERE.

Many of our colleagues tell us in consultations that they
feel just about like that when they receive their own little
message over the telephone, or on a Managed Care company
letterhead, "We're sorry, but our mental health provider
panel is closed at this time, and we have no need for a
therapist in your area." Slam! The gate is closed and the
"No Trespassing" and the "Go Away" signs are posted.

Is this your own experience in your dealings with the
gate keepers? If so, here are what we call Phase II

Marketing Tactics. Phase I strategies haven't yet succeeded in getting your foot in the door/gate. So you shift gears and go into a more creative, aggressive mode of action. Let's talk about what some of those tactics might involve:

1. Keep on knocking. The Chinese symbol for "crisis" is made up of two figures: One denotes "catastrophe" and the other "opportunity." It's no catastrophe, or crisis, when you are turned away by a Managed Care company. It's your opportunity to regroup and make up your mind that you'll not take no for an answer. An attitude of tenacious determination is essential. You must decide to find new and creative ways to knock on those closed gates. So, the first step in Phase II is fixing your mind and maintaining a persevering, persistent, determined attitude. "Knock, and keep on knocking, and it shall be opened unto you."

2. Profile your current patients' insurance coverage to prepare for Managed Healthcare switchovers. Only a few years ago most of your patients were either pay-as-you-go or indemnity insurance plans, right? Not today. You may have some holdouts who still have private insurance plans that pay 50%-80% or less for your services. Within the next few years, however, their employers will doubtless be switching over to Managed Healthcare "pruning" of benefits. You need to be ready to move into action when they do.

On the front of each patient's chart, note what kind of insurance he/she has. Do this as well for those patients who are cash-paying, because they too may have insurance or an HMO that they do not use to cover your work now, but could later when the switchover occurs. Periodically ask these patients about their insurance benefits; any changes in coverage; any new benefits available? The best times to profile their insurance plans is in February, May, July, and November — common times employees are notified of upcoming insurance changes.

Many Managed Care companies taking over a new employer account will offer therapists currently seeing employees the opportunity to "grandfather" in as preferred providers on their panel. Hooray! Here is your window of opportunity to move through those gates before they slam shut.

It's also a strategic time to (a) get to know all the case managers at this company (call them, send them your practice brochure, business cards, announcements of groups or workshops you plan to present), (b) similarly introduce yourself and your work to the patient's EAP or HR people, and (c) find out what other companies this Managed Care Plan serves and market to them vigorously using the strategies in this book.

3. Talk to colleagues who have found favored status with the gate keepers, or who know other therapists who have, either as providers or assessors. Talk to colleagues who are not only preferred providers, but who receive referrals from, and interface with case managers. Preferably they should be colleague friends who do not practice in your neck of the woods.

Ask them how they managed to gain entrance? Which of their specialty areas helped open the gates most? Which case managers have they found most pleasant to work with? And, if possible, would they feel comfortable talking to this case manager about you and your potential value as a provider to the company? Contacts, dear colleague, can sometimes swing big gates wide open. "It's who you know," you know.

4. Make yourself, and your work, visible. Position your reputation and your unique personality in places where case managers and other gate keepers can learn that you indeed do exist. What organizations and associations are they likely to belong to? What workshops and seminars would likely attract them? What conferences probably

interest them? Make the time to attend them and network with gusto. Or what about sponsoring the kinds of meetings or speaking at them yourself to make yourself known? Until you do this you are, to the gate keeper, one of the other 5 1/2 billion passengers aboard Spaceship Earth.

5. Consider every Managed Care new-patient call your invitation to become a new preferred provider. The Managed Care company doesn't need you. They have more therapists on their provider list than they could possibly ever use. So that means you have no power. But the client whom they represent has power. Why? Because they pay their healthcare insurance premiums. Some of those funds pay the Managed Care company's bills, and in turn, the case manager's paycheck. Money is power. Therefore, the needs and requests of the client have more "pull" than yours.

So, when you receive a call from someone who has been referred to you, wants to be your patient, but is covered by a Managed Care company whose gates have been closed to you, don't send them away saying, "I'm sorry, I'm not on your Provider List." Instead, do this. Ask them to first call their case manager requesting that you be approved as a permanent, or at least an *ad hoc* provider. Remind the prospective patient of your area or areas of specialty which may influence the case manager to give you special consideration. Is there anything that you can offer this client that other therapists may not provide? Do you have an ongoing, no-cost support group available? Do you offer group therapy at lower cost? Do you do 12-step therapy? Do you have hours available that meet the person's needs? Help prepare them with specifics to mention to the case manager, and remind them to write them down. The gate keeper may be persuaded.

6. Let prospective patients promote your practice for you. Many times the client is told, "We're sorry, we have providers in your area and our panel is closed." Tell the caller if they get this message to call you back. Then, ask

them who, at their place of employment, is in charge of the employee benefits and healthcare coverage? It may be Personnel or Human Resources or Insurance Benefits. Instruct them to go directly to this person. Tell them that they are experiencing (whatever the problem is), and that they have found a therapist whom they truly believe can help them, and why. Tell them that their request has been turned down by the Managed Care company. Mention that this is causing them stress in having their care blocked, adding another problem to the problem they started out with. Then advise them to ask this person to intervene on their behalf so that "I can get the help I need with a therapist I trust." They can remind this person that the therapist they are requesting has all the educational and professional licensure qualifications needed to serve as a preferred provider.

You'll find that many times this method can swing big gates wide open.

7. Have the prospective patient use the 2-step leverage method on your behalf. A related strategy we've found effective is to have the new caller write a letter to the director of their employer's insurance benefits department The letter essentially says the kind of things just described. At the end of the letter the employee says, "I will be coming in to your office next week to meet with you regarding this matter. Trusting that you will do all you can to help me get the help I need."

What tends to happen is that the head of employee insurance benefits goes into some action phase before the employee shows up. Often the employee arrives with good news awaiting them. Their good news is your good news. The insurance director may have persuaded the Managed Care provider people to open the gates to you, in this particular case, of course. They may grant you permanent provider status, or *ad hoc,* (this-case-only status). Either way you've gotten a toehold on building a trusted provider relationship with case managers, and that can lead to a foothold in getting referrals in the future.

8. Repeat step #6 with the director or manager of the prospective new patient's EAP program, if they have one, or the head of Human Resources (HR).

9. Repeat step #6 with the prospective new client's union steward; or have them go to the president of their union and use the top-down trickle-down approach, putting pressure on the employer, who can put pressure on the Managed Care company, who then "magically" invites you to walk through those gates to become a preferred provider.

10. Use the PEMCO 3-Step Method. Translation: Physician → Employer → Managed Care Organization: Let's assume that someone is referred to you via word of mouth. You are overjoyed till you learn that they have a plan whose gates are closed to you. You call and the gate keepers say, "Sorry, but our provider panel is closed" and, slam! You call the person's EAP and insurance person, and get nowhere. Again, slam. Don't give up. Tell the caller to call or visit her/his physician (if they don't have one, refer them to a physician who knows and trusts your work). Encourage them to complain to their doctor that they are experiencing increased stress because they are not being permitted to consult with you, a therapist who they have confidence in because you come so highly recommended.

The physician then (a) calls you to discuss the case and then calls the employer insurance person, or (b) makes a direct call to the employer insurance program, or (c) writes a strong letter recommending reconsideration of the patient's needs, and approval of this wonderful therapist we all know and love — you. (In turn, you send a letter of "Thank You!" to the M.D., accompanied by your brochure, business cards, and perhaps even a gift certificate to one of the finer restaurants in town).

The physician's medical concerns can exert pressure on the employer (who desires to avoid potential lawsuits, as well as keeping the employee happy). They in turn contact the Managed Care gate keepers and use their persuasive leverage to open the way for you.

Unethical tactics, you say? Sneaky? Crass pushiness? Not at all. It's simply professional guerrilla marketing strategy at its best, and *all done for the patient's best interest.* After all, you're doing more than marketing here. You're going to bat for a person who can benefit from your care. Face it, dear colleague, as the mental healthcare dollar does more shrinking than we do, we had better become increasingly comfortable when we wear that somewhat uncomfortable marketing hat! Few clients or patients are equipped to fight for themselves, are they?

These methods work. But they all may not be suited to your personality or temperament. To succeed in the world of Managed Care, PPOs, HMOs, EAPs, and who knows what future external reviewing "big brothers" await us, you must find the marketing methods that fit you, or, stretch yourself and make them fit!

How to use paperwork to enhance the reputation of your practice

Initial assessment forms, treatment plans, progress updates, ongoing treatment reports, ad infinitum, *ad nauseum.* Years ago when we worked for a governmental agency, we made up our minds that "when we are in our own full-time practice, we won't need all these *forms du jour,* we'll keep it simple." That was the plan. But that was before the advent of Managed Care controls.

We have no choice. The good-old-days of the new client intake sheet, simple progress notes, ledger sheet, check, and deposit slip are over. Linked to every Managed Care patient you see is a minimum of 4 additional, required forms that you must make time for. *God help our forests!*

No need for us to discuss whether all this paperwork is necessary or fair or of clinical benefit to the patient. This book is about hard realities and how to handle them successfully. You can look at all those forms as a curse and complain and spoil the gift of a day, which you'll never have again. Or, you can reframe the issue and consider every piece of paper you send to the case managers or case reviewers as — *an opportunity to enhance your own image by (1) helping them do their job faster and easier, (2) keeping your name out of the pool of provider names who regularly cause case reviewers frustration and aggravation, and (3) delivering all paperwork with excellence on every line.*

Here are some simple ideas that will establish your name and practice reputation with an image of excellence, so that you join the elite provider ranks:

1. Using paperwork to link positive value to your name starts with the right mind-set. During those hell-on-earth early days of adjusting ourselves to the Managed Care giants, we spent many miserable hours groaning and griping, complaining and condemning the "blankety-blank" Managed Care paperwork! If only our patients could have heard us failing to practice what we teach them! But one day we learned through an EAP manager that another case manager had commented to them, "those Brownings are easy to work with; their reports are crisp, in on time, and treatment plans are right on target." Paperwork suddenly took on new meaning to us! We had no idea that filling out all those forms actually served to position our image with high favor in the minds of those case managers.

From that day on, we approached the paper chase with a new vision. You might do well to implement this new mind-set. It has done wonders for (1) our relationship with case reviewers, and (2) saved us from hours of grumbling and griping and murmuring that used to spoil our days. As you sit there at your desk with a stack of Managed Care forms looking you in the face, tell yourself this, or make yourself a sign to read over and over again,

> "This piece of paper is my opportunity to create a sphere of influence as I favorably enhance the image of my work, make myself highly valued, and thereby receive more new clients from each case reviewer. I will complete this communication tool with excellence, to help the case reviewer help my client, and in the process, it will help my practice to grow."

Positive-mental-attitude hype? Definitely not. This is an important tool to make paperwork less painful and referrals more plentiful.

2. Make an appointment with "Practice Paper Marketing." It's our experience that if you let paperwork get done "when you have the time," it won't. Or it will get done late and arrive late, and in some cases, you will miss a key authorization end date. Missing this date can result in your clients coming in for unauthorized sessions, and in turn, you may not get paid for this work! Ouch!

Solution: Take out your appointment book. Block out an hour, or whatever you feel it will take, during which you do all your Managed Care paperwork that is due during that week. And don't allow yourself to make that time optional, open for paperwork only if there's nothing better to do, or no patient needing to be seen. Make it a must. And call it "Practice Paper Marketing." That will help you approach it with the right attitude each week.

3. Create and use a Tickler File System. You'll be dealing with many Managed Care organizations supervising the care of many patients. They all will have different requirements and dates when initial assessment forms, treatment plans, ongoing updates, and other paperwork

are due. You need a simple system for keeping a handle on these gymnastics. Here's what we've found most effective:

Buy a small box with 3x5 index cards inside. Insert in it dividers labeled, "January, February...November December." Insert within these dividers additional tabs marked, "1, 2, 3, 4." Then as you begin (and continue) working with a Managed Care referral, enter on the appropriate month and week card the patient's name, SS#, Managed Care plan, case manager's name and phone, and the form required with exact date due. We make it a policy to return forms *not* on the due date, but *1-2 weeks early.*

Note on this card any contacts you've made with the case manager, or things you want to mention next time you talk to him/her (about the patient, or something personal). During your Practice Paper Marketing time each week, look at that particular week's cards and complete them.

4. Use a countdown code system to monitor authorized sessions. Many case reviewers will not only authorize an end date for treatment, but also a specific number of sessions you may see the patient within a given time period. We've found it helpful for some of our staff therapists to use a special countdown system. Let's say we have 8 sessions authorized within the next two months, by the end of September. We enter right in the appointment book this code, "6-9/30-i." The "6" means that after 6 sessions, do a treatment update report and send to case manager. The "9/30" is the final date after which no further sessions should be scheduled, because the authorization has expired. And the "i" indicates that this patient has authorization for individual therapy only. Why did we use "6" and not "8"? Glad you asked: Because 8 is the total number of sessions authorized. If we do the update 2 sessions in advance, we do not inadvertently run over. And, it keeps our practice image shining brightly as one of the good guys who never misses a due date (and who is often even ahead of the deadline).

5. Use the Sessions/End-Date/Co-Pay Tracking Sheet. Keeping track of the total number of sessions authorized, sessions used to date, the end-date of certified or "certed" sessions is no easy trick. Add to that the changes in the amount the patient must pay in co-payments as sessions accumulate — it's a little like the juggler who must toss-and-catch the raw egg, the bowling ball, and the "live" chain saw all at the same time! If he slips, it's not a pretty sight. If we miss, we can end up working in our self-made "free" clinic.

After many months of trial-and-error experimentation, we have come up with a Sessions/End-Date/Co-Pay Tracking System that works very well, and keeps us from missing changes in sessions remaining, end-dates approaching, or changes in patients' co-payments due. On the following page you'll find a sample of the Sessions/End-Date/Co-Pay Tracking Sheet that we use for each Managed Care patient seen.

You'll note that each session is numbered so that we always know where this particular patient stands per total number of sessions to date.

Also note that the End-Date is entered next to every session so that we never lose track of this cert cut-off point.

The Countdown date is entered in this manner: If the case reviewer has authorized, say 7 sessions; we enter the number "5" in this column. Why not "7"? Because if we enter "5" we cannot possibly inadvertently run over the 7 certed sessions. And, when we come to the end of the 5 sessions we allotted to the patient, we will give a *timely and early update* to the case manager. This enhances our reputation as a cooperative team player. And thirdly, it may help motivate us to wrap up treatment even earlier than expected — ask case managers what they think of that when it happens!

Patient Name _____

Therapist Name _____

Insured Name _____
Insured SSN _____
Case Manager _____
Mgd. Care Co. / EAP _____

Session Tracking Sheet
BROWNING THERAPY GROUP, INC.
Internal

First 10 Sessions					First 10 Sessions (cont.)		Next 10 Sessions					Next 10 Sessions (cont.)		Last 10 Sessions					Last 10 Sessions (cont.)	
Date of Session	Patient Pays	Paid	Call Case Mgr. & Send OTR At 2	At End Date			Date of Session	Patient Pays	Paid	Call Case Mgr. & Send OTR At 2	At End Date			Date of Session	Patient Pays	Paid	Call Case Mgr. & Send OTR At 2	At End Date		
(1)	$8.80						(11)	$17.60						(21)	$26.40					
(2)	$8.80						(12)	$17.60						(22)	$26.40					
(3)	$8.80						(13)	$17.60						(23)	$26.40					
(4)	$8.80						(14)	$17.60						(24)	$26.40					
(5)	$8.80						(15)	$17.60						(25)	$26.40					
(6)	$8.80						(16)	$17.60						(26)	$26.40					
(7)	$8.80						(17)	$17.60						(27)	$26.40					
(8)	$8.80						(18)	$17.60						(28)	$26.40					
(9)	$8.80						(19)	$17.60						(29)	$26.40					
(10)	$8.80						(20)	$17.60						(30)	$26.40					

Authorization period: _____ to _____   No. Sessions: _____

Sample of Session Tracking Sheet for a Managed Care Company that requires progressively increasing patient co-payments.

In this example you'll also note that when the patient covered under this Managed Care contract uses more than 10 sessions, their co-payments increase. This method helps us, and the patient, keep track of these changes. We give these sheets to our patients to monitor their own sessions, but we do not count on them to keep accurate records (most don't). So we do it for them, for us, and for the case mangers.

If this tracking system seems too cumbersome to you, then use it as a prototypical model and construct your own version. And if you can improve on it, please send us a copy of your new, improved version and we'll publish it in the next edition of this book (giving you due credit, of course).

Pull all patient forms for the following day from your "Managed Care Cert Tracking" alphabetical file. Complete this form faithfully at the time of each session. Update your Tickler File as you reach your End-Date or Countdown number. If you have a secretary, instruct her/him to give this Tracking System and the Tickler File high priority.

We hope that this will help you get a sense of being in control of the many demands that your Managed Care partnership necessarily places on your life. Place all those complexities in this kind of order and you can manage it. Let them get out of hand, and they will manage to drive you nuts! Enough said. Now on to more interesting things:

A special tool that demonstrates your "Managed-Care-Friendly" provider status

You have doubtless noted that frequently we have emphasized case managers' affinity for providers who rely on and recommend the use of outside resources. Here is a tool that can help. It can enable many patients to find needed support and assistance. It can bring you new business from the community as these are handed out. *And it shows positive evidence that you are predisposed in the direction of utilizing outside resources — making you "Managed Care Friendly."*

How many times we have wanted at our fingertips the phone numbers for various support groups, helplines, or other resources a patient needs. Using this tool you simply assemble all the local (and national) numbers in one convenient place, print them on a small wallet-sized card, and at the bottom insert some information about your practice and your availability to help.

Here are some groups and services you might want to include (with phone numbers) on your Resource Card:

> AA, Al-Anon, Alateen, ACA, Coda, CA, NA, SA, GA, OA, Incest & Sexual Abuse Survivors, Women's Shelters, Rape Hotline, Suicide & Crisis Hotlines, Women's Hotline, Child Abusers Hotline, Homeless & Runaway Hotline, Child Abuse Reportline, Social Services Referral Infoline, Emergency Food & Shelter, Victim's Hotline, HIV/AIDS Hotline, other emergency numbers

At the bottom of the card you can put a statement like this: *"When you need professional counseling and recovery services you can trust, we are here to help."* Followed by the name, address and phone number(s) of your practice.

Typeset (or produce on your computer) several of these on both sides of a page, each within a neat border. Reduce to wallet-size and then have a printer or laminating service seal it and cut the cards out for you. Have several hundred made, as your budget permits.

You can then mail 10—15 of them to each case manager you know, and those you meet in the future, with a note saying something like, "Thought you might like to have some of our new Resource Cards to give to clients who may need them...Please let me know if you'd like more." Do this as well with EAPs, employer benefits personnel, Human Resources reps, union reps, and others involved with potential patient healthcare. You can also send them to present and former clients, encouraging them to share them with friends. Show them to the proprietor of bookstores in your area which carry recovery literature and they will very likely be happy to offer them as bookmarks on their counters.

CAUTION: It is *not* a good idea to attend recovery meetings and hand these out. The program should not be used to promote anything except recovery. If your Resource Cards are helpful tools, they will find their way into the right hands. Keep a supply of them in your waiting room. Your own patients can be good distributors.

Another valuable tool you can use to distinguish your work with case managers

Many clinicians contact case managers asking to receive new client referrals. All of them are professionally qualified and can do the job. But the therapist who clearly goes the extra mile providing service to the client and to the case manager — that therapist will receive high regard, and elite status on the Preferred Provider List.

Try this to distinguish your practice as pro-active when it comes to understanding and using outside support resources:

Prepare a booklet containing the following:

1. A section containing the names, addresses, and phone numbers (both national and local) for recovery services, support organizations, and other agencies.

2. A section containing a copy of the 12 Steps modified for each of the major recovery groups.

3. A section containing self-tests to help diagnose the presence of alcoholism, incest, abuse, codependency, etc.

4. A section of the best recovery books, workbooks, audio and videotapes.

5. Articles written by you, or others who are given due credit, that encourage a client who may be in denial, who may have a loved one in bondage, how to perform an intervention, what to do if your child has a drug problem, how to start a self-help or recovery group, and so on.

6. A section briefly describing how to select a therapist who can provide quality short-term help, with questions that the patient can ask prior to counseling, how to set therapy goals, and how to follow through with aftercare.

Of course, some statement at the end of this booklet describing your own practice, orientation, staff, location, how to make appointments, and your office phone number.

What to do when provider panels are "closed"

We estimate that in approximately 80% of our work in practice marketing consultation we hear this comment, both in written communications and in face-to-face or telephone consultations:

> "What can we do to get on provider networks and panels in our area? We are told time and time again, 'We are not accepting new providers now because our panel is closed.' Is there anything we can do?"

The answer usually surprises the frustrated clinician. We'd like to share our response to this query with you here in a verbatim transcript of a recent consult. When they report being shut out by a "closed panel" we simply tell them:

> "Yes, there is something you can do, but the first step is not what you can *do,* but rather, it's a matter of what you should *think.* Most therapists make the mistake of believing what they hear. When the provider relations person tells them 'the panel is closed,' they accept that at face value and thus, they quit trying and give up. So, for them, the panel was closed because they stopped pursuing the Managed Care organization.
>
> "But what of the therapists who are told, 'the panel is closed' and, lo and behold, we find their names on the Preferred Provider List of that same Managed Care company sometime later? How did they get their names on those 'closed' panels?"
>
> "Answer: They knew how to translate the provider relations language into English. You see, when they are told 'our panel is closed to new providers,' this in reality means one thing, and that is this — 'Our panel is *partially open* and only those practitioners who do and say and are the right things will manage to get those partially-open gates to swing wide open."

Note that translation very carefully, please. It may be the key that opens so-called closed gates for you. The real meaning of "closed panel" is "partially open panel." The strategies, techniques and ideas in this chapter (mixed well with a good measure of your own creative genius) should help you get "partially open" gates to swing wide the rest of the way.

In truth, of the hundreds of Managed Care organizations in the U.S., there is no such thing as a "closed" panel. Only partially-open networks awaiting those who know how to market themselves and their work wisely. "Wisely" means convincingly meeting the special needs of Managed Care.

That's what Phase II Marketing, and this text, is all about.

Chapter Five

A Short Course in Effective Brief Therapy
from a Managed-Care-Friendly Perspective

A Short Course in Effective Brief Therapy
from a Managed-Care-Friendly Perspective

Brief Therapy that gets results 3 ways:
(1) Patients get symptom reduction and solutions;
(2) Case managers get successful, early discharges;
and (3) You get more new patient referrals

Why is the longest chapter in this book about something that's supposed to be brief? Simple. Because many of us have been so well trained, and seasoned over the years in long-term orientations of therapy that little is known about "brief" therapy. We may know that the length of time is limited, or the number of sessions are restricted, but how do we get results for the patient within that kind of a squeeze?

We decided that in addition to helping you manage your way around Managed Care's complexities, we would give you a not-so-brief mini-cram-course on how to do effective Brief Therapy. The kind of time-sensitive therapy that earns the respect of case managers to enhance your clinical reputation. This is not theoretical fluff. It is a hands-on clinical "toolbox" from which you can pick and choose a variety of techniques we've used for over 20 years. Techniques, incidentally, that get results quickly.

We are offering these methods at the request of many colleagues who tell us that they know they must shift to a short-term emphasis if they are to survive the present realities of external controls, but they just do not feel comfortable with these modalities, in large part because they have never been trained in them, or tried them. Many of them have been trained, and have years of experience practicing psychodynamic, introspective, insight-oriented approaches. They find that these methods have produced results for their patients, and they've never found it necessary to change approaches. "If it ain't broke, don't fix it." Many of these therapists have even looked upon short-term therapies as "simplistic", "undignified" or "quasi-professional peripheralistists." Many clinicians apparently believe that short-term therapy cannot produce long-term results.

In the past, every therapist was free to choose her or his own ideosyncratic preference, developing whatever variety of professional clinical practice that seemed best. That was how it used to be. Now, however, if you expect to work cooperatively with the Managed Care reviewers/gate keepers, your sphere of choices is greatly reduced for you. *Brief therapy* is no longer an option left to the discretion of the therapist. It may become *the only game in town.*

So for those of you who may need some brushing up on the rules of the game, in case you're a bit rusty and haven't played for a while; or for those of you who want to learn to play this new game to win, we can help. What we'll present here is a system for providing goal-focused, time-limited therapy with ideas and techniques that we have found useful over the years. Ours is certainly not the only, or the "best" approach, but we hope that it will give you the framework from which to design a brief therapy model of your own — one that fits your personality and comfort zone (and one that endears you to case managers!).

The approach consists of several important steps:

1. *Establish and commit to a time-limited agenda & expectation*
2. *Quickly establish rapport within a therapeutic trust alliance*
3. *Clearly define a time-lmited treatment agenda for patient*
4. *Neutralize initial resistances*
5. *Collect outcome-focused impairment data*
6. *Quickly assess Treatment Targeted Impairments*
7. *Prioritize impairments according to predicted responsiveness to solution-focused,brief intervention*
8. *Determine a descriptive DSM diagnosis*
9. *Plan for ancillary resources for impairments that are non-responsive to short-term therapy*

10.   Get patient to agree and commit to impairments
      to be eliminated or changed
11.   Define precipitating events or "triggers"
12.   State a working hypothesis and DSM diagnosis
13.   Determine brief treatment modalities appropriate for
      each prioritized impairment
14.   Help the patient formulate an"outcome vision"
15.   Make a verbal or written contract with patient
16.   Distinguish "the problem" from "the patient"
17.   Enable the patient to measure complaint intensity using
      the Scaling Method
18.   Aim for small changes only
19.   Give simple, precise, novel, goal-targeted homework
20.   Change the pattern of the impairments/complaints:
21.   Continue emphasizing the termination date throughout
      treatment process
22.   Assess all therapeutic goals accomplished
23.   Structure and supervise continuing outside support
      resources
24.   Terminate and discharge on the agreed date

---

*1.   Establish and commit to a time-limited agenda and
expectation:* How *you* approach the patient and his/her
problem(s) will have much to do with the patient's
expectation, and the final outcome of therapy. We have
found it helpful to remember Parkinson's Law and to
communicate this to our patients: "The job will get done in
the time allotted to it." If both the therapist and the patient
approach whatever the conflicts, disorders, impairments, or
problems are with the expectation that we have a limited
number of sessions to work through and find solutions for
them, then this tends to be precisely what happens. If, on
the other hand, the therapist believes and communicates to
the patient that "we will take whatever time is needed to
uncover, analyze and discover why you have these
difficulties, in the hope that these insights will effect the
changes you desire," then those changes may result only
after a long course of therapy. The patient takes his/her cue
for expected outcome from the confident, time-limited,

focused agenda of the therapist.

We set this expectation before we even see the patient. Not in specific number of sessions necessarily, but with the firm assumption that we are limited to only brief therapy, so the job must expand or contract to fill that limitation. We want the patient to perceive this attitude early on in the treatment process.

2. Quickly establish rapport within a therapeutic alliance of trust: Rapport doesn't mean everyone is happily smiling like Cheshire cats. It means finding a fluid, flexible, congruent responsiveness between therapist and patient in which both people feel accepted, understood and free to be themselves. We believe that the essence of true rapport is creating a climate in which a person feels "loved as is" in all their precious uniqueness.

How is this kind of accepting/affirming climate created? Each therapist will use him/herself in unique ways. But there are certain guidelines we've found effective in training therapists to build a therapeutic alliance quickly to assure the success of brief therapy. Here are a few suggestions that seem to be most effective:

(a) Avoid the stuffy, formal, holier-than-thou, aloof and detached clinical image. This only increases anxiety, distancing and defensiveness in the patient.

(b) Project a warm, friendly, person-to-person image. Use the kind of words the patient uses every day. Smile. Shake their hand with both hands. Put a hand on their shoulder. Sit naturally, relaxed (and never behind a desk!). Use the patient's first name often. Use the first names of the patient's significant others; don't say, "how long has your husband been doing this?"; do say, "how long has Tom been doing this?" *Never, ever* call the patient "Sir" or "Madam."

(c)   Never begin a session with "problem talk," — e.g., "Can you tell me why you are here and what the problem is?" Instead, find an area of common ground that will put the patient quickly at ease — something the patient can talk about with minimal anxiety or uncertainty. For example, "Isn't this some of the strangest weather we're having?" or "You were referred to me by Alice, weren't you?—She is such a special person; how long have you known her and how did you meet?" *Note:* This kind of warm-up chit-chat makes it easy for the patient to find something comfortable and easy to discuss. We all share the weather in common. She already knows Alice as her friend and has positive associations linked to Alice. The therapist's job is to rapidly link herself or himself to positive associations in the patient's mind. (You might even say something favorable about the case manager who showed concern for them and referred them!). But talking about weighty "problems" too soon tends to heighten anxiety, pain or resistance.

(d)   Use empathic mirroring. Observe carefully the patient's verbal styles — volume, tone, pitch, pace, rhythm, favorite words or phrases, pauses. Try to mirror or make your own verbal patterns reflect theirs. Observe facial expressions, eye contact, tilt of the head, hand and arm movements, feet placement, crossing of legs, gestures, body positions, breathing patterns. Try to mirror these back to the patient in very subtle ways. As your conscious communications influence the patient, these subconscious stimuli can make the patient feel, "Hey, this therapist's not so scary; as a matter of fact, they're a lot like me for some reason...I think maybe I can trust this person!"

(e)   Use the patient's unique verbal styles. Listen carefully to see how a patient conceptualizes her/his world and use that style in future interactions. Does the patient see life from a *visual perspective:* "I see your point," or "It's pretty hazy to me," or "It's crystal clear." Does the patient see life from an *auditory perspective:* "Does this sound right to you?" or "I hear what you're saying," or "that doesn't ring a bell with me." Does the patient see life from a *kinesthetic perspective:* "I think I'm in touch with my own motives," or "I feel I've got a handle on this," or "what he's doing just doesn't feel right to me." Using a patient's representational system can give you a key to the patient's private code, and this can help you rapidly develop rapport to form a therapeutic alliance of trust with them. Practice framing your verbal communications in the system that your patient finds most comfortable to them. The "fit" is a powerful tool for forming empathic bonding.

(f) Verbalize the patient's feelings and needs using his or her own language style. Making statements that are already in the patient's mind, but that they are perhaps unable to conceptualize, builds trust and confidence fast. Such statements as, "You must have felt abandoned when this happened?" or "Even though you said nothing, you must have been filled with rage at that moment?" If you're right, the patient will see you as being really "with" them.

(g) Reassure the patient that there is hope. Statements like, "Even though you've tried many things to overcome these problems, it's not hopeless; not at all; let's consider this 'Phase II'—we'll look at what didn't work, and then find new ways to replace them with what will work—that's what we are here to do together!" We have found that using the concepts of "Phase I" (the period of time prior to therapy until now), and "Phase II" (what takes place in therapy together henceforth) offers patients in brief therapy a new and hopeful framework with which to approach old problems. We emphasize "writing down new rules of the road or guidelines" in Phase II. This method seems to give the patient renewed confidence and hope.

(h) Positively reframe and redefine for the patient. The patient typically views his/her world negatively and hopelessly; "My husband refuses to come in for counseling — there's just no hope for our marriage." If you can help the patient see their pain and their despair in a new light, your own credibility grows dramatically; "I can appreciate how you must feel, but you know, if you change only one part in a system, the whole system changes, doesn't it?...Well, you're here, and as you and I make some important changes, your whole family can be changed!"

(i)   Evaluate the outcome of patient's previous therapy. Ask about previous therapies and therapists.   Which were successful?   Which were not successful?   What made the difference?   What did the patient like most about previous therapies that got results?   What kind of results?   What did other therapist(s) do that displeased patient?   *(Never, ever make derogatory, critical remarks about other therapists or therapies.   Instead, find something positive to link your own work to, encouraging patient to build on past successes. And define the patient's current decision to enter therapy as a "new phase", a chance to build on past successes, inner strengths, and to start over.*   Even if the patient has little good to say about her or his previous therapist, you can do two things: (1) compliment them sincerely for having the courage to work on their problems, and (2) point out that perhaps in time something important may surface from that earlier therapy.

(j)   Therapist enthusiasm and conviction of successful outcome is contagious.   Show sincere excitement about the possibility of the patient's "new life" being just up ahead. Be enthusiastic about the privilege of being part of it!

3.   *Clearly define a time-limited treatment agenda for the patient:*   Within a trusting bond of the therapeutic alliance, the patient should be told early on that a limited number of sessions is available in which to accomplish the objectives of therapy.   The patient may have been in long-term therapy in the past.   If so, their expectation is that you will provide the same kind of treatment.   It is crucial to establish a goal-focused mind set in which the

patient's expectation is shaped to anticipate outcome in very few sessions. Doing so forces both therapist and patient to be focused and goal-oriented at every session (and between sessions).

One way to handle this would be to say, "Alright, since we only have about 8 sessions to get control of your anxiety attacks, we'll need to first define the specific events and thoughts that tend to trigger these feelings..." *Note:* Why 8 sessions? Even if the Managed Care reviewer authorized 12 sessions, an experienced brief therapist knows that the tighter the limits we place on ourselves to help the patient get results, the sooner those results will be realized.

Suppose we help the patient get control of these panic attack symptoms in 8 sessions (as expected). How do you think the patient feels about you as a therapist with results like this? How do you think the case reviewer (who certified 12 sessions) feels about you as a referral resource? *Less is definitely more!*

4. Neutralize initial resistances: In brief therapy we do not have the luxury of weeks or months in which to overcome the barriers and resistances the patient brings to the therapeutic relationship. We have to disarm them quickly so we can get on with the business of solutions.

When the patient shows disappointment or disapproval with some aspect of the therapist himself or herself, that attitude must be openly discussed, accepted, and the patient affirmed and encouraged to progress anyway. The patient may say they expected an older therapist, a therapist of a different sex, a therapist with a different degree or license, a therapist of a different race or nationality, or even a therapist with a different appearance or office decor.

The key here is for the therapist to do three important things: (1) verbalize, using the verbal and non-verbal styles of the patient, the patient's own unspoken concerns, (2) create an accepting, "safe" milieu for the patient in which the resistance is okay, and (3) propose an experimental phase in which the patient controls the decision to continue, or not to continue.

For example, here is a verbatim transcript of resistance that was successfully neutralized by a male therapist who received a referral from a case manager of a woman who was suffering from depression secondary to recent memories of childhood sexual abuse. The therapist specializes in the treatment of this disorder and was most effective with both male and female patients on a short-term basis. Note how gently he handled the three steps of disarming resistance:

> "It seems to me that you're having a hard time feeling relaxed and at ease sharing with me what your problem is. I'm wondering if you might feel a bit uncomfortable working with a male therapist? After all, some of the things that have happened in your past are very personal and I know are delicate matters to deal with. I can understand perfectly how you feel. A lot of people feel this way. But how about this: Suppose you try to just discuss what you can with me to see if we can find some definite solutions, and if you still feel you'd like to see a female therapist, I'll be happy to help you with a referral to a skilled female therapist who can help. Does this sound okay with you?"

The same reflecting, affirming, and empowering strategy can be used with most forms of resistance. The only difference, however, is when working with those with addictive disorders, chemical dependency, or obsessive-compulsive disorders. The key difference in these cases is the presence of a denial system that must be quickly dealt with. The first two phases of neutralizing resistance by mirroring the concerns of the patient and affirming the patient are used. The third phase, however, is one of unswerving confrontation of the denial. Here, for example, is how a therapist handled a male patient referred by an EAP

manager for assessment of multiple absenteeism and interpersonal conflicts in the workplace:

> "From what you've said, Jack, it's clear that you're dealing with
> a load of pressure on the job, and the fights you are having with
> Karen are increasing your stress. It's got to be everything you
> can do just to get through each day. At the same time, Jack,
> we've got to face some important facts—can I tell you what they
> are?...Number 1 is that you're using alcohol to cope; number 2 is
> that you never have knock-down, drag-out fights with Karen
> unless you've had something to drink, and number 3, your ab-
> sences at work seem to all be related to your drinking. Yes, I can
> help you make your relationships at work better, and yes, I can
> help you make your marriage happier. No problem. But if we
> work on those things without you getting help for your alcohol
> problem, it'll all be for nothing, like building a sand castle at the
> beach and a wave comes in and washes it all away! I don't want
> that to happen to you and to your family. So, let's talk about the
> most important first step, and that's getting you some help with
> your drinking behavior. We'll work on those other issues later."

If denial is not handled directly, firmly, and with
resolve, the patient will waste many sessions — driven by
his/her denial — trying to get you to deal with everything
but the main problem. It is our opinion that it is unethical
and actually harmful to the patient's life, if they are clearly
diagnosed as CD or addicted, to proceed with any other
intervention until a recovery program is initiated.

After building rapport through reflection and
affirmation, the brief therapist must press for an all-out
decision for a recovery or rehab program, using motivation
to resolve other problems as leverage to do so.

Another case requiring the therapist to disarm the
resistance is the patient who comes with what we call
"gun-to-the-head-motivation" — a supervisory referral for
counseling in which the employee has no choice ("get help
or good-by"); a husband sitting in the consultation room
because of his wife's ultimatum ("get help or get out"); a
rebellious teenager defiantly coming in to "please" his
parents ("get help or else"); or the referral from a lawyer

who wants to impress the judge in an upcoming hearing ("get help or get more time in the slammer"). In these recalcitrant patients, the therapist must deal head-on with their questionable commitment to the process. Here's how one therapist effectively handled an angry, "get-help-or-get-out" husband:

> "Hey, let's you and I talk straight, okay? It's obvious to me that you're POed and don't want to be here, right? I can understand that, and I'd probably feel the same way if my wife put this kind of pressure on me. I'm glad you are up front with how you feel about being in counseling, so we can be honest with each other. But as long as you're here, why not make the time really pay off for you? You chose to be here, so you can choose what you'll get out of it for *you!* And, if Joyce is happy in the process, fine. But I'm not here for Joyce; I'm here for you. So, since you've decided to spend this time with me, you tell me what specifically you'd like us to work on so it's time well spent. Give me three things you'd like to get out of this — what's number 1...?"

Too tough? Too pushy? We don't like this role either. But with some kinds of resistance, if you don't step boldly into the mood of the resistance, you'll fail to win the patient's trust, respect and cooperation. In the above example the therapist was not only successful in enlisting the commitment of the patient to therapy within one session, but in the following 9 sessions successfully helped this couple develop new ways to defuse domestic violence.

Openly, directly neutralizating resistance must be one of the primary objectives in the first session of brief therapy.

Some patients are referred for brief therapy because of some physical symptom or symptoms. Their own physician or the employer's doctor or EAP rep may believe that their problems are not physical in origin, but emotional or psychological in origin. The patient is referred to you for assessment and treatment. The patient sits in your office, but thinks it's "a waste of time" because they want a physical, not some psychological explanation, and medical intervention. They're only going through the motions with the therapist. If the therapist doesn't handle these motives assertively, much time will be wasted over many sessions.

Consider, for example, this active intervention with a patient referred by a Managed Care case manager for the brief treatment of what her doctor believes may be a psychosomatic headache condition:

> "I can imagine that you must be concerned about these headaches you've been having. It's so hard to concentrate on anything when your head is pounding, isn't it? And I hope you'll continue seeing Dr. Jordan to try to find out if there's anything physically wrong—that's really important, and he's an excellent doctor. He's also concerned, I'm sure as you are, about what things are going on in your life that may be producing tension or stress for you. As you know, I'm sure, tension and stress can only intensify your headaches. If you and I can pinpoint some of what we call the "triggers" that make your headaches worse, and find ways to show you how to get control of those stressors, we may be able to help reduce or even eliminate some of your headaches. This will work in conjunction with what you and Dr. Jordan are doing. How does this sound to you?...Now let's talk about a typical headache and trace some of the possible stress triggers one by one..."

Some important things to note in this successful alliance with a reluctant, unmotivated, resistant patient: (1) the therapist makes no attempt to persuade the patient that his headaches are not physical; (2) the therapist attempts to validate Dr. Jordan's value to the patient; (3) in so doing, the therapist attempts to positively link herself to Dr. Jordan's favorable reputation in the patient's mind; (4) allowing the patient to "decide for himself" whether the symptoms are physical or not, this frees them both to explore possible psychological causes; and (5) energy in the sessions can now be shifted away from attempts to "prove" that no psychological causes exist, to a precise focus on possible stressors as what we call "Treatment Targeted Impairments," which is why the case manager referred the patient to us in the first place.

Suppose a brief therapist bypasses neutralizing resistance and goes straight for focused symptom reduction? It is highly probable that the patient will expend her/his efforts consciously and unconsciously sabotaging therapy progress. A competent brief therapist is well advised, therefore, to ask him/herself, *"What are the blocks, defenses, walls, attitudes, beliefs or conditions that need to be disarmed in order to enlist this patient in a cooperative therapeutic alliance free from resistance or sabotage?"* The items on this list are as important as the list of symptoms targeted for treatment intervention.

5. *Collect outcome-focused impairment data:* In traditional psychotherapy the therapist undertakes an historical assessment of the patient's internal and external "world" in order to diagnose (1) the reasons for the presence of the disorder(s), and (2) descriptive criteria of the disorder itself. Important information? Yes, but not the "stuff" the brief therapist is after.

In brief therapy we are after *the specific reasons the patient hurts and why they require treatment.* We look for objective, demonstrable, observable, measurable behaviors or statements of thought patterns which can justify treatment. And that treatment must have a significant probability of successful outcome.

Coming at the data-gathering, diagnostic work from this perspective helps the brief therapist keep her/his work focused on only those problems that are within the realm of Managed Care's short-term treatment focus. Otherwise we could assemble a catalog of symptoms, disorders and conditions that would be massive, and thus considered "unresolvable." The patient could be disqualified for treatment altogether under the "medical necessity" parameters of Managed Care. Our job is not to engage in exhaustive diagnostic workups, but to *pinpoint and describe in observable, measurable, behavioral terms*

*conditions that can be resolved within the context of brief
therapy.*

To assist in keeping this perspective clearly before us
during the assessment phase, we have found it helpful to
refer to each observable condition as **Treatment   Targeted Impairments (TTIs).** "Treatment" because our emphasis is intervention leading to change. "Targeted" because
those interventions are focused. And "Impairments" as
opposed to underlying, abstract disorders or maladies.

TTIs are the outward expression of certain DSM-III-R
diagnoses. They specifically describe a lessening, worsening, weakening, deteriorating, or reduction in the patient's
ability to function adequately. At the same time TTIs offer
the potential for strengthening, repairing, and improving
the patient's internal and external condition. TTIs are both
behaviors and statements about behaviors and thought processes by the patient.

Treatment Targeted Impairments also provide the therapist and case reviewer with an operational frame of reference with which to communicate and document the problem, the treatment plan, and the final outcome of treatment.
TTIs give therapist and case manager objective behavioral
"handles" by which to describe DSM-IV mental disorders in
outcome terms.

The bottom line is this: *Information linked to solution.*

Here are some examples of fuzzy, traditional diagnostic
labels that we have turned into operational TTIs:

Traditional Label	Observable Treatment Targeted Impairment
Suicidal ideations —	"Hopeless" thoughts & statements
Dysphoric mood —	Statements of being "depressed, empty, heavy"; strained speech, tearfulness
Low self-esteem —	Allows others to hurt her/him repeatedly; statements about being "no good/worthless"

Poor ego strength —   Unwilling to set limits with others; non-assertive behavior; fearful self-talk

Substance abuse —   Drinks alone, 9 beers per day, vodka on weekends; rage & violence when drinking; 2 DUIs; multiple work absenteeism

As you can see, describing the criteria of mental disorders in terms like these keeps us focused on behaviors or verbalizations about the patient's internal world. In turn, this kind of thinking lends itself easily and naturally to selecting active treatment modalities to correct, restore, and reestablish the emotional and social health, with maximum adaptive functioning for the patient. We help the patient most, and please case reviewer best, when we use treatment-focused, outcome-friendly TTIs.

Collecting behavioral data in TTI terms significantly enhances treatment intervention choices. But before we can treat we must justify the need for treatment using DSM-III-R classifications (or its latest revision). A way to become more comfortable describing the conditions in the DSM-III-R in TTI terms is to try this. You'll need two books:

DSM-III-R (Revised Edition) Case Book; American Psychiatric Assn.,1989, and *DSM-III-R Training Guide; Reid & Wise; Brunner/Mazel, 1989.* Select diagnoses that are most commonly referred by Managed Care reviewers: i.e., depressive disorders, anxiety disorders, obsessive-compulsive disorders, substance abuse, marital problems, panic disorders, and so forth.

Read the focused discussions of cases in the *Case Book.* Take note of all objectively observable descriptions of each person discussed under each diagnostic category. Then turn to the same diagnosis in the *Training Guide.* Read the case vignettes, discussions, essential features, associated features, and predisposing factors. Pay particular attention to the diagnostic criteria list. Again note the specific behavioral/verbal observations that support the diagnosis.

Then, try to succinctly summarize each diagnosis in

explicitly measurable terms, as you would if documenting this condition or explaining it over the phone to a case manager. Remember: Your goal is to enable the patient to get help. To do this you must justify the medical necessity for treatment to the case manager in language that points directly to treatment modalities that promise (1) a short-term change in the problem, (2) a positive redefinition of the problem by the patient, or (3) a positive change in the solutions used by the patient to handle the problem.

Consider these examples of a correct and incorrect approach used by a therapist responding to a case manager's question, "What is the client's diagnosis?" The patient is a 32-year-old female who has been experiencing tension and worry for the past 8 months that is now interfering with her work performance.

> *INCORRECT:*   "She's exhibiting free-floating anxiety that may be related to suspected unfaithfulness of her husband, but we'll need to rule out other possible underlying causes. She has been experiencing this distress for the past several months. The diagnosis is Generalized Anxiety Disorder."

> *CORRECT:*   "Her initial diagnosis is Generalized Anxiety Disorder, 300.02. She reports almost daily concern and worry over her husband's suspected extra-marital affairs. She states that she fears being "abandoned" by him. Physical symptoms include getting fatigued easily and eye twitches. She reports very frequent urination and there is no urinary infection. She also states that her hands are always cold and sweaty, and sometimes she develops shortness of breath. She says that most of these symptoms occur when the thoughts of her husband's unfaithfulness come to her mind and she feels helpless. In addition to referring her for medication eval, I think that the treatment plan must help her structure ways to confront him, and learn effective ways to manage her fearful thoughts."

You are the case manager. Which therapist do you think you would have more confidence in? Which clinician helps you quickly justify treatment as a medical necessity? Which therapist would cause you to believe that solution-focused, time-limited results are most likely? Which therapist do you think gets that case manager's next referral?

Study carefully what each therapist reports to the case manager.   Avoid the vague, obviously psychodynamic errors of therapist #1. And note the precision of therapist #2, the order of presentation, and how treatment strategy is mentioned simultaneously in describing diagnostic material, *even before it is requested.*

Practice writing your own "incorrect—correct" scenarios with other commonly encountered diagnoses using the two texts mentioned above. It can make the difference between receiving "Certified" and "Non-Certified" sessions.

6.   *Quickly assess Treatment Targeted Impairments:* The Managed Care case reviewer is impressed by the therapist who knows how to sift out the wheat from the chaff, narrowing down problem areas, and selecting brief treatment approaches to resolve them.   The therapist equipped with a framework or guidelines with which to do this kind of "sifting" and "focusing" finds himself or herself in an enviable position.

You will find a step-by-step diagnostic approach which we call a *Treatment Targeted Impairment Assessment* in the next chapter.

7.   *Prioritize impairments according to predicted responsiveness to solution-focused, brief intervention:* Following the precise delineation of patient problem impairments, the next step is to define those that are within our scope of care — care within an acceptable Managed Care context, as described earlier.

Obviously we cannot adequately offer treatment within a brief framework to resolve schizophrenia, a sociopathic disorder, or chronic adjustment disorders. Other supportive plans must be made for these patients (to be discussed later). What is necessary is that we rank those conditions that lend themselves most readily to short-term amelioration.

Here are some questions to help make these decisions:

Which problem/complaint is most severe or poses suicidal risk?
Which impairments pose a threat to the well-being of others?
Which condition is most immediately dangerous?
Which condition is most debilitating for patient or family?
Which problem/complaint is now causing patient the most pain?
Which problem/complaint is causing the most pain to loved ones?
Which condition interferes most with self-care abilities?
Which condition impairs attention or concentration most?
Which conditions most interfere with ability to perform at work?
Which impairments interfere most with treatment follow thru?
Which impairments interfere most with patient's daily ability to
    handle family, financial, work and personal responsibilities?
Which impairment is most apt to respond favorably to medication?
Which problem/complaint most concerns case reviewer?
Which impairments am I adequately skilled/trained to treat?

Answers to these questions will help you quickly outline those impairments you have pinpointed in order of priority for intervention. A suicidal or homicidal risk obviously must be attacked before reports of anxiety attacks. Reports of child molestation must be dealt with before anger issues. Alcohol abuse must be handled before the therapist tackles secondary marital conflicts. And so on.

It is a good idea to let case managers know that you have carefully assessed and prioritized those conditions that can be adequately handled on a time-limited, focused basis. In doing so you will be telling them that you are part of the "team" and thinking in terms of early discharge success, not long-term psychotherapy.

8. *Determine a descriptive DSM diagnosis:* One question that every case reviewer will ask you is, "What is

the patient's diagnosis?" In order to justify the medical necessity of treatment, they expect the provider to give in verbal communications and in written documentation, the precise, unequivocal diagnostic data on the DSM-III-R (or DSM-IV) multiaxial system. The 5 axes of the multiaxial classifications are:

Axis I: Clinical syndromes and additional Codes & V Codes
Axis II: Personality disorders & developmental disorders
Axis III: Contributing medical/physical illnesses & conditions
Axis IV: Severity of psycho-socio-behavioral stressors
Axis V: Highest level of adaptive functioning in past year

The brief therapist formulates the DSM diagnosis in the same way other therapists do this, and so we will not spend time here going over something you already know full well. However, in the chapter dealing with designing an effective treatment plan, we will discuss these 5 axes from the point of view of giving the case managers what they want, what they need, and in the form they need it.

When two patients qualify for the same DSM diagnosis it simply means that they have very similar clinical presentations. It does not indicate that they have the same causal conditions, socio-cultural influences, symptom consequences, or motivational pressures. And the diagnosis tells you nothing about which treatment modality will work best with each patient. As a matter of fact, you may have 4 patients who are all accurately diagnosed "Major Depression, Recurrent, Moderate Stress". All four patients may receive entirely different brief therapy interventions, even though they share one diagnosis.

Therefore, determining the DSM diagnostic classification is primarily for purposes of justifying treatment necessity not for purposes of making treatment decisions. The Treatment Targeted Impairments Assessment schema presented later, will give you all the diagnostic data you need for making diagnosis-related intervention decisions..

For purposes of requesting and then justifying a given modality of service, the Axis IV classification/rating is most important. For example, if a provider believes that the patient requires short-term, in-patient hospitalization, a high level of stressor severity would be necessary (5 or 6). On the other hand, if weekly or bi-weekly brief therapy is indicated, a lower level severity rating would be chosen (3 or 4).

The DSM Axis IV Severity of Stressors Scale is best used for this rating. The zero to 6 scale for ranking stressors related to the patient's complaints looks like this:

Degree of Stress	Code	Examples of Stressors	
		Acute Events	Enduring Circumstance
	0	Inadequate information	Inadequate information
None	1	No acute events	No enduring stressors
Mild	2	Argument with wife	Daily fights with wife, debts
Moderate	3	Threat of layoff	Kid taking drugs, hates job
Severe	4	Received divorce papers	Fired from job, car accident
Extreme	5	Death of loved one	Unfaithful spouse, sexual abuse
Catastrophic	6	Suicide/homicide attempt	HIV/AIDS, cancer, rape, stalker

When determining the diagnosis, remember that the level of severity rating you select will be used by the case manager to approve or disapprove your treatment plan. If, for example, you show "Generalized Anxiety Disorder" on Axis I, Axis II None, Axis III None, Axis IV 1, and Axis V 85 (a very high level of functioning), there is good reason to question why this patient is even in your office. *For most patients in the early stages of treatment, their Axis IV rating will range between 3 and 5;* rarely a 6. An Axis IV rating of 1 or 2 may be more appropriate for a patient nearing the end of treatment (if we've done our job well, that is!). And again, we will have more to say about this in the chapter on effective treatment plans.

9.   *Plan for ancillary resources for impairments that are non-responsive to short-term therapy:*   With the limited constraints imposed on us and on our patients by the realities of Managed Care, we cannot treat, or offer to treat, all impairments diagnosed.   But we cannot ignore these conditions, or push them aside, leaving the patient on her/his own to "somehow" manage them.   That would clearly be unethical, in our opinion.

Here are some thoughts to help you assist the patient in obtaining help for conditions or problems outside your time-constrained   interventions.   Mobilizing   outside resources helps form a total treatment plan:

What impairments indicate the need for medication evaluation?
Which conditions indicate possible psychiatric hospitalization?
Which complaints indicate the need for medical hospitalization?
Which conditions indicate the need for detoxification?
Which condition indicates the need for legal intervention?
Which impairment requires social service intervention?
Which impairment indicates the need for spiritual help?
Which condition indicates the need for educational help?
Which impairment suggests the need for vocational help?
Which condition is outside the purview of my own clinical
     expertise and requires intervention by another therapist?

(in each item identified, what are specific resources available)

What resources are available under the Managed Care plan?
What resources from patient's employer? (with his/her consent)
What resources are available from local agencies/organizations?
What resources are available from county agencies?
What help is available from state facilities?
What help is available from private professionals?
Which well-known colleagues could consult or treat patient?
What family resources can assist the patient?
Which friends can assist the patient?
What hotlines or helplines can patient call if in crisis?
What resources are available from free support groups?

The last item on this list is one you should pay close attention to.   In many instances you can find free support groups within the community to come to the aid of the patient. Case reviewers respect any clinician who helps the patient depend more on outside resources than on therapy or the therapist alone. And in each of the above resources, the therapist needs to care enough about the welfare of the patient to get actively involved in making specific, direct referrals; even if this is above and beyond the "letter of the Managed Care law." There is still plenty of truth in that old truism,

"It is in giving that we receive."

10. Get the patient to agree and commit to impairments to be eliminated or changed: Selection of the specific targets for brief therapy helps both patient and therapist stay goal-focused. With time restraints in mind, each session can bear down on solution, rather than drifting or rambling into other areas of concern. These areas may be interesting to both therapist and patient, but may represent needless excursions into issues that dilute outcome-based treatment.

Although this is a logical step, we have found that getting the patient's agreement as to which problem, complaint, or impairment will be dealt with in sessions can arouse some resistance. This is particularly true for patients who have had therapy in the past and were fairly free to "move at their own pace" or explore dynamic issues related to their past over an indefinite period of time. With patients who have also experienced excessive control at the hands of others in their lives, a "controlled" method of intervention stirs uneasiness, if not fear and rebellion.

How to handle this kind of resistance? We have found it best to reassure the patient that:

1. Their concerns and needs are understandable and important.
2. The things accomplished in prior therapy can be built upon.
3. Within the time restrictions of their present plan, they can relieve stress and become stronger in specific areas.
4. This will very likely transfer to and produce strength.

confidence, feelings of security and/or competence in other areas.

5. As treatment progresses and goals are reached, we can discuss how other aspects of their lives are being changed.

6. It is also fortunate that they have insurance coverage that allows us to work on their most pressing issues — while many people today have even more limited coverage, or no coverage at all.

Most patient resistances to time-limited, focused therapy are effectively neutralized using this approach, or something like it. Once overcome, the patient and therapist can then focus their energies throughout the brief counseling process toward achieving treatment goals. Once there is agreement and commitment, therapist and patient become partners with the case manager seeking solutions.

11. Define precipitating events or "triggers": The patient is helped to identify the situations, circumstances, and people who are integral parts of causing or maintaining the problem behavior or impairment. Using a "backward chaining" or "rewind" approach, the patient is assisted to trace the ultimate pain or problem, step by step, link by link, backwards to identify events and people who trigger the *thought processes, the feelings, the choices, and the resultant consequences of the problem impairment.*

Emphasis on *thought chains* as opposed to *feelings,* per se, gives the therapist and patient observable, hands-on material by which to structure new reactions — first in the patient's thought life, and then in her/his behavioral responses.

12. State a working hypothesis and DSM-III-R (or IV) diagnosis: At this point in the process, you should have sufficient information about the patient's past history, behavioral excesses, deficits and assets, verbal and cognitive styles, triggers, systems and self-control factors, and also the patient's behavior in the sessions to form a clear statement about what you think defines the real problem(s). Once you are able to formulate your clinical hypothesis, then translate this into "English" and inform the patient of your conclusions (or educated speculations).

Here are ten rules of the road or tested tips to help the patient gain a therapeutic understanding of the problem (to perceive the problem as "fragrance" and not "odor":

1. Use language familiar and easily understandable to the patient — Avoid all psychological jargon or "psychobabble."
2. Try to emphasize patient's strengths and assets along side descriptions of problematical issues.
3. Help the patient reframe or redefine problem areas in terms of accomplished solutions, e.g., "*when* it's no longer happening, *what will* you do?"
4. Help patient clearly link past influences, relationship triggers and consequences with cognitive responses and choices.
5. Help patient describe complaints in terms of unmet *needs* rather than failures, disasters or catastrophies.
6. Discuss goals of treatment rather than labeling patient's condition with a clinical diagnosis.
7. Link solution, need-meeting hypotheses to specific treatment plans and procedures to be considered.
8. Use tentative words, like "probably,""possible,""it may be that," and other non-dogmatic words to allay patient resistance, and to leave room for diagnostic revision as you go along.
9. Check to see if patient shows any confusion over what you have shared, and clear up misunderstandings or doubts.
10. Help patient see you as entirely allied to their healing and solution, and not an extension or "agent" of Managed Care.

Apprising the patient of your clinical hypotheses is an integral part of both the diagnostic and the treatment process. It can also help you get a firm fix on factors maintaining the problem behavior, and help you relate the patient's needs more accurately to the case manager.

Formulation of the DSM diagnostic criteria is then done as you would normally perform it.

13. Determine brief treatment modalities appropriate for each prioritized impairment: Space does not permit a catalog of treatment techniques and methods available to the brief therapist. Suffice it to say that those chosen for each designated impairment should meet the following conditions. The modality should be:

- Appropriate to the identified condition or problem
- Ethical and within approved professional standards of practice
- Tailored to the physical, emotional, socio-cultural patient needs
- Within the patient's intellectual and motivational limitations
- Acceptable to patient's spiritual or personal values orientation
- Effective if utilized within a short-term intervention only
- Predictive of symptom reduction or removal and not just insight
- Targeted toward direct problem solution under patient's control
- Aimed at observable, measurable objectives
- Acceptable to the patient and/or her/his loved ones
- Effectively enhanced by outside "homework," if possible
- Effectively enhanced by outside support resources, if possible
- Within the expertise of the therapist
- Apt to receive approval by the case manager

We'll say more later about how to link treatment methodologies to Treatment Targeted Impairments in your documentation and telephone communication with case managers.

14. Help the patient formulate an "outcome vision": Patient expectation of change is closely related to the ultimate results in treatment. If the patient can be encouraged to describe the best possible scenario — i.e., what will life be like when the complaint is resolved — the probability significantly increases for successful attainment of therapeutic goals.

The patient needs to be "primed" in order to build her or his confidence in their own ability to use memories, imagination or fantasy as a tool in therapy. Here are three steps that we have adapted and modified from Milton Erickson's and Steve de Shazer's "crystal ball method":

(a)   Ask the patient to try to recall pleasant memories from their *distant past.* Some event or relationship in which they felt completely good about themself, competent, and something in which others accepted and approved them. Get them to describe this as vividly as possible. "How many rooms were in your house?...Can you describe them?...What did she look like?...Can you picture how you looked?"   This can be done in the course and context of gathering past history data.

(b)   The patient is asked to describe events in the *recent past* that were pleasant, that were in some way surprising or unexpected, and that resulted in the patient receiving positive responses from others. Can the patient recall any experience in which there was some measure of victory or success over the problem or complaint, no matter how small? Who, what, where, when, how, what surroundings can he/she recall? Sights? Sounds? Smells? Sensations? Movements? Feelings? Thoughts? Responses?

(c)   What people in the patient's life are able to handle the kind of problems and complaints that trouble the patient? What has the patient observed about how they effectively do this? Describe their attitudes? The things they say? Their relationships? What makes them so successful? How does the patient feel about them?

After this creative preparation, the patient is guided to attempt a "vision for outcome". To motivate the patient toward a therapeutic vision for success, we use a series of solution-focused questions.   Note carefully the use of phrases like *"what will you do when..."* , *"when the problem is over, what..."*, *"what do you suppose they will do when.."*, *"when you change, how do you suppose you will..."* — instead of the doubt-inducing, *"if* you change, how *could* you..."*, etc. Such phrasing is crucial to inspire and motivate the patient to attempt change.   Note, too, that these questions are themselves therapeutic interventions, and tend to quickly help establish a climate for goal setting.

The questions we find most useful include:

Suppose after we talk, your problem magically disappears, as if some miracle occurred; how would you know it was gone?
When the problem is gone, what will your life be like?
When the problem is gone, what will you be doing instead?
How will your family know when the problem is gone?
How do you suppose others who know you will recognize that it is gone? What do you think they will say? Do? Think?
What will you do when you don't react like you did before?
In what ways will your life be different when you can do this?
How do you think your new skills will change your closest relationships? Your responses to them and theirs to you?
When you're able to do that, how will your thoughts be different? How do you suppose your feelings be different?
How will your future change when you're in control of this?
When you've made this change, how will you relate differently to the things that happened to you in your past?
Describe what you think your self-image will be like when you make these changes?
How will your self-control be changed after successful therapy?
Imagine people's reactions to you when you overcome the difficulties we've been talking about: how will people treat you?
How do you suppose their changes toward you will affect your responses and your relationships with them?
Try to imagine how you will describe the same problems you have now when you're able to manage it on your own easily?

As the patient uses the visioning or "crystal ball" method for predicting outcome and the changes to his/her life, in effect they are owning and committing to the treatment process on a level far deeper than merely intellectual assent. We've found it helpful to have the patient actually write out this kind of vision in response to a list of the kind of questions just mentioned. The motivational force of *seeking the pleasure "seen" in the vision is a potent stimulus for patient commitment to work in therapy, both in and outside of treatment.*

15. Make a verbal (and/or written) contract with patient: The patient is then asked to commit, with the therapist, to 5 things:

(1)   the measurable goals of treatment (with criteria)
(2)   the frequency of appointments
(3)   the number of sessions
(4)   the necessity of homework/home-therapy assignments
(5)   the termination date

It's not necessary to write this agreement down, but it helps some therapists stay on target and resist the temptation to return to their old habits of dynamic, unfocused psychotherapy. A contract specifying target behavioral changes, time limits, number of sessions, and discharge date pushes and pulls therapist and patient toward one thing — the one thing the patient has come for, the one thing the case manager has referred him/her for — that one thing is *change.*

Many therapists find this step a bit threatening. But when you commit to each of these objectives early-on in the treatment process, you will find yourself holding fast to outcome objectives, the patient will work harder both in and outside of sessions, and satisfactory discharge will occur in more and more cases. And, obviously, case managers will smile on your work; as new referrals find their way to your practice.

16. Distinguish "the problem" from "the patient": One important distinctive characteristic of the brief therapist is how the problem is defined. In long-term therapy the therapist typically sees the patient *having* the problem. In successful brief therapy, however, the therapist and the patient form an alliance and join together to find solutions to a common problem. The focus then shifts to the patient, not just the patient's problems. Most patients feel very much alone in their frustrated efforts to find solutions. In brief therapy they find someone entering into their world to help them — someone armed with skills and attitudes and strategies to bring about change they could not achieve on their own.

Communicating to the patient that it is "us against it" instead of "me against the problem in you" helps reduce resistance and build rapid patient cooperation in the treatment process.

17. Enable the patient to measure complaint intensity using the Scaling Method: Most patients typically feel overwhelmed or helpless to solve the problem which brings them to therapy. They often feel even more at a loss to understand it. If, early-on in treatment, the therapist gives the patient a conceptual framework by which to measure the complaint, the patient is equipped with more than a rating device. A measuring tool can help the patient (1) realize a sense of security in understanding the problem, (2) experience a sense of power in "getting a handle" on the problem, and (3) develop the ability to control the intensity of the problem.

A 10-point subjective rating scale is used. The patient is asked to think about the complaint and then assign a specific numerical rating to it. For example, the patient is instructed, "Let's give some specific numbers to the problem you're having. Let's say that at it's most unbearable point it's a 1; and at 10 the problem is completely non-existent, that you're handling things great, and have no need for therapy.. Where would you rate yourself *right now?*" It is surprising how many patients quickly come up with a specific number, and how few patients struggle to determine an exact rating.

In addition to asking the patient to rate where they are on a scale of 1-to-10 at the time of intake, we can ask them to rate "where do you think you will be on the scale when you no longer need therapy?" For example, at intake the patient typically says, "I'm at a 3 now," and when asked their estimated discharge rating, they usually report, "about a 7 or 8." Notice we have them thinking early on in their treatment about fulfilled goals, successful outcome, and satisfactory discharge.

When the patient predicts a successful-outcome rating, we can then ask, "What do you suppose you will be doing (thinking, feeling, reacting) when you reach 7?" The patient then enters into projective exploration of solution-oriented behavior.

We can also use the scaling method to help move the patient along, step by step, from one level of wellness to another. The patient who reports, "I'm at a 4 today" after her third session, can be asked, "what do you suppose you will be doing this week to get from 4 to 5?" (Notice that we set very *small* steps, from 4 to 5, and not from 4 to 9, to help the patient postulate realistic behaviors they can achieve).

The 10-point scale can also be used to help the patient empathically predict the attitudes and behavior of those who may be instrumental in their problem or complaint. For example, a wife whose husband refused to come for counseling was asked, "Let's suppose John were sitting right here with you, and suppose I were to ask him to rate on the 10-point scale just how interested he is in becoming the kind of husband you need him to be — what do you suppose he would say? or suppose I asked him how determined he is to make this marriage work? What do you think he would answer?" Once we get her to assess his rating, we can then move to the interim solution question, "OK, if he's at a 3 now, what do you think would be going on in your relationship to move him from 3 to a 4 — how would you know he was at a 4?"

These questions enable the patient to predict positive outcome, and to get a visual picture of the solution process. It's sometimes useful to actually display in graphic form the 10-point rating scale, asking the patient to circle or check the appropriate number coinciding with his or her assessment of the complaint. For example:

On a scale of 1 to 10, please rate the seriousness of the problem right now:

1	2	3	4	5	6	7	8	9	10

Unbearable,
Unable to cope,
Desperate for help

No problems,
Handling things great,
No need for help

This is a wonderfully simple and exciting way to get patients to participate in exploring and setting interim goals, and then committing to them. We use this device on our intake questionnaire for new clients to help set expectations for measuring and aiming at solutions in treatment. More will be said about this in the chapter on outcome research.

18. Aim for small changes only: When therapist and patient attempt to bring about major changes in the patient's life in time-limited therapy, they risk failure. Most brief therapists believe that the patient's world is a "system" and that any change, no matter how small, will bring about changes in the rest of that system. With a positive therapeutic alliance built, impairments identified, and a defined course of therapy agreed to, the stage is set for giving the patient a series of success experiences all leading toward the final goal of treatment. In the behavioral "fading" mode of successive approximations, the patient is helped to plan and carry out a series of thoughts and actions that bring about change. Each success experience leads to increased confidence in the therapist and in herself or himself to take the next little step.

19. Give the patient simple, precise, novel, goal-targeted homework: Giving therapeutic, goal-directed assignments to be carried out outside the consultation room is one of the hallmarks of effective short-term therapy. One case manager told us recently (and this is verbatim):

"One of the ways I evaluate our providers is to ask for details about homework used with the patient to reach treatment goals. I find that many therapists get very vague and go into a fogging mode with me. When I hear this, I know right away that no homework is being used, and, in turn, that this provider probably doesn't really understand what brief therapy is all about, or what managed care requires."

Right from the "horse's" mouth! With that perception of this clinician, how many new clients do you think the case manager will refer to him in the coming weeks? This therapist may be an outstanding practitioner, well known and highly respected among his colleagues. But without a grasp of the mechanics of brief therapy, that reputation will have little impact on those blank places in his appointment book and empty waiting room!

Case reviewers know when a clinician talks a good game, and they know when a therapist actually plays the "game" according to the rules. If you hope to succeed at providing the kind of brief therapy that wins case managers and influences referrals, homework is a non-optional *must.*

Not only does homework speed results, but it has other important advantages. Outside assignments linked to what goes on in the sessions causes the patient to depend less on the therapy or therapist, and more on him/herself. Homework builds confidence in self-discovery. Disciplined efforts to resolve the problems/complaints occur with increasing frequency. And others in the patient's life observe her/him making changes in attitude and response to the problem; which in turn, impacts those relationships.

Homework should be: goal focused, directly or indirectly linked to session content, clearly explained to the patient in terms of how it relates to symptoms, and at every step tied to outcome objectives. Assignments should be used as springboards by which to launch the upcoming session, and to give it momentum. Homework assignments should be *written down by the patient in 1, 2, 3, simple, easy-to-accomplish steps.*

Some typical examples of brief therapy homework that have been used with Managed Care patients include:

• A wife who flew into rages when her husband refused to talk out problems was assigned letter-writing to release her bottled-up frustrations. • A man with a checking obsession was instructed to check for 8 hours straight without stopping and to observe his thoughts and emotions during the procedure. • An alcoholic man promised his wife he would quit drinking and told *her* to pour all liquor down the drain; which she happily did. The therapist sent the couple to the liquor store *together* to buy a brand new bottle of vodka, take it home, and while she looked on, *he* was to pour it down the toilet. • A woman caught in the web of an affair which caused her deep depression, was told to make a list of all the damaging consequences to her, the marriage, and the future of her children, and to read that list when she was tempted to call her lover. • A pornography addict, filled with guilt and causing his wife pain and grief over their non-existent sex life, was given the task of *taking his wife to the porno shops, and movies, and clubs he attended secretly alone,* and to review the assignment openly with the wife and therapist in the next session.

Patients may be instructed to keep logs, journals, charts, behavioral observations, thought/feeling tracking records, fill out questionnaires, workbooks, write letters, or take detailed notes on reading assignments. We have found that patients get far more out of outside reading if (1) they must take careful notes on what they read, (2) relate what they read to their current difficulties, (3) must bring this written matter into the next session(s) and openly share it with the therapist. For example, an alcoholic isn't asked how his meetings are going, but may be asked, "can you share with me what you wrote down for the first 3 steps you agreed to do for your outside home therapy?" *(We believe that when the 12 Steps are worked within the therapy context, that open sharing is therapeutic because it is actively humbling and creates accountability, thus preventing denial and relapse).*

The array of ideas is endless. The important feature of each of the above effective interventions is that some active change was introduced into the patient's system that resulted in positive impact in the patient's problem. And note that many homework assignments are *novel, surprising* or *unexpected.* This cuts through the control tactics and sabotage-moves brought in by many patients — especially the "trained" or therapy-wise patients. The patient is encouraged to "step out of character," to take small risks, to try something a little "off-the-wall." This kind of surprise-homework disrupts the patient's rigid, unhealthy control tactics and can begin to break the power of the underlying attitude the patient holds toward the symptom or impairment. Where logic or reason has failed time and time again, novel homework can succeed.

Surprise or novel homework can also help motivate patients to do prescribed homework where follow-thru is unlikely. The patient is told to "surprise yourself and see what happens," when they doubt whether they can (or will) do the homework recommended. This seems to relieve the performance anxiety/resistance, and often moves the patient to compliance. For example, a 42-year-old woman was experiencing severe depression and agitation due to her husband's ongoing adulterous affair. The husband wanted to remain in the marriage, but was "unable" to stop seeing the other woman. The homework we prescribed was not popular: We told her that to break the bond of the other woman with her husband, and to reposition herself as a real factor to be dealt with (and not just a "myth"), she must confront the other woman.

Obviously, she was frozen with fear of doing this and reported an inability to do the homework. We responded with the following:

"That's perfectly understandable. Many women in your position feel exactly the same way—this takes real courage. But they find that unless this step is taken, no change happens and the adultery goes on and on. So, try this: Don't try to force yourself to do it. Just surprise yourself. Many women find that when they take the pressure off, "somehow" the right opportunity presents itself, and, guess what? They confront the other woman and set some realistic boundaries. So don't put pressure on yourself to *make it happen,* just *let it happen.* Watch what happens and surprise yourself."

The next session, no change. But two sessions later found this precious lady beaming with victory. She had "impulsively" found herself driving down the street where the other woman lived, pulled into her driveway, and went right up to the door. Three hours later the girlfriend no longer saw our patient as a myth, but someone to be reckoned with. We are happy to report that that marriage is still together. The affair is long over, and our patient's self-esteem continues to grow. The element of surprise made it possible for her to "somehow" take a risk that she couldn't have taken had she tried to force herself to do so.

What about those *excuses du jour?* No matter how creative you become in prescribing homework, you will hear this day in, day out, "Oh, I forgot my journal," "What a week I had!—I just didn't have a minute to do my logging," "I've got to be honest; I just started my homework out there in the waiting room." Ten thousand excuses, not one good reason, and no results. We believe that if the therapist ignores or permits the non-performance of therapeutic homework, he or she contributes to the patient's dilemma. The patient wants to resolve the problems, and at the same time they do not. If we do not insist on, or assist the patient in following through with home therapy, we reinforce and strengthen the pathological, problematical side.

What can you do when the patient CHOOSES NOT TO DO homework? (Note the emphasis, please, on *chooses!)* No matter how creatively ingenious the excuse may be, it is best to consider it for what it is — a choice to continue giving the problem power. We call it "feeding the monster." Why feed it? Why not starve it out with action? Here are

10 things that work well to motivate the patient to choose to follow through with assignments:

1. Review carefully and openly unkept assignments before doing any other work in the next session.
2. Disarm and neutralize alibis and excuses. Examine precisely all decisions that the patient made during the interval between sessions to avoid follow-thru (and label them *decisions, choices")*.
3. Spend some time in the session doing homework that was undone.
4. Encourage patient to observe, day by day, her/his skillful efforts to avoid, resist, and deceive self with reasons to fail at homework. Make them expert observers of self-sabotage.
5. Encourage patient to "sabotage" the home-therapy and report back on what they learned about their "ability to choose *not* to do what could change the patterns or reduce symptoms."
6. Make future sessions contingent on homework completion.
7. With the patient's consent, encourage patient's significant others to get involved (but avoid codependent enabling or shifts of responsibility).
8. As a last resort, assign patient to a "therapeutic vacation" (or as it's called in industry, a "Decision Making Leave") — they return when their level of motivation and commitment to "work" at homework is no longer dormant.
9. Evaluate the appropriate "fit" between the homework task assigned and the patient's ability to perform it; i. e., "Is the unmet assignment related to patient's *"inability to perform it"* or *"unwillingness to comply?"* *"Could we facilitate the success of homework by breaking assignments down into smaller, easily performable pieces?"*
10. Evaluate your initial rational and motivational explanation of the homework tasks; e.g., "Did I make the task(s) clear, simple, and linked to some payoff/benefit for the patient?; or, did the patient perceive it as 'busy work'?"

You will note here a decided absence of any discussion of the patient's *feelings* about the rightness or wrongness of homework. You are correct. Experience in brief therapy has taught us that exploration of feelings on this issue (1) sidetracks both therapist and patient from the key issue, which is *choice,* and (2) lures both into endless, long-drawn-out journeys into the realm of dynamic long-term therapy (which is a mine field in the land of Managed Care!). So, it's safer to stick to the business of *getting the patient to accept responsibility* for the home assignment they agreed to do.

And be sure to inform case managers about your motivational moves to get homework done. Give them details about your home therapy interventions, steps you take to get that work done, and do so in case documentation, and over the phone or on voice mail. They will appreciate your commitment to action-therapy to get results on the patient's behalf.

20. *Change the pattern of the impairments/complaints:* Solution-based brief therapy aims at direct intervention into the performance and the context of the presenting complaint or impairment of the patient. The most effective way to do this is to initiate the patient's making some *very small and seemingly insignificant change in thinking, talking, or acting out the problem.* The idea is to alter the performance of the problematic behavior in some way, thereby altering the context, thus changing the patient's perception and definition of the complaint itself. Here are some examples of *prescribed pattern-altering interventions:*

(a) *Change the timing of the complaint:* Example — A patient with severe anxiety attacks was instructed to "schedule" time for these attacks every evening between 7:30 and 8:00 p.m.; to bring them on, increase their intensity, decrease their intensity, and chart out her observations.

(b) *Change the rate or frequency of the complaint:* Example — A client who had an ongoing dread of earthquakes was told to "schedule" time every other day to simulate "the big one" while lying in bed, to imagine the sounds and sensations of the event, and to shake himself to simulate the onset and termination of the event while restructuring his thoughts to maintain self-control.

(c) *Change the duration of the complaint:* Example— A married couple agreed to use a timer to limit their "fights" to 5-minute intervals. They were to "fight as usual" and then write an evaluation of what occurred, focusing on how they personally contributed to the problem. Fights that typically lasted hours were reduced to 5-minute "mini-fights."

(d) *Change the location of the complaint:* Example— A chronic cigarette smoker was advised to keep her cigarettes in the trunk of her car, her matches in a hat box in the top of her closet, and to smoke only on the side of the house near the trash cans.

(e) *Change the sequence of the complaint "chain":* (the complaint chain is the series of stimulus-response events leading to the ultimate performance of the problem). Example — A chronic gambler agreed to write down on a 3x5 card all thoughts and feelings about placing bets or going to the track. He further contracted with his wife to call her (or leave messages on their answering machine) describing all gambling-related thoughts. This interrupted the "secret" pattern that led to relapse.

(f) *Add at least one new or novel behavior to the complaint chain:* Example — A high-level executive who was referred by management through his EAP manager was on the verge of losing his job due to conflicts with colleagues on the job. He was instructed to (1) paraphrase in his own words, paragraph-by-paragraph, Dale Carnegie's book, *How To Win Friends & Influence People;* (2) when he was aware of a tension level over 3 (on a 10 point scale) he would find a reason to excuse himself for a few moments; (3) he would then privately read his summaries of Carnegie's people-winning techniques, choose one, then (4) return to the tension-producing relationship and practice this technique; and finally to (5) rate his success in "winning" (instead of alienating) this person.

(g)   *Break down the complaint chain into small, easily-manageable steps:*   Example — In a domestic violence case, the batterer contracted to monitor the "distant early warning" cues, to tell himself or read to himself (on a 3x5 card) the statement, "Am I going to allow my father to live his life thru me, to abuse my wife like he did my mother?", then to make a conscious decision to be like him or to unhook and "live my own life!" This intervention disrupted the automatic pattern of living out the old childhood script, and triggered a healthy rebellion — refusing to be like his father by resisting spousal abuse.

(h)   *Link the performance of the complaint to some aversive, burdensome, or painful behavior:*   Example — A man with severe insomnia was advised to get out of bed and clean his oven or polish the silver or scrub the shower or clean the toilets rather then staying in bed, tossing and turning, tormenting himself trying to fall asleep.

(i)   *Shift focus from a "doom and gloom" negative expectancy to a "catch 'em doing something right" positive response pattern:*   Example — Parents (who were well-read in parenting self-help literature) reported that their 8-year old son "always gets into trouble and causes problems because he craves negative attention because he has poor self-esteem." The perfectionistic, critical couple were instructed to "for one week, observe anything — no matter how small — that Timmy is doing right or good, and write it down on an index card, not saying anything to Timmy." This was reviewed on the following session. They were then instructed the following week to "just pretend you don't notice his negative behavior, but just for a few weeks gently point out to Timmy anything you see him doing right or good."

21. Continue emphasizing the termination date throughout treatment process: Some brief therapists make it a habit to mention the agreed-upon termination date at every session: "Now, we have 7 sessions remaining, so let's plan carefully the homework you'll need to do, and how we will structure your next session, so we are sure to stay on target; is that acceptable to you?" We believe, on the other hand, that this need not be a rigid rule. We typically mention the number of sessions during the first 3 sessions (typically at the end of each session in order to motivate for homework), and at each of the last 3 sessions.

Informing or reminding the patient that "we have so many sessions left to get the job done" has several important advantages for the brief therapist:

1. The patient's motivational level to "work" is increased, both in session and in homework/home therapy.
2. Both patient and therapist begin and remain goal-focused.
3. Both patient and therapist maintain an expectation of time restraints that consciously and subconsciously pull them toward resolving problems/complaints within that time.
4. It causes the therapist to select treatment strategies and techniques that produce results within a brief context.
5. It assists the patient to work through separation anxiety on an ongoing basis, not flooding in at the end of treatment.
6. It encourages the therapist to become more proactive in the mobilizing of outside resources for after care, helping the patient to wean herself or himself from dependence on therapy and move toward self-sufficiency.
7. It influences the therapist's written and telephone communications with case managers, and in turn, case managers' favorable perceptions of the therapist.

While discussing this issue with a colleague, she expressed an important concern: "Wouldn't the mentioning of the termination date or how many sessions remain stir up patient anxieties, and possibly create a recurrence of symptoms that have been showing improvement?" Great question, and the kind we hear at seminars and workshops.

We have observed over more than two decades of clinical practice that separation anxiety and symptom recurrence are far less common if a brief therapy modality is faithfully followed. These problems are minimized if both end date and number of sessions are addressed during the first 3 sessions, and are clearly linked to goal setting and how goals will be measured. It's much like the student who knows, and is informed repeatedly, that the final exam is on Friday, May 20th, at 8 a.m. Interesting, isn't it, how the student finds herself or himself prepared and ready on that Friday morning? God knows we all had enough of these kind of experiences!

We have also observed that repeated focus on end date and/or total sessions allowed helps motivate the patient to become actively involved much sooner in outside support resources. Such shared support helps encourage both therapist and patient to rely on growth experiences beyond the consultation room, from the very outset of treatment.

Discussions with our more analytical colleagues indicate that they experience more intense levels of separation anxiety, negative transference, and symptom return. Another good reason to embrace the short-term, brief therapy orientation, yes?

22. Assess all therapeutic goals accomplished: The best measure of treatment goal outcome is the report from the expert herself or himself — *the patient.* The starting point for most counseling and psychotherapy is the complaint or presenting problem reported to the therapist by the patient. In most long-term therapy, however, the therapy process soon departs from that focus and a pursuit of related (and often unrelated) issues is undertaken. In brief therapy — the kind Managed Care reviewers prefer — therapy begins, *continues, and ends* with the patient's complaints and problems.

Treatment success, then, or lack of it, is best judged by the same person or persons who came in evaluating the problem. They should go as they came — the expert on how the impairment affects their life. At intake we take their word about the problem as the definitive statement about its nature. Why not accept their word for it as treatment progresses and ends, and as time passes following discharge?

We have found that there are essentially 3 reliable ways to measure brief therapy outcome from the patient's reports: (1) The patient's definition/redefinition of the problem; (2) The patient's behavioral description of the problem; and (3) The patient's attempted solutions.

In a later chapter we will discuss a system for performing reliable outcome research using these categories. In that chapter we will present specific measures that you can use to pre- and post-test patients at the time of intake, at termination, and months after discharge to assess treatment success.

23.   *Structure and supervise continuing outside support resources:*   Here's an area of treatment terribly neglected by traditional therapy. Think about your own graduate school training. How many courses, text books, or professors emphasized the use of support groups, recovery groups, bibliotherapy, the use of tapes and videos as treatment tools, workshops, seminars, or for that matter *any* interventions outside the purview of counseling *per se?*

In the world of Managed Care and in the brief therapy arena, we must focus from the very first session on discharge planning. This means that our treatment plan must (1) aim at problem behavior reduction or control, and

(2) assist the patient in arranging an environment conducive to maintaining maximum adjustment and functioning after discharge, to prevent relapse. This is especially important because the patient in most cases returns to the same environment that, in the past, has reinforced and been linked to the problem.

The support groups listed on the Resource Card discussed in a previous chapter of this book provide a good listing of excellent outside resources. If the patient can be persuaded to become active in appropriate groups of this kind, using therapy sessions as both motivator and source of accountability, by discharge the patient should have established confidence in them and should be deriving some benefit. It is unwise, in our opinion, to wait until the last few sessions to recommend outside help. Attrition rate is much higher as motivation is weaker. Start early, asking the case manager to assist in reinforcing these recommendations.

Patients also appreciate contacts from their therapist after treatment has been terminated. A letter or phone call to check on the patient's welfare, progress, and benefits derived from support resources — these have strong motivating value. We recommend such communications take place 2, 6, 8 weeks, and perhaps every few months after discharge. It is important, of course, to exercise good discretion, carefully guarding against any dual relationships for at least 2 years after treatment. Letters or calls should reflect the same professionalism that characterized your work during treatment. *(NOTE: It is not our style, nor our comfort zone, to get so clinically formal; but in the past few years several therapists have lost their licenses for dual relationships with patients. Therefore, caution seems advisable).*

24. Terminate and discharge on the agreed date: No need to expand on this. If the patient obviously shows worsening of the problem behavior, arrange for an extension with the case manager. But when you do, be prepared to start from scratch. Indicate why goals were not reached? What methods did not work, and why? What new strategies will be attempted, and how will progress be assessed? The brief therapist monitors effectiveness of treatment at each session and does not wait until the end date or last session to draw conclusions. If patient's problem or complaint does not seem to be responding to treatment, *report this early on to the case manager.* If you wait until extension is requested, you will be shooting yourself in the foot. It's quite difficult to greet any new patient referrals in your waiting room that way!

Do all you can to discharge the patient by the agreed upon termination date, with an outside recovery or support program in full swing. Inform the case manager *in advance* of your intention to discharge patient on the expected date, then inform them again when you do it. Remember, each time you communicate with the case manager about a successful patient discharge, and a happy patient, you sharpen the image of your practice value in her/his mind.

What you've just reviewed here is a proven framework for the kind of solution-focused brief therapy that Managed Care reviewers appreciate. It gets results. Goals are set and reached within a time-limited context. Treatment is tightly focused on impairments and problems that can be measured as they change. And the patient is progressively helped to become more self-sufficient and less therapy-reliant. In all of this the patient gets what he or she came seeking in the first place. The case manager gets the outcome desired when they made the decision to refer the patient to you. And what do you get besides the satisfaction of seeing the patient's life changed for the better? You get more opportunities to practice brief therapy, because you get more referrals. Many therapists "talk about" brief therapy, telling case reviewers what they want to hear. And there are those who know how to "do" brief therapy, using procedures like those outlined here. "Talk" doesn't impress a case manager. But results do.

In the final analysis, brief therapy is not just *"less of the same."* It is much more than just time-constrained therapy, or limited-sessions treatment. Brief therapy, as we define and practice it, is an effective method for restoring the joys and pleasures of life to a greater number of suffering human beings. Human beings who, incidentally, just happen to find themselves under the "care" and "management" of the healthcare system of the future. And so, if we want to "manage" to "care" for more and more of these people, we must become skillful at providing high quality, solution-focused, brief therapy.

Chapter Six

A System for Assessing "Treatment Targeted Impairments" Within a Brief Therapy, Managed-Care-Friendly Context

Personal Notes

Chapter Six

A System for Assessing "Treatment Targeted Impairments" Within a Brief Therapy, Managed-Care-Friendly Context

What follows is a proposed framework which we believe will make brief therapy more understandable and successful outcome more attainable for most clinicians, regardless of their orientation or clinical comfort zone. Within a Managed Care context, we have found this approach highly effective for rapidly pinpointing five important spheres: (1) areas in which treatment interventions are needed (and not needed), (2) specific targets of the interventions, (3) measurable goals of each intervention, (4) appropriate treatment methods to be utilized, and (5) precise scales for measuring outcome.

Using a Managed Care framework, we have adapted and expanded our Treatment Targeted Impairment Assessment (TTIA) from the classification model proposed by Kanfer and Saslow's "Behavioral Diagnosis" in C.M. Franks, *Behavior Therapy: Appraisal and Status,* McGraw-Hill. You may wish to experiment with this approach, expanding or condensing it to fit your own needs and style. The beauty of this system is that it helps quickly pinpoint problem, treatment, and outcome decisions. The 10 key areas of the TTIA system are summarized here, followed by a step-by-step explanation of each assessment:

I.	BEDA ASSESSMENT OF PROBLEMS/COMPLAINTS.
II.	CLASSIFICATION OF PROBLEM/COMPLAINT.
III.	ASSESSMENT OF SUBSTANCE ABUSE.
IV.	ASSESSMENT OF PATIENT'S SELF-CONTROL.
V.	ASSESSMENT OF SYSTEMS AND SOCIAL RELATIONSHIPS.
VI.	VERBAL/COGNITIVE STYLE ASSESSMENT.
VII.	BIOLOGICAL/PHYSICAL ASSESSMENT.
VIII.	MOTIVATIONAL ASSESSMENT.
IX.	SUICIDAL/HOMICIDAL RISK ASSESSMENT.
X.	MOLESTATION/ABUSE ASSESSMENT.

I. BEDA ASSESSMENT OF PROBLEMS/COMPLAINTS *(BEHAVIORAL EXCESSES/DEFICITS/ASSETS)*

Using this system we examine all outward behaviors and verbal reports of internal cognitive processes from two perspectives: ***excesses or deficits.*** For example, "excessive assaultive behavior toward wife," or "deficient concentration on the job." The vantage point of the patient's social system from which each element is described is very important in defining excesses and deficits. If the patient's wife is the source of the assessment measure, for example, we might say that he "demonstrates excessive assaultive acting out." If, on the other hand, the abusive husband is the source of the measure, we might say, "patient demonstrates a deficit in physical self-control and positive self-talk." The excesses/deficits approach gives us two ways to objectify and measure complaints and outcome.

Using observable excesses or deficits helps the clinician make the decision about selecting the best starting point for various treatment interventions. It also helps prioritize those interventions, and thereafter helps assess progress as therapy proceeds. Finally, we can know if we have reached therapy goals, and precisely communicate with case managers (who, in turn, can use this data to justify a satisfactory discharge of the patient). Excess-deficit measures also give us tangible measuring devices to perform outcome studies of our own success (or lack of success) in brief therapy. We'll say more about outcome studies later.

A. ***Behavioral Excess:*** A behavior or group of behaviors reported by the patient, or another informant, to be problematical, causing the patient pain or the loss of pleasure is considered an impairment *excess* if it is described as occurring with excessive (1) intensity, (2) frequency, (3) duration, or (4) violating socially acceptable boundaries.

Examples of these four behavioral excesses might include the following:

Excessive intensity — Combative or physical assaultive acting out
Excessive frequency — Compulsive drinking, drug use, gambling
Excessive duration — Prolonged excitement, daily worry or dread
Violates social boundaries — Child molestation, incest, sexual exhibitionism, arson, drunk driving, domestic violence

Those behaviors just listed are more obvious examples of presenting complaints that should be labeled as excesses. Some of the more subtle excesses might include: workaholism or social isolation. The workaholic fails to meet the needs of his/her family due to excessive intensity and duration of work behavior. The socially isolated housewife may justify neglecting the needs of her children and husband by all the housework requiring her time. In both cases the intensity, frequency and duration measures should be used.

B. **Behavioral Deficit:**   A behavior or group of behaviors is described to be a problem because it fails to occur (1) with adequate intensity, (2) with sufficient frequency, (3) in the appropriate form, or (4) under socially acceptable conditions.

Some examples might include the following:

Deficient intensity — Social withdrawal, reduced concentration.
Deficient frequency — Absenteeism, chronic fatigue, insomnia.
Deficient form — Crying in public, reduced eye contact.
Conflicts with social expectations — Verbally unresponsive, impotence, nudity in public, starving behavior, ungroomed.

Describing a patient's behavior in terms of the failure to occur sufficiently or appropriately gives the therapist a precise tool for planning treatment, and for later measuring treatment outcome. For example, if a depressed patient reports increasing social withdrawal due to a reported fear of social rejection, the therapist can undertake a brief course of assertive training. Patient reports of social involvement, and changes in cognitive self-talk and increased comfort levels would clearly indicate progress toward a successful therapy outcome.

C. *Behavioral & Social Assets:*   A review is made of the patient's arena of strengths and available resources that can be mobilized to support or even initiate a therapeutic program for the patient. Here are some assets in the patient's life to be considered as adjunct tools available to the therapist:

What are some of the patient's talents, skills or natural gifts?
What does the patient do well (or has done well in the past)?
What intellectual strengths does he/she have?
What personality or emotional qualities does she/he have?
What adequate or strong social behaviors are present?
Are there key spiritual resources in the patient's background?
Which significant others are important to the patient?
Who are patient's circle of supportive, close friends?
What financial resources can patient rely on?
What work activities have been rewarding to patient?
What recreational activities have been special to the patient?
Are there any creative activities that the patient enjoys(ed)?
What places has the patient enjoyed?
What events have been meaningful to patient?
What kind of music "lifts" the patient's spirits?
What kind of art appeals to the patient?
Are there any crafts or projects that patient has enjoyed?
What support groups is patient a part of now, or in the past?
What life-accomplishment(s) is patient most proud of?
What media or entertainment does patient enjoy most?
What makes the patient laugh?
What is (was) the patient most thankful for?

During the intake process it is just as important to assess these assets or strengths as it is to determine impairment excesses or deficits. Why? Because the brief therapist knows that to initiate new, healthy behaviors, or to decrease old, problematic behaviors, treatment will be more effective if it can incorporate people, events or behaviors in which the patient already shows competence and positive self-evaluation. There is a kind of transfer effect from the kind of items on the list just given and a linking of those assets with patient attempts at change. Case managers also appreciate (and are often surprised) when a clinician takes the time to focus on client strengths. They know that this kind of thinking promotes clear, goal-focused outcome planning (a refreshing change from the "pathological" mind set of many psychodynamic orientations).

II. CLASSIFICATION OF PROBLEM/COMPLAINT.

A.   As assessment of the patient continues, assign each problem or complaint behavior to either Behavioral Excess or Behavioral Deficit (as described above).

B.   Which persons or group encouraged or coerced the patient to come in for therapy?

C.   Which persons or group objects to the patient's behavior? Why?

D.   Which persons or group supports the problem behavior? How?

E.   What consequences does the problem behavior have for the patient?   For significant others?

F.   What are the possible consequences to the patient if the problem behavior were removed?   Consequences to significant others?

G.   Under what specific circumstances and conditions does the problem behavior occur (biological, time, place, social, relational, vocational, symbolic, etc.)?

H.   What payoffs, rewards or satisfactions (secondary gains) would occur if the problem or complaint were to continue?   What payoffs, rewards or satisfactions would the patient experience if, through therapy, the problem or complaint was removed or positively changed?   What positive or negative consequences would occur for significant others if, through therapy, the problem behavior were positively changed or removed?   How would positive change in patient behavior cause discomfort for significant others?   What would patient's life be like if therapy produced no change whatever?

I.   What new problem is most likely to occur if patient's therapy is successful and problems and complaints are changed or removed?

J.   Is the patient capable of providing sufficient information on her/his own to form a treatment plan, and to assess outcome later; or should significant others be enlisted in the process? Who? How should they be brought into the treatment process (conjointly in the office, via speakerphone or telephone, tape recorded input, letters, questionnaires, etc.)?

Answers to these questions help give the therapist a handle on environmental influences that can promote or hinder progress and therapeutic gain. They should be taken into account when planning for discharge, and used to support the patient's progress and changes after discharge.

III. ASSESSMENT OF SUBSTANCE ABUSE.

A.   How does patient respond to the question, "Is alcohol or drug use causing any trouble or problems at all or in any way affecting your life?" How would patient's significant others or spouse respond to this question?

B.   When this subject is posed, how does the patient exhibit denial? Minimize? Rationalize? Resist? Protest? Blame? Divert attention? Justify self? Lie? Withdraw?

C.   What is the pattern of drinking or using? Amount? Frequency? When used? What kind? How obtained? Used alone or with whom? Openly or hides it?

D.   What problems has substance use/abuse caused for patient?   DUI?   Other legal involvements? When and to what extent? What work problems related to substance use/abuse? What health problems?   What financial or property problems?

E.   How does alcohol or drug use affect loved ones? How does patient's report differ from reports of significant others?

F.   How is patient's personality or behavior changed when using or drinking? How are attitudes changed? How does verbal treatment of others change? How does he/she respond to others' needs differently?   Patient's responsible actions when sober/clean vs. under chemical influence?   Contrast patient's reports vs. significant others' reports of these issues?

G.   Which significant others have the power to influence patient's abusive drinking or using?   Are any ultimatums being applied?

H.   What efforts has patient made in the past to get help or control/stop the use or abuse?   For how long clean/sober? How did relapse happen?

I.   How is co-dependency or enabling occurring?   Who is involved?   How do they interact with and support patient's use/abuse?

J.   Patient's history of family alcoholism or drug use?   How does patient describe parents or other substance abusers in childhood?   Does patient see any similarity between her/his own use/abuse and family history of use/abuse?   How does patient react when this is proposed?

K.   How does patient react to confrontation about use/abuse issues? Education about substance abuse? Proposed treatment or rehab?   Proposed support, recovery, or 12 Step groups?   Antabuse?

L.   If an intervention is indicated, who would be the most important people in the patient's life to participate?   Who has the greatest influence on the patient's decisions?

M.   If chemical dependency is not controlled, what other problems or complaints are likely to become worse?

N.   If patient is resistant and entirely unwilling to get help for substance abuse, what can therapist do to influence patient or leverage him/her into accepting help? People? Events? Self-tests? Therapy? EAP? Case manager? Books? Tapes? Videos? Meetings? Phone calls from other addicts? Phone calls from loved ones? CAUTION: *Be careful to observe the patient's right to privacy and confidentiality as you consider mobilizing these resources on his/her behalf.*

O.   If patient is willing to get involved in recovery, how can therapy be closely integrated with and supportive of her/his recovery program?   How can 12 Steps be integrated into treatment

plan?   Journaling?   Workbooks?   Reading "big book"?   How can
therapist provide ongoing accountability?

     P.   How can case manager be enlisted to motivate patient to
follow through with recovery and after care?

     Q.   What people or groups are most likely to undermine or
sabotage patient's recovery?   How can therapist head this off in
order to preserve patient's recovery?

     R.   What local support groups can therapist suggest to help
establish a solidly founded and balanced   recovery program for the
patient?

     S.   How should therapist handle relapse during treatment?
How can relapse prevention be handled?   What significant others
can therapist mobilize to prevent relapse?

It is our personal and professional opinion that if a
patient is referred for treatment, and substance abuse is
clearly diagnosed, no interventions should be planned or
undertaken until and unless the CD issues are handled first.
Even if the patient is displeased about this decision, most
case managers are savvy in the CD arena and will
appreciate your astute handling of this matter, and will
support your decision to treat the abuse first.

If you are not skilled in diagnosing substance abuse and
its effective treatment, we recommend strongly that you
make this, if not your specialty, an area of expertise in your
practice.   If you misdiagnose a patient whose life is out of
control due to CD, not only will all the work you do
therapeutically be for naught, but most case managers may
be reluctant to refer to you in the future.   Now that we
must deal with Managed Care realities, diagnosing and
treating substance abuse is no longer optional.   The
assessment framework we have just presented has been
immensely helpful in our own practice.   We hope it will be
in yours.

IV. ASSESSMENT OF PATIENT'S SELF-CONTROL.

A. In what situations and under what conditions is the patient able to control the problem behaviors? In what ways does he/she achieve this control by manipulating self or others?

B. Has the patient developed the ability to avoid, evade or escape situations that tend to trigger the problem or complaint? Or does the patient rely on substitutionary or replacement thoughts or behaviors to avoid problem behaviors occurring? How does she/he do this?

C. How do patient's self-reports of self-control and how others see it compare or contrast? How does patient's verbalized intentions match his/her actual behavior and their consequences?

D. What conditions, persons, or changes in events tend to impact or influence the patient's ability to control the problem behaviors?

E. Have any negative or aversive consequences occurred to cause the patient to choose self-control (e.g., arrest, jail, divorce, rejection, ostracism, etc.)?

F. How can the patient's efforts at self-control be used to structure an effective treatment plan? What people in the patient's life can be enlisted to support these steps? Is medication indicated to help stabilize these steps?

When case managers review ongoing treatment plans and summaries they want to find some indication that the provider is helping the patient rely on outside resources, as well as his or her own inner strengths. You should try to mention somewhere in your reports something about the patient's self-management assets and how you plan to enhance them.

V. ASSESSMENT OF SYSTEMS & SOCIAL RELATIONSHIPS.

A. How is the patient's problem/complaint entangled in marital, family, generational, spiritual, vocational, educational, or community interrelationships?

B.   Which people or groups have the most influence over the patient's thinking and actions?   To whom is she/he most responsive?   Who contributes to or provokes or antagonizes problematic behavior or thinking?   How does the patient's problematic response to these people influence patient's thoughts, actions, or reactions in other situations?   For example, a woman whose mother "runs her life" and dominates her, finds herself treating her children similarly, compounding her own depression. Treatment would therefore focus on her relationship with the mother, her self-messages, as well as with her relationship with the children.

C.   In these relationships, how does each person get positive payoffs or secondary gains that cause the problem behaviors to continue.   For example, husband and wife provoke one another to rages in order to (1) avoid their fear of intimacy, and (2) to validate their own childhood memories of family discord.   How can these payoffs be replaced or rearranged?

D.   What are the patient's verbal expectations of these people?

E.   What do people closest to the patient expect from him or her in terms of words or behavior?

F.   Is there any consistency or match between the patient's and the expectations of those closest to him or her?

G.   How can these significant others be integrated in a therapeutic way in the treatment plan and process?

H.   Which of these important people are most likely to sabotage the patient's progress and changes?   How can (1) they be helped to join the therapeutic alliance, or (2) their influence over the patient be neutralized or reduced?

I.   Do patient's complaints reflect directly or indirectly specific stressors from his or her interpersonal system?

J.   Have patient's (and significant others') attempts to resolve the problem become part of the problem system?

K.   To bring about maximum cooperation with the treatment program, can leveraging the patient's systems produce better motivation than simply dealing with the patient alone?   Which specific people can be brought in to motivate patient's progress?

VI. VERBAL/COGNITIVE STYLE ASSESSMENT

The brief therapist does not have the luxury of months (or years) of interacting with the patient to gain a clinical impression of how the patient's internal world works. The time-limited constraints of Managed Care mean that we must more quickly get a picture of the cognitive processes that motivate problematic behaviors, and in turn, help the patient modify those processes in order to change those behaviors.

We have found that the following verbal/cognitive schema serves this purpose well. It is a reliable way to get a clinical understanding of the patient's internal representations, mental strategies, and self-talk that seem to perpetuate problems and complaints.

A.   What are their beliefs about life? What is the patient's philosophy of life?   What are her/his statements about life's meaning? Purpose? Primary goal? Why do we exist? What makes man different from animals or objects?

B.   What are their beliefs about themselves? What words would they use to describe their appearance? Worthiness/unworthiness? What makes them special?   Unique?   Important?   Different? Good/bad? Loveable/unlovable?   Significant/insignificant?   Which people in their lives contributed most to these attitudes?

C.   What are their beliefs about the future? What words does the patient use to describe his/her expectations about the future? How do they describe their life one year, five years, ten years from now? How are they responsible, or not responsible, for those outcomes? How are others responsible? How is chance or luck responsible?

D.   How were they programmed to think as a child? What words come to mind, or labels used to describe them when they were growing up? What names did parents call them? Names siblings and friends called them? What predictions were made about them, e.g., "You'll never amount to anything." How do they use those same labels as thoughts against themselves today (how are they replaying those tapes, reliving those scripts)?

E.   When they made mistakes or messed up in some way as they were growing up, how were they criticized?   How were their siblings criticized?   What specific words were used?   How do they use those same words today (replaying tapes, reliving scripts, "obediently" being loyal to the same old family rules)?

F.   In what ways are they modeling or imitating the behavior and patterns of the authority figures who raised them?   How are they a clone, xerox copy, or duplicate of those people?   Are they conforming to molds others have prescribed for them?   If they duplicate these people's lives, can that validate or make their own pain right?   Do they want to hand this pattern on to their children? —*These questions tend to provoke the patient to "rebel" in healthy ways to find their own solutions.*

G.   In what way(s) is the patient like his or her mother?   Unlike her?   How are they like their father?   Unlike him?   What words do they use to describe mother/father that they also use to describe self?

H.   What is the patient's verbal style?   Vocal pace?   Rhythm?   Tempo?   Tonality?   Emotionality?   Volume?   Pauses?   Interruptions?   *(Mirroring vocal styles can significantly enhance rapport).*

I.   Is the patient's verbal/cognitive style *visually oriented?* — "I see what you mean;" *auditorily oriented* — "Does what I'm saying sound right to you?"; *kinesthetically oriented* — "I feel she doesn't grasp what I'm saying."   *Tailoring therapeutic interventions to the sight/sound/touch perceptions of the patient can dramatically build therapeutic alliance and motivate follow-through.*

J.   What are the patient's personal pronoun patterns?   *I* statements?   *You* statements?   *He, she, they* statements?

K.   In what ways does the patient control the relationship by withholding verbal communication?

L.   In what ways does the patient use victimization language?   Self pity? — "Why me?"   Powerlessness? — "Why this?"   Fatalistic helplessness? — "Why now?"   General helplessness? — "It just came over me."   Self-limiting? — "I can't."   Blaming? — "They just won't let me."   Boundaryless? — "I had to go along with him."   Abandoned? — "No one was there for me."   Betrayed? — "And after all I did for them!"   Martyr role? — "I gave up everything I had."

M. How does the patient use fogging ("I'm not sure"), or confusion ("I'm lost"), or ignorance ("I don't know"), or amnesia ("I can't remember") to evade taking responsibility?

N. In what verbal ways does the patient demonstrate extreme, all-or-none, black-or-white thinking? In what contexts does she or he use words like "always, never, all, none, every, completely, totally," "I just died", "I was devastated", "I was destroyed," "It's ruined my life."

O. How can I use this data to create a congruent fit or match between therapeutic interaction with the patient and her/his cognitive styles?

P. How can the treatment plan use reframing, redefining, and confrontation to enhance awareness of these patterns to help the patient reshape internal representations of the problem, and change ineffective mental strategies for coping?

VII. BIOLOGICAL/PHYSICAL ASSESSMENT

A. Are there any physical limitations that might negatively affect the patient's problem behavior (e.g., poor hearing, limited vision, hypertension, hypoglycemia, etc.)? How do these limitations initiate or maintain the problem behaviors? Can the patient's perceptions about these limitations, or his/her perceptions of others' attitude toward them, be changed in therapy? How?

B. How did these biological limitations occur? How did they impact his/her self-estimate, self-image, and the resultant relationships with others? Was anything ever done to correct the limitations? By whom? Results?

C. Did patient's parents suffer from any physical or emotional limitations? Impact on patient's childhood? How does patient relate this to her/his present problem or complaint?

D. How will these limitations affect potential outcome in therapy? How should the treatment plan take them into account? Is medical consultation indicated?

Referral of patient for medical consultation is considered by case managers to be desirable because of

Managed Care's commitment to assure quality, as well as cost-effective, healthcare. In your documentation and updates to case reviewers be sure to show how you are assisting patient in any biological/physical need.

VIII. MOTIVATIONAL ASSESSMENT

A. Why did the patient make the decision to seek therapy? What persons or groups influenced the patient to do so?

B. Has patient had prior positive experiences in therapy? What benefits and positive changes does patient report from prior therapy? What characteristics of earlier therapy and/or therapist does patient favorably report?

C. What does patient say negatively about prior therapy or therapists? What happened, in the patient's opinion, to cause lack of success? (It is important to listen very carefully to patient's responses to this and B. above so you avoid making the same mistakes, and build on what good another colleague was able to accomplish in the past).

D. Does the patient describe friends or significant others who have had positive experiences in therapy? What specific reports influenced or impressed the patient most?

E. Which of the following tend to be most effective in motivating patient to initiate or maintain healthy behaviors: Friendships, approval of others, career advancement, recognition, sympathy, money and ability to buy things, good health, good looks, security, sexual satisfaction, intellectual achievement and competence, control over others, being controlled by others, group membership, championing a cause, spiritual victory, family respect, athletic achievement, future financial security, avoidance of loss, avoidance of physical pain, avoidance of rejection, avoidance of loneliness.

F. Under which specific conditions do these motivators cause healthy behavior?

G. Which persons or groups in the patient's life have the most influence for good in the patient's life? Which are most likely to cooperate with and be included in the treatment plan (with the patient's consent)?

H. What are the major negative or aversive motivators for the patient (1) in the past, (2) in the here and now, (3) in the future? What are her/his fears? Dreads? Worries?

I. What are the positive motivators that we can use to enhance patient's commitment to treatment goals and to anchor him/her in new, healthy behaviors? What are the best aversive or negative motivators that we can use in treatment to help the patient unhook from problematic behaviors and attitudes?

IX. SUICIDAL/HOMICIDAL RISK ASSESSMENT

A. What response does patient give to the question, "Have you had any thoughts of harming yourself or others?"

(1) If "yes" to "harming others," who? Thoughts/fantasies? How? When? Why? Any actions taken as yet? If not, how has patient exercised self-control?
(2) If "yes" to "harming yourself," how long? Thoughts and ideas? Specifics of plan(s)? Informed anyone/who? Prior history; recent and distant past? Precipitating factors/people? When most intense?
(3) *Rate Lethality 0 — 10.* 0—2 = No Danger; 3—4 = Vague Ideas Only; 5—6 = Vague Plans And No History; 7—8 = Specific Plan With Family History; 9—10 = Specific Plan With Recent Acting Out, With/Without Family History.

B. Prior family history of (1) physical violence/abuse? (2) Suicidal talk/behavior by parents? Siblings? Grandparents? Other relatives? Specific acts? If parental violence/abuse, did patient witness it? How often? Specific acts? Impact on patient? Who else did parent(s) abuse? Did patient witness this? Impact? If family members took their own life, who found them? Impact on that person?

C. If patient fears loss of control, what would be impact on her or his life if they "lose it"?—To loved ones? To marriage? To children? Job? Impact on the future? Legal ramifications?

D. If patient has acted out, how has this affected his/her relationships with others? Guilt? Shame?

E.   What family, loved ones, friends, clergy, or other professionals should be called in to reduce danger to self/others?

F.   What professional interventions are indicated?   More sessions per week?   Psychiatric hospitalization?   Rehab?   Day treatment?   Psychiatrist?   Medication?   Medical doctor?   Other therapist consult?   Group therapy?   Support groups?   Emergency hotlines?   Authorities?   Social services?   Safe shelters?   Legal help?   Consult with case manager?

G.   What outside homework/home therapy can be prescribed to facilitate self-control and self-care?   Books?   Tapes?   Videos?   Workbooks?   Workshops?   Conferences?   Recovery groups?   Victim survivor groups?   Retreats?   Church groups?   Social groups?   Special interest groups?   Educational experiences?   Health activities?   Recreational activities?

H.   How should case manager be informed of lethality and plan?

X. MOLESTATION/ABUSE ASSESSMENT

A.   How does the patient respond to the question, "Have there been any problems with the children?   Problems with discipline?"

B.   How does the patient respond to the question, "Have you had any experiences of abuse or physical violence or sexual abuse of any kind in your life or your children's life?"

C.   How does the patient respond to the question, "Are there any periods of time in your life that seem to be missing, that you can't remember, or are totally gone from your memory?"   Which years?   (Explain to patient that this may be due to trauma causing pain, shame, shock and loss of memory to protect self; that therapy is a "safe place" to allow these memories to surface slowly).

D.   How does the patient respond to this question, "Are there any experiences in your life, both now and as you were growing up, that seem to cause you guilt or shame?"

E.   Are there any necessary legal interventions, such as reporting child abuse/molestation, that should be taken?   By telephone?   In writing?   How should this be documented?

(1) If actions are taken, how can patient be informed of this in such a way to preserve the therapeutic bond while at the same time fulfilling legal sanctions and protecting the victim(s)?

(2) If actions are taken, how can patient and the family be helped to prepare emotionally for the investigation and/ or interventions?

F. How can therapist actively, aggressively get involved in protecting the victim(s)?

G. How should therapy plan assist the victim(s) to stop and avoid further abuse? How can return to perpetrator be prevented using cognitive, behavioral, interpersonal, and legal measures?

H. Is there anything therapist can initiate to encourage perpetrator(s) to get help? (This is important because in many cases the victim returns to a relationship with perpetrator, and, the perpetrator is a suffering, tormented, needy human being, who often is a victim him/herself).

I. How should case manager be apprised of these findings?

Other areas of interest to some therapists include an assessment of the following: Sociological, socio-cultural, and in-depth geneological data; strength of patient's will and decision-making patterns; emotional patterns; intellectual functioning; memory and imagination/fantasy constructs. We have found that the Treatment Targeted Impairment Assessment that we have presented here gives the solution-focused brief therapist enough — *perhaps more than enough* — information about the patient's life to construct a highly effective, focused, time-limited treatment program.

It also provides important details that will help the clinician provide the kind of data that Managed Care case reviewers want most. Too many clinicians fail to provide such "hard" data in their documentation and updates. When a therapist integrates this kind of specificity into communication with case managers (succinctly, of course), they distinguish themselves as valued providers, and are likely to find themselves on the most valued, "elite" provider list. And what does that mean? It means two things: (1) You will have the opportunity to provide high quality brief therapy; and (2) It means more referrals.

Chapter Seven

Telephone Etiquette:

Some Tips on Making Your
Phone Communications with Case Managers
More Effective & Persuasive

Personal Notes

Chapter Seven

Telephone Etiquette:
Some Tips on Making Your Phone Communications with Case Managers More Effective & Persuasive

Most of the case managers whom we have worked closely with over the past several years we have never met face to face. For all we know, and for all they know, we could be dealing with 7 foot 2 inch giants, or 4 foot 3 inch dwarfs. But there is one thing we do know: We have come to respect one another's work, and we know how to efficiently help one another do our respective jobs to help hurting people.

We have never personally met most case managers because our relationship has been built, from the very beginning, over that little wire stretched from their telephone to ours. A powerful tool in dealing with Managed Care.

Yes, a lot of data is shared via paperwork with case reviewers (as we all know only too well!) — initial assessment reports, treatment plans, updates, extensions, and discharge reports. But we build our image as one of their valued providers, or tarnish our image as a *provider non grata* in many cases over the telephone.

The material in this chapter is worthy of careful consideration, especially as your future relationship with that organization rests on how successful you are at implementing these fundamentals. Keep in mind that your phone relationship with *one* case manager can affect — positively or disastrously — your relationship with all the other reps in that organization! Why? Because case managers talk among themselves, at meetings and informally, about which providers are rendering the best service to the patient, and to the company. A provider who helps them do their job more effectively and efficiently gets known very quickly. And those who mishandle their contacts with case managers get known just as fast.

So, dear colleague, take heed. Here are a few ideas and strategies that have worked well for us over the years in building positive, cooperative, and respectful working relationships with case managers. Like most fundamentals, they're not difficult, they're just essential.

Avoid the adversarial attitude

The other day we did an interview in which we were asked to talk about the future of the private mental health practice. Our comments, as you might expect, were quite optimistic, and we had a lot of good things to say about the benefits of Managed Healthcare as it related to the practitioner who knows how to partner with them. The interviewer said, "Of the several interviews I've done with other psychologists, you are the first one to say *anything* at all favorable about Managed Care!" The interviewer went on to say, "I just talked to one female therapist in Los Angeles who said that she 'despised and detested' everything about Managed Care!"

"Despised" and "detested." Now there's a therapist who needs to read this book. But although her words reveal an extreme reaction of rigidity, we find that many therapists share her hostility. We typically hear things like, "I don't like someone telling me how to treat my clients." "Who are they to tell me how many sessions it takes to treat a depressed patient?" Or, "I don't know if I'm going to allow my client's confidentiality to be violated by some mis-managed non-care big-brother watchdog company!" Oh yes, change is painful, isn't it?

If any of these clinicians got on the phone to attempt a relationship with a Managed Care rep, their "Well, how are you today" chit chat would be a thin disguise for their real heart-felt attitude. This is true especially as many case managers are highly trained, perceptive clinicians themselves. When a razor blade has been sugar coated, they know the blade is there. And if they "read" a hostile attitude beneath other social niceties, how do you think their image of you and your work impresses itself into their mind?

So, before you pick up the phone to call a case manager, you might do well to examine your Managed Care Attitudes. And if you find any "stinkin' thinkin'" (similar to the examples cited above), adjust your conceptualization of the whole process. You want to be perceived as an ally, not an adversary.

Here are some simple ways to adjust an adversarial attitude. If at first you don't agree with them, meditate on them until the mind is adequately converted.

Managed Care is here to stay; for me to be, I'd better join them.
Managed Care makes it possible for hurting people to get help.
Without Managed Care many companies would offer no mental health benefits whatever for their employees.
Although fees received from Managed Care are below my standard fees, a reduced fee is better than *no fee at all.*
Although the paperwork is a necessary reality, it helps me stay on goal, and impact case managers with my expertise.
The case manager is dedicated to authorizing medically necessary care for my client, not obstructing it.
The case reviewer is a professional colleague of mine.
Since economic realities place limits on treatment, we can work together to plan the best help possible for my patient.
The case manager is a good resource person to locate other professional services my client may need.
My relationship with this case manager not only benefits my patient, it's also a good potential source for new referrals.
A positive, cooperative partnership with case managers helps to create a bridge between the community and my practice.

Favorable positioning on their provider list saves me hundreds,
even thousands of marketing dollars I don't have to spend.
Without "Managed" Care there would be no care for this client,
and my appointment book would be mighty sparse.
The case manager is an ally both to my patient's life and the
life of my practice.

Brainwashing? Yes it is, for some. No doubt about it. But well worth the price of sacrificing our negativity. With concepts like these occupying the mind, you will communicate a cooperative team spirit to the trained ear on the other end of the telephone. The case manager's ear, who is trying to figure you out — "Is this therapist one of 'us'? Do they understand time-limited therapy? Are they Managed Care friendly? Can they help us do our job?" To the extent to which you demonstrate yourself cooperative and "Managed-Care-friendly" in these areas, your value as a preferred provider increases.

Once you've adjusted your attitude from adversary to ally, go ahead and pick up the phone. And add to that mind set the following important fundamentals, as well:

Getting in step with the case manager's needs

There's the story of the therapist walking down the street on her way to do a lecture at a Managed Care seminar. Up ahead she sees a homeless beggar coming straight for her. She knew that he was going to ask for money, she was irritated at his disrupting her thoughts, and when he finally stopped her abruptly asking for the money, she shook her head and said no. He walked away muttering something about people who are stingy. Both people were upset by the encounter.

On another street another therapist was on his way to the same seminar. He had a mind full of questions he wanted to ask at the small Q&A group following the seminar. He hardly noticed a homeless beggar sidling up to him asking for financial help. Without thinking, the therapist got out his wallet and gave the man $5. Both people got what they wanted. The therapist's thoughts were not disrupted. The homeless man got money for food.

Observe the important lessons in this story, and the important difference in the two beggars' approaches. The first man got nothing and got nowhere because he *abruptly forced his way into the therapist's world, making no attempt to get in step with the therapist, and thus the two were going in two different directions.* The second homeless man got what he wanted because he *adjusted himself to the world of the therapist, got smoothly and seamlessly in step with him, and gently asked for what he wanted without disrupting or forcing his way in.*

The essential point in your telephone communications with case managers is this: Always start from the point of view or the "needs point" of the case manager. How can you get in step with them as you make this call? As you do with your patients, try to empathically enter into the world of the rep as you prepare to talk to them.

Think about their job demands. One case manager recently told Marion, our secretary, "When I got to the office today I had over 50 messages on my voice mail!" Fortunately, Marion is a treasure, and is highly skilled at getting in step with people. She said, "Oh, I can appreciate that; one of those days, huh?...I'll talk with Dr. Browning and we'll get back to you in a few days because what we need to talk to you about certainly can wait." The case manager told me later how grateful she was for Marion's thoughtfulness.

All case reps are not that busy (we hope), but they are pressured by too many cases to manage, too few hours in the day, not enough energy, and providers calling who have not read this chapter. To distinguish yourself at the outset of *every contact,* get in step with their pressured job. Ask this question if you get them on the phone:

> "Hi Allan, this is Dr. Browning, I'm calling about a client;
> *is this a good time for you to talk?"*

Notice the second line. It's a mistake to launch in with "Hi, I'm calling about Jane Jones and she's been in to see me for six sessions now, and I want to update you on her progress..." etc., etc. That's the abrupt beggar method.

It's wise to get their assent first off that this is the best time for them to talk, and if it isn't, I want to yield to their needs to tell me when a better time would be; thus, "...is this a good time for you to talk?" This is definitely the best approach to use to demonstrate respect for their time.

Even if you are in a hurry or stretched pretty thin by time pressures to complete your phone calls within 2 minutes in between patients, don't let your pressure cause you to intrude abruptly into their pressure-cooker world. When you ask that "is-this-a-good-time-to-talk" question, you send an important message about you to them. The overt message is that you are courteous and respectful. The underlying message is this: "This therapist respects my time; how refreshing...I enjoy dealing with providers who care about my time demands." Your name from that point on (all other things being done well, of course) is associated in their mind with "I enjoy dealing with providers like _____" (fill in your name). When it's time for them to make a referral of a client who needs a provider in your location, well, you know the rest of that story.

Be prepared with the kind of data case managers need

Because their time is limited, don't make the same mistake many providers make. Case reps get too many calls like this: "I'm calling about Jane Jones and I want to give you an update on her treatment." The case manager asks as she/he punches up the computer screen, "What is the client's social security number?" Therapist, "Oh, can you hold on a few minutes; the case file isn't on my desk and I'll have to look it up..." Not smart.

What is smart? Case manager, "What is the client's social security number?" Therapist, "332-24-5718, that's 332-24-5718, and in case you have more than one Jane Jones, her middle name is Marie." Note that this therapist comes prepared to *help the case manager do her job,* knowing that before anything can be done on the patient's behalf, this information is essential.

Notice, too, that the therapist, slowly repeats the number for the rep, in case it was not clear the first time, and, gives one more piece of useful data, the middle name, to avoid any possible confusion or time-wasting hunting on the computer. (We actually called in about one patient with a very common name, and believe it or not, there were four patients with the identical name in the computer!). The case manager appreciates any help with identifying data; it saves him/her a lot of time and needless questioning.

If the rep has to question 8 out of 10 providers, most of whom are ill-prepared, how do you think their concept or image of you and your work is affected when you give them what they want, and more besides?

In addition to identifying data, you should be ready to give them other important information, such as:

Date patient was first seen.
DSM-III (or IV) diagnosis on all 5 axes (including GAF).
Medications for reduction of which symptoms; name of M.D.
How many sessions seen to date.
How many sessions missed, if any.
Reasons for no-shows or cancellations, if any.
Goals of treatment, linked to treatment targeted impairments.
Progress toward goals and interventions used.

Any resistances or problems attaining timely goals.
Specific homework assigned and follow-through.
Outside resources you are prescribing and follow-thru.
Number of sessions used, requested, and time remaining.
Update on probability for discharge as planned; with date.

You don't have to give all of this, certainly, And you shouldn't. But it is a good idea to have these points ready at hand, and succinctly outlined, should they request any of it. When this kind of preparation meets their kind of expectations, the result is that your image of professional competence is greatly enhanced (especially in contrast to many providers who are not similarly prepared).

Mention case manager's prior comments about the patient

It is important to think of the case manager as an ally, committed with you to the best possible care of the patient. One good way to communicate this attitude is to bring up in the course of discussions about the case something they may have said about the patient during earlier contacts with you. We have found this helpful even while they are waiting for their computer to locate the patient's file. For example,

> "While you're locating her case, I want to just mention that your hunch was right on target. You said that you suspected that he might have a substance abuse problem. After a lot of denial and firm confrontation, he admits to daily use of crystal meth..."

This is not manipulative flattery. It is giving *sincere credit where credit is due.* You are simply acknowledging anything that the case manager may have said in reference to the patient that has proven valid or helpful to your treatment and understanding of the patient.

How can you remember these kinds of comments? We recommend keeping a "Case Manager Contact Sheet" in the patient's case file, or separately in your desk. Each time you contact the rep, jot down their comments verbatim, with the dates made. Then, when you update the rep their comments are ready at hand.

A real benefit of this principle is that the case manager is treated as part of the treatment team, not merely as a gatekeeper with veto power.

Ask for the case manager's opinion

In the same spirit as the last point, it is helpful to consult with the case rep regarding his/her treatment ideas and recommendations. Too often they are related to as stern-and-stingy guards, blocking the way to treatment. Or they may be thought of as mere order takers.

Yes, they are gatekeepers with responsibility, and yes, they do order or authorize care. But if you deal with them on those levels, you create emotional distance between you. How do you talk to a colleague with whom you are consulting on a case? How do you relate to another professional whom you know to be as committed to the patient's welfare as you are? This is precisely the way you should communicate with the patient's case manager.

Ask a sincere question about what brief therapy methods they are familiar with that may have worked in cases like this? What do they think of a certain method you are considering using? How do they feel about this or that homework assignment you have tried? How do they suggest you might intervene with a family member who continues to sabotage treatment?

You are not asking them to tell you how to treat the patient. That's your job. You are asking them for their professional opinion on *one important clinical issue.* Professionals on the same "team" do this kind of thing.

Avoiding a dogmatic attitude

When you describe your treatment plans for the patient, be flexible and tentative as you are formulating your impressions of the patient and considering possible intervention strategies. This is especially true during the early stages of care. You don't want to be perceived as mechanical—treating all anxiety attacks the same way, all depressions with the same techniques. Brief, yes; rigid, no.

The wrong way: "This client is obviously depressed and should be started on antidepressants right away, as well as given the Beck Scale."

The better way: "It seems to me that, as you thought, the patient is clinically depressed.   We may want to consider referral for antidepressants, but first I want to assess some of the precipitating family factors that might be maintaining her feelings of helplessness..."

Similarly, when you are not prepared as yet to rank-order or prioritize impairments, say so: "There are 3 significant behaviors that seem to need immediate attention; they are 1... 2... and 3....   During the next session I plan to pinpoint which complaint we'll attack first, and I'll let you know on my next update, if that's okay with you?"

Can you see the difference? Can you feel the difference? The case manager will. The objective is to come across as balanced and moderate, not unsure, wishy-washy, or indecisive. There's a huge difference!

Be precise, succinct and brief

The case rep is not interested in the kind of update or case description that you might present to a group of colleagues during a case presentation. "The patient is a 32-year-old, well-groomed, married female who is well-oriented in all three spheres, with normal affect, judgment is ..." Do this and you will stress to the limits their own frustration tolerance level! Keep it brief, crisp, and to the point. "Her diagnosis is Major Depression, recurrent, with the primary stressors an abusive husband and a runaway daughter...There's no suicidal behavior, but significant social withdrawal, which does cause her absence from work."

That's what Managed Care reps want. Give it to them that way. If you have to write it out and then edit it before calling them, do it. They will remember you as a provider who knows how to make their job more efficient, and who knows how to get the job done right, in a time-sensitive manner. That's the kind of reputation you want.

Don't be afraid to admit your weaknesses

What do you do when the telephone rings and a case manager is graciously referring you a new patient? Rejoice, right? Not if the patient presents a problem or condition outside your professional skill purview. You could attempt treatment and do the best you can. But results will speak for themselves, the patient may be displeased, and your reputation with the rep will suffer.

Better to admit your shortcomings and weaknesses. Two instances occurred recently that will illustrate this issue. A case manager called and referred a 15-year-old boy to me (C.B.) for treatment of anxiety attacks. Tempted, definitely? I had not received many referrals from this particular case manager and here was my opportunity to meet his needs. Even more tempting when he said, "He needs to be seen right away, wants a Christian therapist, and I think you'd be good for him. When could you see him?"

Hanging there upon the horns of the dilemma I had to make a choice. My area of expertise (and preference) does not extend below the age of 20. A 15-year-old troubled teen needed someone who (1) likes working with teenagers, and (2) who possesses the skills to help him. Hanging there on those horns I decided the truth would make me free, "I really would like to help him, but we all have our gifts, as you know; and one of my areas of definite weakness lies in working with kids. He needs someone who can really get results for him, and I'm just not what he needs...But could I suggest so-and-so as an excellent choice?"

The risk was that I might displease the rep because he was in a bind and really needed a therapist now. The outcome? He thanked me for my honesty, for the recommendation, and has since referred several other patients — who fortunately were all recovered from the condition known as "adolescence."

On another occasion a patient referred by another Managed Care company that we were "courting" complained that I was not dealing with her "feelings" to the extent that her previous non-Managed-Care therapist did. She vehemently resented the brief therapy format. Decision time: Do I shift gears and go into "dynamic gear," or do what I am expected to do by the case reviewer who referred her? What would you do?

I explained to her the realities we both were constrained by within her insurance plan, complimented her prior therapist's skills, and referred her back to the case rep for reassignment to another therapist. Risky because her report back to the rep would doubtless be a stinging rebuke of my lack of sensitivity to her needs. But it was worth the risk. In both my verbal contact and documentation of the case in writing, I explained that the patient was unwilling to work within a brief orientation. In spite of the patient's displeasure, the case manager was both surprised and pleased by the way this problem was handled. And no doubt this story will make the rounds at that Managed Care company.

We share these true stories to encourage you to go ahead and take risks. Admit your flaws, foibles and fumbles. Case reviewers admire providers who have the courage to be vulnerable and acknowledge powerlessness at times. They appreciate providers who have the integrity to work within the limits of Managed Care. They do not admire providers who try to be all things to all "men" or those who will do just about anything to curry their favor.

Don't be afraid
to ask questions

You will be dealing with more than one Managed Care company, and many case managers within those companies. We have found over the years that each company requires something different from the provider, and even the reps within the same company often want and expect very different things as they handle a case. For example, in one large Managed Care company, one rep will routinely authorize 7 sessions for almost every case referred, and wants only a voice mail memo that the patient came in, followed by a treatment plan. Another rep in the same company will only authorize 1 session, then wants a personal call from us with diagnosis and treatment plan, and only then will she authorize sessions — and then only 3 at a time.

You cannot say that at XYZ Managed Care company all the case managers have the same requirements or expectations. Often the reps have a lot of autonomy and even enjoy adding their own special "twist" to dealing with providers. They may want phone contacts to be handled differently, documentation to be sent at various times, or varied types of updates given. The only way to be sure is to *ask questions.*

Of course, your first question will be directed to the director of provider relations: "What is the procedure to make application to become part of your provider panel?" This sounds simple, doesn't it? But it is getting more and more difficult. How frustrating it is to call a Managed Care company only to be confronted by a "canned" computerized menu message. Many Managed Care companies are using them. As you run the numbers you often cycle back to where you began, never making contact with a human being, much less finding out how to become a provider.

The best way around this is to press the menu number for case-manager-updates for active clients. You will very likely get a real, live homosapien (pulse and all) who will know the ins and outs of becoming a provider. Ask them who to talk to? Their extension to bypass the infernal menu? Any suggestions for making application? Any specific specialties needed at this time? And tell them something about your work, while you have them on the line. Who knows — you may find some inside support.

When you then contact the director of provider relations (or whatever their title may be), be sure to tell them that you were referred to them by so-and-so, whom you've just talked to. It's always helpful to introduce yourself (an unknown) with an accepted name as part of the team (the known). Then get specific about what to do to join the panel.

If they say, "We're sorry, our panel is closed right now and we do not need a therapist in your area," then go back to the basics you received in the beginning of this text and persist until the gates swing open.

Getting back to your interactions with the many varied case reviewers. The *only way* to know precisely what a given case manager wants, expects and demands is to ask them. Here are some simple questions that will give you good guidelines to follow with each rep:

When is the best time for me to call you? Any particular days?
When is your busiest time, so I don't call and bother you?
How do you want to receive updates on clients you refer to me?
Can you give me some guidelines about when to use your
     voice mail versus when I should talk to you personally?
What kind of info do you need when I call about a client?
How often do you want updates on a client? By voice mail, by
     personal call, or in writing?
Is it okay for my secretary to update you, or would you prefer
     that I call you personally? Does this apply to voice mail also?
When you call me, how soon would you like a call back?
When you refer a new client to me, will you have the client
     call me, or do you want me to call to set the appointment?
Do you want a call after the first visit, first 3 visits, how often?
How much DSM diagnostic data do you want by phone? Axes?
What's the preferred number of sessions and length you prefer?
What forms do you need sent in for documentation and when?
Is there a number or beeper where I can more easily reach you?
How should I handle a client emergency when your office
     is closed?

There is no such thing as a silly question. Ask them anything you need to know. You can also ask about how billing is handled, who to talk to about billing, how to get a new member of your group on the panel, how to handle medication or hospitalization evaluations, etc. Assume nothing; ask everything. Will this annoy the case rep? Yes, if they are pressed for time. But remember, your first question was, "Is this a good time to talk," followed by, "I have some procedural questions so that I can be sure to give you the kind of information you need."

And what about the scary question about getting new referrals from them? Do you dare ask it? By all means. *"Can you tell me the best way to work with you so that you can have confidence in my work and feel comfortable referring to me as a regular provider?"* Many therapists get on preferred provider panels only to receive few or no referrals. Why? Because they are afraid to ask that question. Don't be afraid — as a good book title proclaims so well, "Feel The Fear And Do It Anyway." Sometimes it is as simple as the concept: "You have not, because you ask not."

Ask and you will receive — Useful guidelines about the rep's individual expectations, and yes, perhaps even more referrals. And be very sure to write down on a "Case Manager's Profile Sheet" their ideosyncratic preferences so you can stay in step with them. The dividends will be well worth this little research project.

Use humor to enhance your image

Case managers deal in serious issues all day long. They also have to interact with many therapists who put them in an adversarial role. They also deal with patients who want care that must be denied. And they have higher-ups looking over their shoulders seeing if they are helping the company justify their existence. That's serious; too serious.

One of the ways you can distinguish yourself is by weaving some light touches into the fabric of the case updates over the phone. "Laughter doeth good like a medicine." Look for opportunities to bring them that kind of medicine. Humorous (but tasteful) comments about your work. Something that pokes fun at yourself. A good cartoon. An anecdote. Something surprising. Something paradoxical. Something cute the kids said/did.

These should be like times of refreshing that you bring to the case rep. No more than a minute or two so you don't use up their already-pressured time. They'll look forward to your call; an oasis in a dry land of clinical stuffiness.

And try to remember those important off-hand remarks they share with you from previous conversations. If they mention their vacation, ask how it was, what they did, what they enjoyed most? If they mention a conference they plan to attend, ask what stood out most for them? If they are out ill, ask how they are feeling and say something to lift their spirits.

Keep in mind that under that gate keeper identity is a

person who needs a break in their daily routine. Link your name with clinical excellence in brief therapy, and someone who has a way of bringing "sunshine" into people's lives.

Leave clear, complete voice mail messages

If the case rep says that they prefer voice mail messages (and most do in order to save time), try to leave messages that communicate a complete idea. Don't just say, "Hi, this is Dr. Browning, my number is (310) 799-6655, please call me back." That message requires the case manager to play phone tag or telephone tennis with you, and that is frustrating and time wasting.

Instead, leave a message that stands on its own and gives them enough information that can save them from having to return your call. For example: "Hi, this is Dr. Charles Browning and I want to give you an update on client Sally Saint, SS# 123-00-4567, that's SS# 123-00-4567. She was referred on June 14th for problems with co-workers on the job. She was seen on June 16th by me, her diagnosis is Dysthymia 300.04, client refuses meds, and the primary impairment seems to be anger outbursts triggered by the pressures of single parenting. Plan is to teach her how to manage anger via journaling and cognitive restructuring techniques, and to help her learn positive discipline strategies; I'll use a workbook as homework for this. She's also agreed to join a single-parents support group in her church. I'd like to see her every other week, and discharge after 6 sessions, if all goes as expected. I'll update you after her 3rd session. Hope this gives you all the information you need, but if you need to call, my number is (310) 799-6655, if you need any other info. Have a terrific day! Thanks, bye."

That message contains it all. They can enter this data into the patient's file in their computer and avoid the hassle of trying to call you back between patients. Most case managers will appreciate this thorough, efficient and considerate phone method, and in turn, you'll receive certifications more quickly and more painlessly.

On the other hand, there are reps who don't want that much information. They may want it only in direct communications with you. They may want it only in written documentation. They may want less or more data. How do you know what they want? Ask each rep to instruct you as to their preferences. Write this down on your Case Manager Profile Sheet and follow that format.

The hot topics and magic words case managers appreciate

Don't spend time describing syndromes, personality dynamics, characterological defects, ego functioning, or underlying etiological factors. As interesting as these may be, especially if you've been analytically trained, they reveal to the case manager that you will probably have a tough time being comfortable on the Managed Care Team, playing by Managed Care rules.

The topics you select for your brief discussions on the phone with case managers tells them a lot about what you are like in the consultation room with a client they refer to you. They entrust you with a patient because they believe that you can help them do their job — providing time-sensitive, goal-focused treatment to bring wellness to the patient's life. They don't want fuzzy clinical abstractions that suggest long-term or supportive therapy.

So, what should you talk about? Talk about those *behaviors that are observable and measurable.* Talk about behavioral and cognitive *excesses and deficits.* Talk about *impairments* that are clearly *linked to treatment intervention.* Talk about *goals and solutions.* And talk about any *homework assignments* that you have used to find solutions and reach goals. Managed Care reps know that one of the hallmarks of quality brief therapy is an ongoing reliance on outside homework. Even if the rep does not ask you directly about homework, you can be sure that most of them will be listening to see (1) if you mention homework as an instrumental part of your treatment plan, (2) how you relate outside homework to accelerate successful discharge, and (3) if you use homework to help the patient maintain therapeutic gains after discharge.

Thus, dear colleague, your homework is to learn to use more homework. How do you learn this skill if your orientation has been primarily session-based intervention? The best way perhaps is to read books and journals published by our behavior-therapy, cognitive-therapy, active-therapy, directive-therapy, problem-solving-therapy, decision-making-therapy, and brief-therapy colleagues. You'll get a wealth of good ideas that you can experiment with and then fit into your own therapeutic style.

Consider authors like Wolpe, Lazarus, Beck, Stuart, Meichenbaum, Haley, de Shazer, Watzlawick, Weakland, and Greenwald. And even though he comes at it from the point of view of hypnosis (which we are not recommending as a brief therapy approach), most of Milton Erickson's works are invaluable — he was a genius at inventing rapid, solution-focused homework to individual patient impairments. Erickson can teach us much about creatively tailoring homework to patient's ideosyncratic needs and situational dynamics.

Spend time reviewing the chapter on assessing treatment targeted impairments. You will find this, we believe, helpful in talking about the kinds of observable phenomena case reviewers will be listening for. The core language of the Managed Care "team" centers on these issues.

10 "little things" that make
big impressions on case managers

The tips and suggestions we have shared with you in this chapter thus far, if carried out, will certainly have positive effects on how you and your work are perceived in the mind of case managers. There are 10 other so-called "little things" or subtle things that can also help establish your name as a *preferred* -preferred provider. Consider:

1. Always try to return case managers' calls within two hours.
2. If you are unable to do so, have your secretary, or a trusted colleague (or your spouse) call on your behalf to let them know when you will be getting back to them, and to take a message for you, if it is urgent.
3. When you leave a voice mail message, or talk with the case manager's assistant, always leave your name, phone number, beeper number, best time to reach you, and a BRIEF description about why you are calling.
4. If you send the case rep a fax regarding a patient, do so only if the rep can stand by and personally receive it to guard patient's confidentiality.
5. If you want to update the rep on more than one patient at the time you call, ask if this is a good time to do so, or should you call at a better, more convenient time?
6. Do not ask secretaries or others to call for extensions or to relate important treatment details to case managers; providing them with dates of service, diagnostic codes, and other less urgent matters may be fine — Ask the case manager to define these parameters for you.
7. Some case managers prefer that you personally call clients referred to you, not assigning this to a secretary. Be sure to ask them how they want clients contacted.
8. Any time you can do it, opt for leaving a complete, clear voice mail message instead of personally talking to the rep, adding, "I hope that this will save your time in not having to play phone tag calling back. Thanks!" (or something similar to this). This courtesy will be appreciated.
9. Many times case managers are transferred or assigned to other caseloads and another rep is assigned to handle your client. If this happens, ask the rep you have formed a good working relationship with to "put in a good word" for you with the new rep. This can enhance continuing referrals.

10. When a new rep is assigned to you, make it a weekly goal to make some phone and written contact with them in order to quickly establish their confidence in your work.

As we noted earlier in the text, like paperwork, even though phone communication with Managed Care reviewers takes time, redefine that time. It is useful time to enable the patient to get the help they need. It is a time to help the case manager understand the needs of the patient more thoroughly. And, it is time invested in the growth and stability of your practice as the case manager develops increasing trust and respect in you and your work.

In essence, that instrument on your desk with all those buttons and wires is, in actuality, *a first tool in the treatment process.* Your telephone, used skillfully with case managers, can enable a potential patient to find his or her way into your office — *your* office, because your name continues to be at the top of the preferred provider list. Without the influence of the telephone, the patient may never even know that you exist, and end up in someone else's office.

Use it wisely.

Chapter Eight

Writing Effective Treatment Plans:

The Do's, The Don'ts,
The Strategies and Methods
For Preparing Convincing Documentation

Personal Notes

Writing Effective Treatment Plans:

The Do's, The Don'ts,
The Strategies and Methods
For Preparing Convincing Documentation

Every — not most, but *all* Managed Care organizations require written documentation of services rendered by providers. They call those forms by many names. For example, on the desk in front of us we have a sample of the required reports from 10 Managed Care firms. At the top of each form is the name of the Managed Care company and its description:

> "Initial Outpatient Treatment Report"
> "Subsequent Outpatient Treatment Report"
> "Ongoing Treatment Report"
> "Assessment Form"
> "Clinical Plan"
> "Outpatient Treatment Plan"
> "Progress Report"
> "Request For Clinical Services"
> "Outpatient Mental Health Treatment Summary"
> "Mental Health Verification Form"
> "Request For Treatment Authorization"

A rose by any other name would still smell as sweet. A treatment plan by any of these names is still a *treatment plan*. In these early stages of Managed Healthcare each firm appears to be trying to set the standards for quality external review of mental health services. Because we have no clear-cut standards as yet, it's whatever works best for each company while providers and firms alike struggle to form our identities.

But no matter what they call these reports, each and every company wants some form of a treatment plan or summary in writing. Your value as a trusted member of the Managed Care team is judged in large part by how well you handle treatment plans. That is the purpose of this chapter — to help you get comfortable getting out paperwork that gets results.

The 6 basic ingredients of a good treatment report

Although they are called by many different names, most case managers want essentially the same things in the treatment report.

The all-important basics: You might be surprised how many clinicians tarnish their otherwise sparkling image by neglecting the fundamentals. Ask any case reviewer and they will tell you that each and every one of these "basics" rank high on their "must" list:

1. All identifying data about the patient is filled out completely and accurately, including Social Security Number.
2. The report is clearly printed or typed.
3. The correct form is submitted.
4. All appropriate sections are completed.
5. Only those items requested are completed, in a straightforward, decisive manner.
6. The form is returned to the case manager on time.

The basics are crucial. Go over this list once again, please; your reputation as a cooperative team player hangs on it.

How to avoid making the most common (& most costly) mistakes

Like the fundamentals listed above, there are a few other important details to observe.

(1) Use the correct patient name: You may be seeing a couple or a family who have more than one authorization

for care. Both husband and wife may have a given number of individual and conjoint/family sessions certed. One or more of their children may be authorized. When submitting treatment reports be sure to check to see if that particular patient (1) has sessions remaining, and (2) if there is an "end date", be sure it has not been exceeded.

(2) Carefully note number of sessions authorized: Some Managed Care organizations print out on the initial treatment form the number of sessions authorized. Be sure to note this number and enter it on whatever system of record-keeping you use. Then keep careful track of how many sessions are utilized and *be sure not to schedule sessions beyond this number.*

(3) Carefully note the end date: Most companies certify a given number of sessions. Others, however, not only certify total number of sessions but also an "end date" at which time no further services are permitted without further authorization. Many therapists, overlooking this important date, continue rendering services beyond this date because they know they have not exhausted the number of sessions authorized. Don't let this happen to you! We have personally lost hundreds of dollars when members of our staff have made this mistake (and we are not guiltless ourselves — ouch!). Many case reps are understanding and have been known to extend the end date as a professional courtesy. But others, unfortunately, are "letter-of-the-law" strict taskmasters and say, "I'm sorry, but no services were authorized beyond that date and no payments are possible." No matter how effective your work was on the patient's behalf, if you "forget" the end date, you may live to regret it (at the bank).

(4) Send the forms to the correct company: Here's another mistake that many therapists, including ourselves, have made, to their dismay. All the fundamentals are met and each item of the treatment plan is filled out in careful detail. The form is then mailed and no response from the

case reviewer.   No session authorization. No response, either, from those who send out your paycheck.   Why? Because that beautifully-filled-out-meeting-all-the-rules report was mailed in error to the *wrong Managed Care company!* Humanity strikes again. When you are dealing with several companies and DOZENS of reports, it's easy to make this blunder. If you mail the correct form to the incorrect company, it can take weeks, even months, for this error to be discovered and the form returned to you. And occasionally they do not bother returning them. We would do well to heed the sage advice of the old machinist who said, "Three times measure ... one time cut" (thanks to Fred Pilone for this piece of wisdom).

(5) Use correct postage when returning documents: Here's another mistake you might think is too trivial to occupy space here. But again, we've made this one too, and in so doing have had unnecessary delays in sessions certed and payments received. When you mail 10 or more forms, be sure to use the correct amount of postage. Otherwise, it will be returned to you days later undelivered.

(6) Don't trust faxes: Most faxes tell you that the transmission went through and was received, or not. We have had reports from case reps that nothing whatever was received, even though our fax told a different story. If you do fax a treatment report, be sure to *follow up by mailing the original or "hard copy."* Be sure, as well, to (1) check to see if the case manager wants a report faxed, and (2) put a statement of confidentiality on your fax cover sheet to protect yourself from legal ramifications (remember: lots of lurking lawyers love lucrative lawsuits).   Here is one example of wording that can be used on faxed documents to protect your patients, and to protect yourself:

> **WARNING:**
>
> **CONFIDENTIAL COMMUNICATION**
>
> The information contained in this fax transmission is private, privileged and confidential, intended only for the professional use of the recipient(s) named below. If you are not the named recipient, or their authorized agent responsible for delivering this message unread to the named recipient, you are hereby notified that you have received this document in error, and that any review, copying, distribution, or dissemination of any part of this transmission is strictly prohibited. If you have received this fax in error, please notify us immediately by calling (310) 799-6655 and mailing the fax to: Browning Therapy Group, Inc. 3662 Katella Avenue, Suite 226, Los Alamitos, CA 90720. Thank you for your courtesy, respecting the privacy of this important communication. *Have a special day!*

This should protect you and your patient even from lawyers looking for loopholes. But the ultimate assurance of your fax reaching the right person is to fax the document only to the case manager at a given time when he or she personally receives the transmission at a specified time.

One member of our staff tells of one experience that demonstrates the risk of faxing treatment reports. She was asked by an assistant to a case manager to "just fax us the treatment report." This she did, checking with the assistant who assured her that, "yes, we received the fax." Weeks later she learned from the case manager herself that no fax was ever received, and nothing was entered in the client's computer file. No sessions, therefore, were authorized — the case manager assuming that we had fallen down on the job and had failed to do the treatment report. Fortunately, this had a happy ending. We mailed the original documents and thereafter sessions were authorized. We also learned an important lesson that we share with you here: *If you fax any documents (even when asked to do so) always mail the original on the same day.*

If these steps are not taken and mistakes are made, it can cause undue delays in sessions being authorized, more work is created for both you and the case manager, the patient can experience unnecessary frustration, *and* your check may be delayed or not find its way to you at all. This should be enough to motivate us to carefully attend to details.

The kind of treatment reports case reviewers appreciate most: Section-by-section strategies

As we've pointed out before, your professional image and the reputation of your practice are measured to a large degree by how you handle communications with case reviewers. You can avoid many of the most common mistakes made by other providers by following the suggestions just presented. And you can further enhance your value to case managers by observing other important considerations when completing treatment reports.

Each company uses its own ideosyncratic paperwork. We do not have the space here to present them all. So we've reviewed the forms from many local and national Managed Care firms, and isolated those sections of treatment reports that they seem to have in common. From our own clinical experience, and consultation with case managers, here are strategies that should help you submit treatment plans and case summaries that score high marks with even the fussiest, most compulsive reviewer:

1. "What is the patient's diagnosis?"

There's no need to spend time here discussing clinical aspects of formulating accurate differential diagnoses. You doubtless need no help with this. Instead, we'll point out the key concerns of case managers as they examine the 5 axes of your diagnostic picture of the patient.

Axis I (Clinical Syndromes): There are two primary causes for rejection or non-certification under Axis I: (1) A condition not severe enough to qualify as a true mental disorder, and (2) Conditions too severe for brief therapy amelioration.

There are specific diagnoses which have a high probability of disqualifying your patient for coverage by Managed Care companies. If the primary diagnosis you select for Axis I is a V code, most Managed Care reps will not certify for treatment. For example, V codes such as these almost always bring quick rejections: Academic Problems V62.30; Occupational Problems V62.20; Phase of Life / Life Circumstances Problems V62.89; Social Maladjustment V62.4; Adverse Effects of Work Environment V62.1; Childhood or Adolescent Antisocial Behavior V71.02; Malingering V65.20; or Legal Circumstances V62.5.

These classifications are considered uncertifiable because, by their very definition, V codes represent conditions that are not clearly due to mental disorders. One Managed Care company's treatment form specifically states, "DSM-III-R Diagnosis: To Include At Least Axis I Dx: *(No V Codes)."* Most, however, make no mention of this, but you use V codes at your own risk.

Of all the V codes, the most common error made by providers is to list on Axis I "Marital Problems V61.10", "Other Specified Family Circumstances V61.80", or "Parent-Child Problems V61.20". The *DSM-III-R* clearly states that these conditions are *"not apparently due to mental disorder."* Keep in mind that the case manager is not only responsible to oversee utilization, but to assure that only those services covered by the patients benefits will be certed. V codes may be of clinical interest and merit some attention or treatment, but *they are not typically covered by the patient's insurance plan.*

In light of this reality, how should you handle patient's with V code diagnoses? Take, for example, a marital conflict that is the primary cause for the patient seeking treatment. In most cases it is highly probable that a diagnosis of depression, dysthymia, or an anxiety disorder is present. This may become your primary or principle diagnosis for Axis I, with the V code diagnosis standing as a secondary choice. If you can, in all ethical good conscience, use this primary-secondary method with V-code patients, do so. Otherwise, refer the patient to other resources for help, and inform the case manager that the patient does not meet criteria for your services.

The second concern is diagnostic classifications that are too severe to merit certification. In the case manager's judgment, such conditions are unlikely to respond to brief therapy interventions. Examples of such conditions might include: Transvestic Fetishism, Severe 302.30, Depersonalization Disorder 300.60, or Schizophrenia, Paranoid Type, Chronic 295.34. Obviously, to affect significant change in 20 sessions or less in patients manifesting symptoms justifying these diagnoses would border on the miraculous (and "The Miraculous" is not a common expectation of most case managers! — And if you promise, or even hint, that you expect to do the "miraculous," you will soon find yourself on the "Non-Referral, *Provider Non Grata* List).

So, avoid both extremes. Select realistic, "brief-therapy-friendly" diagnoses. And if you cannot, then assist the patient in finding appropriate help elsewhere.

Axis II (Personality & Developmental Disorders):
Keeping in mind the reason Managed Care exists in the first place, your primary concern here is this: The case reviewer will cert only those conditions that can realistically be expected to respond to short-term treatment. If your primary diagnosis is, for example, "Schizotypal Personality Disorder, Severe 301.22" or "Histrionic Personality Disorder 301.50"`, what would your conclusions be if you were a case manager, responsible to certify only those conditions that could be effectively treated in short-term, symptom-reduction therapy? You would be less than favorably disposed to certify a course of treatment for this patient, wouldn't you? And so will most case managers you approach with such diagnoses on Axis II.

The bottom line, then? If your patient manifests severe personality disorders, or other developmental problems that are clearly outside the purview of brief therapy (e.g., "Mental Retardation 318.00"), refer them to more suitable help, informing the case manager of their needs and your actions. If, on the other hand, they have other symptoms that can effectively be treated in brief therapy, indicate this in your Axis I diagnoses. Then treat them accordingly (assuming, of course, that the personality or developmental disorders would not preclude this kind of intervention due to their severity).

Axis III (Physical Disorders & Conditions): Most of the time you will find yourself writing this on the line designated for Axis III classification, "No known diagnosis". Occasionally, however, you will note physiological conditions in the patient. Standing alone, they do not justify certification for brief therapy, but can account for mental disorders related to their presence.

Some examples include: "Epilepsy, Traumatic", "Essential Hypertension, Severe," "Hepatic Disease, Alcohol Related," "Tension Headaches," "Bleeding Disorder Secondary to Ingestion of Anticoagulant." Such conditions obviously are linked to Axis I diagnoses, which merit certification.

Some physical conditions when present can disqualify the patient for services. One such diagnosis is "Alzheimer's Disease." Whether presenile or senile onset, most case managers will not cert for this condition, but work with you to make a more appropriate referral for long-term medical and/or custodial care. Some big-hearted reps will, however, authorize a brief course of family therapy if an Axis I diagnosis is also given (e.g., "Primary Degenerative Dementia of the Alzheimer Type, Presenile Onset, Uncomplicated, Moderate 290.10").

Recently we were confronted with a thorny dilemma with respect to Axis III patients. Shortly before writing this chapter a case manager referred a couple to us for treatment of depression. On intake both husband and wife revealed that, "We both are HIV positive and want you to promise that you will not reveal this to anyone." Here we clearly have an Axis III diagnosis with Axis I complications. But how do you respond to the patient's primary need for privacy to protect their personal lives, and their jobs? We feel very uncomfortable consciously withholding the Axis III diagnosis on documentation, and even more uneasy reviewing the case with the case manager, without reference to the real source of the patients' depression.

We consider the patient's right to privacy, and their need to protect their security, a precious thing. From our own value system, we also believe that dealing truthfully in all we do is ultimate. What to do? What would you do? We'll leave this struggle to you, your conscience, advice from your professional association (and perhaps advice from your lawyer).

We all must come to grips with this kind of challenge. The HIV and AIDS patient will find their way into our offices in increasing numbers. How can we handle their special needs, and maintain our own ethical and moral integrity? As Peggy Oquist, a member of our staff, pointed out so well, "This is truly an issue of our times."

Another member of our staff, Jesse Trice, M.A., specializes in therapy with AIDS patients. His recommendation is, when your conscience will not allow you to omit the Axis III diagnosis, to put this: "A serious debilitating illness." Should the case manager ask the nature of this illness, the therapist can reply, "I'm sorry, I am not at liberty to discuss this at the client's request."

Axis IV (Severity of Psychosocial Stressors): In our review of the treatment reports of 15 Managed Care firms, we find that 9 of them require Axis IV ratings. In most cases we recommend that you give case managers only the information requested. But Axis IV ratings present a different case. Even for those companies not requiring the stressor-severity ratings, we suggest you give it anyway.

If you use the Treatment Targeted Impairments schema proposed in this text, the level of stressor severity is instrumental to treatment intervention selected and used. For this reason, we suggest you write in the primary Axis IV stressors description and rating in the diagnosis section. This communicates to the case reviewer that you have done a thorough job of assessing the key symptom targets for treatment, and understand their impact on the patient's life.

For purposes of review: The Axis IV Psychosocial Stressors are rated on a 7-point scale as follows:

Severity of Stressor Rating Scale

0	1	2	3	4	5	6
No Info	None	Mild	Moderate	Severe	Extreme	Catastrophic

Where there are multiple stressors, we recommend rating and describing the 2 most severe stressors causing symptoms or impairments. Stressors should be defined according to how they affect the patient over the past 12 months as: *Acute* — lasting less than 6 months; or *Enduring circumstances* — lasting 6 months or longer.

The stressor(s) must be clearly related to the following:

1. Stressful event causes a new impairment or symptoms,
2. Causes recurrence of previous impairment or symptoms, or
3. Causes exacerbation of existing impairment or symptoms.

In addition, the severity of the stressor is judged by (a) how much negative change the stressor causes to patient's life, (b) how much the patient defines the stressor as aversive or painful, (c) how much control the patient has over the stressor, and (d) how many stressors are affecting the patient at any one time.

The most common types of stressors include these:

1. Relationship   (break-up, marriage, separation, divorce).
2. Family/Parenting   (birth, runaway child, family discord).
3   Developmental   (puberty, PMS, menopause, retirement).
4. Psychological Trauma   (rape, molestation, disasters, death
    of loved one).
5. Physical Illness/Injury   (auto accident, surgery, cancer).
6. Financial   (bankruptcy, loss of job).
7. Occupational   (threat of layoff, retirement, transfer).
8. Living Circumstances   (move to new city, forced move
    to apartment from house due to divorce).
9. Legal   (DUI, arrest, lawsuit).

Here are two examples of Axis IV descriptive ratings:

Axis IV: _Psychosocial Stressor — Spouse abuse;_
           Severity 5, Extreme. (enduring circum.)

Axis IV: _Psychosocial Stressor — Threat of job layoff;_
           Severity 4, Severe (acute event)

Axis V (GAF — Global Assessment of Functioning): All 15 Managed Care companies require the GAF rating under the diagnosis section of the treatment reports. Most of the case managers we have worked with over the years want to know this number in addition to the Axis I diagnosis. We have had some case managers call us after receiving a treatment report with this question, "Can you explain why the client's GAF is 45?" You should be careful and accurate when assigning this rating to your patient.

For purposes of review: The GAF scale is a composite estimation of the patient's psychological, social and occupational functioning. The GAF is a continuous scale ranging from 1 (persistent suicidal or homicidal risk) to 90 (the patient is essentially symptom free).

Two GAF ratings should be given. (1) The *current level of functioning,* which can serve as a baseline to measure how effective therapy has been; and (2) *The highest level of functioning in the last year,* which can be used to measure follow-up outcome as compared to patient's pre-therapy functioning.

A brief version of the GAF Scale that we find helpful in filling out treatment reports is presented here:

Short Version of GAF Scale

Range of Rating	Composite Rating	Description of Level of Functioning
81-90	85	Minimal or absent symptoms; normal daily concerns.
71-80	75	Only slight impairment; symptoms are transient.
61-70	65	Mild symptoms, but functioning generally well.
51-60	55	Moderate, occasional symptoms.
41-50	45	Serious symptoms (e.g., suicidal ideations).
31-40	35	Impaired reality testing, or major impairment in several areas, such as mood, thinking, judgment, family relations, work, school.

21-30	25	Behavior influenced by delusions & hallucinations, or serious impairment of judgment, communication, or inability to function in most areas.
11-20	15	Some danger of harming self or others, or unable to care for self, or gross communication impairment.
1-10	5	Persistent danger of harming self or others, or completely unable to care for self, or serious suicidal attempt with clear expectation of death.

Here is an example of Axis V GAF ratings on two different treatment reports:

Axis V: Current _45__
          Highest in past year _75__

Axis V: Current _78__
          Highest in past year _75__

The first example is typical of a patient seen at intake who is experiencing an acute stressor. The second example might represent the GAF for the same patient upon discharge after a brief course of treatment.

We note that many Managed Care treatment reports do not specify "current" and "within the past year" designations. We recommend that you write in these classifications anyway. Doing so will demonstrate your attention to detail, and can illustrate the severity of current impairments as well as how successful therapy has been at a glance.

We hope that this review helps you approach the multi-axial diagnosis section on treatment forms with a bit more confidence, and with some feel for what case managers are looking for.

2. *"Is the patient on medication?"*

Many clinicians (with the exception of psychiatrists) have relied on cognitive, behavioral, or insight modalities to bring about therapeutic gain, and have only rarely resorted to medication to help their patients. There is much good to be said for this, and a non-drug means to the desired end is admirable.

But how does the typical case manager look at the use of psychotrophic medications to manage symptoms? Do they look with favor on a therapist who does not refer the patient for medication evaluation? Do they appreciate a treatment plan that shuns medical support in favor of a straight-out behavioral approach? The answer is categorically *no*.

Case reviewers carefully consider your responses to items like these:

"Has a medical evaluation been requested?"
"Has medical evaluation been completed to date?"
"If the patient is on medication, give name, dose, start date:"
"Why hasn't a medication evaluation been requested?"

They believe that brief therapy is apt to be more effective in meeting treatment goals sooner if medication is used as part of the treatment plan. Why? Because Managed Care focuses on symptoms. And symptoms can be controlled by medication much more rapidly than by any other means. "Symptom reduction," "Managed Care," and "medication management" are often synonymous terms.

So, most of us have had to adjust our tendency to shy away from the use of psychopharmacological agents. In a day when we believe in and say things like, "Say No To Drugs," when it comes to approaching the Managed Care client, we might want to reconsider this motto. From Managed Care's perspective, it would seem that to "Say Yes To Drugs" (the right ones, of course) bodes well for early successful discharge.

Two common diagnoses trigger, in case reviewers' minds, the need for medication evaluation: (1) anxiety disorders, and (2) depressive disorders. Let's say a case manager sees an Axis I diagnosis of "Generalized Anxiety Disorder 300.02" on your treatment form. When they look under the section "Medication Consultation," they see that you have filled in "None." The question that comes to their mind is, "Why not? ... Couldn't some form of tranquilizing medication serve to help relieve symptoms?" Or a patient with a "Major Depression 296.32" diagnosis also has "None" written in the medication blank; the rep asks herself or himself, "Couldn't antidepressant meds help reduce symptoms in this client?"

These questions should come to your mind before it comes to theirs. If we are to become cooperative members of the Managed Care team, we need to become more medication-friendly. (And we must confess that this has been one of the tougher adjustments we have had to make personally and professionally as we embraced the Managed Care realities — having prided ourselves for years providing effective, brief, drug-free therapy with our patients). But, when in Rome, speak Italian. When working within the Managed Care team, make referrals for medical evaluations.

What we have tried to do is to refer appropriate patients to psychiatrists and other medical doctors who are known to be conservative in how they prescribe meds. The psychiatrists on our staff, and those in the community who get our referrals, are not heavy-handed when it comes to prescribing meds, and work closely with us to help get the patient off drugs and self-sufficient as early as possible. If you are going to introduce meds more and more into your treatment plans because it is expected of you, then find doctors committed to making themselves obsolete. Better still, when you find them, ask them to join your staff to round out the kind of group practice Managed Care holds in high esteem.

3. "Was the patient hospitalized in the last 6 months?"

Keep in mind that the questions you are asked on the forms you complete from Managed Care firms are asked for specific reasons. They are not random inquiries. As you respond to each question, try to come at it from the case manager's needs and perspective.

Case managers do not want to authorize or cert a treatment plan that has a high probability of failure to meet focused treatment goals within a time-limited context.

If a patient has recent history of psychiatric hospitalization, then brief therapy may, or may not be indicated. The case manager will also need to know the details of the course of hospitalization, and discharge after-care planning. Medications prescribed will be important as well.

Similarly, if the patient has had recent detox or rehab inpatient care for substance abuse, this has important implications for brief intervention. The case rep will need to know the course of hospital care and aftercare planning.

Whenever your patient has had either psychiatric or substance abuse hospitalization, provide details of (1) the course of inpatient care, (2) discharge planning prescribed, and (3) how you plan to build on what has already been undertaken, including relapse prevention strategies.

The case manager also wants to see how you recommend, rely on, and insist on the patient using outside support resources in addition to therapy itself. Be certain to outline a specific plan for homework, family intervention, and the use of 12-Step and other recovery groups in the case of CD patients.

A note about hospitalizing a Managed Care patient: It is essential to do all you can to plan a treatment program for the patient that precludes costly hospitalization. Sometimes, however, this is not possible. If you feel the patient requires inpatient care, the case manager will want the following steps taken:

1. What are the objective, measurable justifications demonstrating the medical necessity for inpatient care?
2. What are the possible consequences to patient or to others if inpatient care is not utilized?
3. Has patient had a thorough medication consultation to reduce symptoms or impairments?
4. Can some lesser level of care be used? For example, partial hospitalization, day treatment, residential rehab, more frequent intensive outpatient treatment.
5. Does the inpatient program understand Managed Care?
6. What are the plans for outpatient brief therapy aftercare?
7. What are the plans for aftercare support resources other than therapy?
8. What members of patient's social system need to be enlisted as part of aftercare plan to help maintain adjustment and prevent relapse?

Also, you should always get the case manager's pre-authorization for inpatient admission, unless there is a clear suicidal or homicidal risk at hand. You should also ask the case manager to recommend those facilities that she or he has used with confidence in the past, rather than referring the patient to a facility of your choice. If you have used a particular hospital program that you believe is "Managed Care friendly" (i.e., has a reputation for short-stays), tell the case rep about it, but defer to their recommendation.

A word about CD patients: Most case reviewers will look with suspicion on any treatment plan for a diagnosed case of substance abuse that attempts to treat any mental disorder, symptoms, or impairments without first addressing the need to structure a therapeutic recovery program for the patient. Yes, such impairments must be dealt with, but *only* when, and if, the patient and his/her family system are actively involved in a plan to manage the addiction. The only exception to this would be a high lethality suicidal or homicidal diagnosis. Even in such cases, after crisis intervention is undertaken, addressing the CD issues and designing a recovery program is the next step to take, followed by management of the precipitating causes of the crisis behavior.

4. *"What is the proposed modality of treatment?"*

Most treatment plans will ask you to choose from a list of several treatment interventions, such as: "Individual Therapy — 30 minutes 90843; Individual Therapy — 50 minutes 90844; Family/Couple Therapy 90847; Group Therapy 90853; Management By Medication 90862; and Other Interventions (explain)."

The choice of "Individual Therapy — 50 minutes" does not need any discussion here. This is the most commonly used category by providers. But the provider who keeps the needs of the Managed Care rep in mind will use a more creative approach to modality selection.

To keep the patient's care cost effective, case managers appreciate therapists who utilize "Medication Management" to reduce the severity of impairments or symptoms. They also like to see entries under the "Other" heading that lists homework, outside workshops, conferences, and support groups to help patient maintain adjustment and wellness.

Don't neglect these important modalities used often by the effective brief therapist.

Under this section the case manager also wants to see 3 other things: "Start Date; End Date; and Frequency of Sessions." The start-date is obvious. The end-date tells the rep that you are planning for discharge from the very outset of treatment. This tells them that you are not thinking in terms of long-term care, nor are you counting on extensions. But you are thinking in Managed Care terms — successful early discharge of a satisfied patient.

The other most important feature in this section is the "How Often" or frequency question. Most case managers give high marks to providers who space out sessions toward the intermediate and latter phase of treatment. This indicates clearly that the therapist is attempting to wean the patient from dependence on the clinician or upon therapy. Seeing the patient every 2 weeks, or once monthly toward the end of treatment is good, both for the patient, and for your reputation.

5. *"What is the primary approach to be used?"*

This section is much more than what it appears to be. Most treatment reports ask you to check off or select one of several approaches you plan to use in treating the patient:

☐ Crisis Intervention
☐ Supportive Maintenance
☐ Focused Symptom Reduction or Behavior Change

☐ Psychoanalysis, Awareness, Insight
☐ Major Personality Change
☐ Assessment and Referral Only

Many therapists, in their haste to get the paperwork behind them, whip through the forms checking off the above items without asking themselves one important question: What does this response tell the case manager about my proposed work with this patient? What does this response suggest about my therapeutic orientation?

What this is in reality is a kind of "litmus test". How you handle this section gives the case reviewer a sense of your therapy style. It also indicates, with a high degree of validity, how you think, and how successful you might be, as part of the Managed Care team.

For example, there are 3 items in the above selection list that are definite "red flags" for any case manager with a pulse. Can you identify the 3 items (without looking at the list below)?

The 3 high-risk items are:

(1) ☐ Supportive Maintenance,
(2) ☐ Psychoanalysis, Awareness, Insight, and
(3) ☐ Major Personality Change

A therapist who checks "Supportive Maintenance" reveals that he or she plans to practice non-goal-focused therapy that has a high probability of long-term care. A clinician who selects "Psychoanalysis, Awareness, Insight" has set off an alarm that will disqualify him/her as cooperative with the Managed Care objectives, and can expect to be dropped pretty quickly from the provider list And any provider who chooses "Major Personality Change" similarly indicates by this action an unrealistic expectation for outcome based on the patient's limited benefits. It is highly unlikely, aside from some miraculous intervention from above, that a "major" personality change can be affected within a brief therapy framework.

To avoid these red flags and alarms, avoid selecting items that point to long-term or unrealistic treatment. If the patient needs supportive care, help him or her find such assistance elsewhere. If they need or request deeper, insight/analytical care, help refer them for such care elsewhere. If they have major personality disorders, limit yourself to those manifestations that can be realistically addressed in brief therapy (see the chapter on assessment of Treatment Targeted Impairments).

Is there *one* item that you can always count on to bring "music" to the heart of most case managers, and at the same time enhance your own professional image in their mind? The answer is "yes." That item, as you probably have already deduced, indicates your orientation to brief therapy.

The crucial item includes some reference to the following:

❑ Focused Symptom Reduction or Behavior Change

The only exception to this, perhaps, is "Crisis Intervention." Aside from this modality, you will never go wrong selecting "Focused Symptom Reduction" on treatment forms. This is also the item of choice when treating substance abuse cases. You're on safe ground there. You may be on shifting, sinking sand when you venture elsewhere.

6.   *"Rate Severity of Symptoms"; "Suicide Risk"; and "Physical Violence"*

We will assume that your clinical training well equips you to handle these items. They appear on most treatment forms and require no special discussion here.

7.   *"The Treatment Plan — What are the treatment strategies and techniques to relieve target symptoms?":*

Some reports simply ask for the "Treatment Plan," others want the "Treatment Goals," and still others require the "Treatment and Progress" details. Regardless of what it is called, case managers want you to *briefly* describe the interventions you plan to use to reduce, relieve or change the patient's impairment, problem or complaint that brings them to therapy in the first place.

Numbering, step-by-step, the way you intend to deal with the patient's problems is the simplest method. We find that using a numbered, succinct list in short phrases keeps us from rambling, and tends to minimize fuzzy thinking.

The best way to give you a good feel for this method is to present actual treatment plans that have received favorable comments from several Managed Care reps. This certainly is not the only way to present good treatment plans, but it demonstrates for you one proven system that has shown itself to be highly effective.

The treatment plan guiding your clinical work should include many of the 24 steps outlined in the Brief Therapy chapter of this book. Establishing a time-limited agenda, forming a trusting therapeutic alliance, assessing impairments, neutralizing resistances — these are common to every treatment plan. Successful outcome depends on careful implementation of these techniques. However, space on the treatment form is limited, so you will have to boil your written plan down to a few key steps you will take in meeting the patient's needs.

What follows are several sample treatment plans for specific diagnoses for your consideration:

Treatment Plan for Substance Abuse

Treatment Targeted Impairments:
1. Alcohol dependence, moderate.
2. Major depression, acute episode.

Goals of Treatment — to be met by (discharge date):
1. Determine the need for (a) detox, (b) rehab, (c) meds.
2. Take history & enlist the involvement of spouse/family.
3. Neutralize denial; determine motivators to leverage compliance.
4. Help pt. identify triggers in self & others.
5. Help pt. identify destructive impact of alcohol on family & work.
6. Supervise pt. participation in 3+ recovery/12 Step meetings/wk.
7. Assign workbook homework to get at causal factors.
8. Cognitive & behavioral methods to deal with depression.
9. Plan for outside recovery resources to promote sobriety & prevent relapse.

Treatment Plan for Sexual Addiction

Treatment Targeted Impairments:
1.   Pornography addiction.
2.   Marital/relationship dysfunction.

Goals of Treatment — to be met by (date of discharge):
1.   Enlist wife in therapy sessions to detach enabling.
2.   Expose all deception, hiding, & scheming to undo denial.
3.   Help pt. understand effects of addiction on self & marriage.
4.   Homework: Pt. to take wife to all porno bookstores he has previously visited secretly (to break power of secrecy obsess.).
5.   Burn all porno with wife present; save ashes in plastic bag as memorial symbol of finality; keep bag in prominent place.
6.   Assign homework: reading, workbook, letters of confession, admission, disclosure, requests for forgiveness.
7.   Supervise pt.'s involvement in 2+ SA meetings/wk; motivate wife to participate in weekly Al-Anon meetings.
8.   Homework: tapes on improving marital/sexual happiness.
9.   Educate pt. & desensitize for normative sexual functioning.
10. Help pt. identify & unhook from traumatic causal events.

Treatment Plan for Dysphoric Mood

Treatment Targeted Impairments:
1.   Depression, social withdrawal, hopeless/helpless verbal reports.

Goals of Treatment — to be met by (discharge date):
1.   Refer for antidepressant meds eval.
2.   Increase cognitive appraisal and reports of strengths, assets.
3.   Broaden pt.'s alternative options.
4.   Help pt. express repressed anger in constructive ways.
5.   Homework: Letter writing in journal to targets of rage.
6.   Homework: Outside involvement in anger workshop series.
7.   Pt. will be able to identify triggers of mood swing & verbalize

8. Pt. will demonstrate a 50% reduction in depression per Beck Depression Inventory compared to intake scores.

Treatment Plan for Domestic Violence*

Treatment Targeted Impairments:
1. Assaultive behavior, verbal & physical, toward wife.
2. Self-hate ideations, verbalizations.
3. Acts out frustrations, poor impulse control.

Goals of Treatment — to be met by (date of discharge):
1. Help pt. increase awareness, understanding & acceptance of self as batterer.
2. Help pt. identify and clarify his role & responsibilities as a husband.
3. Help pt. develop appropriate ways to respond to stress, by breaking thru denial, rationalizations & violent ideations.
4. Educate the pt. on the cycle of violence, his role within the cycle.
5. Help pt. develop self-control by identifying ways to break the cycle of power, control & tension, pinpointing the precipitating cues or signals.
6. Help pt. develop appropriate ways to manage his anger, and develop coping skills to reduce tension & stress.
7. Develop skills to assist him to break down the sexual, social, & psychological patterns which perpetuate rituals of intimidation, threats & verbal attacks that lead to violence.
8. Help pt. learn appropriate negotiation & communication skills.
9. Help build pt.'s wounded self-concept by simple bibliotherapy homework to build his confidence in strategies for effectively handling frustration, anger, feelings of failure, guilt, & embarassment.
10. Pt. will be able to use cognitive-behavioral solutions to improve his interactions with wife, children & employer, even at times of high tension or frustration.

---

* Treatment plan developed by Jesse M. Trice, M.A., 1993

Treatment Plan for Panic Attacks

Treatment Targeted Impairments:
1. Panic attacks, no apparent causal event
2. Obsessive worrying, fears

Goals of Treatment — to be met by (discharge date):
1. Assess need for anxiety-reduction medication evaluation.
2. Help pt. gain belief in her ability to take control of her life.
3. Compartmentalize obsessions to 1 hour daily.
4. Homework: massed practice listing all worries, fears, dreads in writing for 1 hr. on even days; odd days read aloud and burn and flush ashes.
5. Homework: keep a 3-column daily log (a) describing panic event, (b) specific automatic thoughts, and (c) the false beliefs.
6. Homework: affirmation book; writing self-affirmations; daily meditation on affirmations during non-obsession times.
7. Help pt. understand anxiety triggers, past & present.
8. Pt. will be able to redefine/reframe panic attacks and to "go with" instead of "resist" anxiety.
9. Pt. will have several alternative options when symptoms occur.
10. Pt. will report at least 30% anxiety reduction post-test as compared to pre-test scores.

Treatment Plan for Work Dysphoria

Treatment Targeted Impairments:
1. Dread and total avoidance of workplace.
2. Social withdrawal, uncommunicativeness.

Goals of Treatment — to be met by (discharge date):
1. Assess need for medication eval to manage depressed mood.
2. Help pt. specify exact nature of work aversion.
3. Consult with pt.'s EAP rep to assist in preserving job.
4. Consult with wife to assess other contributing stressors.
5. Help pt. plan a comprehensive vocational testing to give hope.

6. Teach cognitive affirmations to help pt. manage negative thoughts on the job.
7. Work with EAP to promote possible job transfer.
8. Enlist support of family/friends to encourage pt.'s changes.
9. Homework: ventilation of feelings to relieve helplessness.
10. Homework: monitor automatic thoughts, false beliefs, and replace with reframed alternative definitions.
11. Homework: Bibliotherapy, *"What Color Is Your Parachute."*

Treatment Plan for Incest/Molestation Victim*

Treatment Targeted Impairments:
1. Dysphoric mood, hopeless/helpless thoughts, verbalizations.
2. Sexual dysfunction, fear of intimacy with husband.
3. Fear of employer's authority, impaired concentration on job.

Goals of Treatment — to be met by (date of discharge):
1. Assess need for meds to manage depression & anxiety.
2. Homework: bibliotherapy readings on incest victims who openly, courageously tell their stories to build pt.'s confidence.
3. Journaling homework to encourage pt. to express her shame, rage, guilt, confusion.
4. Journaling homework: letters to perpetrators and parents.
5. Bibliotherapy homework: *"Beyond The Darkness"* recovery workbook integrated into sessions to help build pt.'s self-worth & confidence in her own value, specialness, and spiritual strengths.
6. Encourage pt. to freely talk out and role play feelings of rage & shame toward perpetrators.
7. Develop specific plan for confronting perpetrators.
8. Role play, write cognitive rehearsal script for confronting abandoning parents.
9. Homework: letters of forgiveness-release following open confrontation of parents & perpetrators.
10. Attend incest-survivors workshops.
11. Active participation in incest-survivor support groups.
12. Homework: begin 12-Step workbook for victims of sexual abuse.
13. Homework: create list of assertive behaviors (to overcome people-pleasing codependency) and carry out at least 1 per day.
14. Enlist involvement of husband to support pt.'s changes.

15. Educate pt. & husband on normative sexual behavior using *"Intended For Pleasure"* with homework assignments.
16. Maintain bi-weekly phone contact with pt. post discharge to encourage follow-thru with above recovery plan, & to allay her fears of abandonment by therapist.
17. Send pt. self-help articles once monthly post discharge.

---

* This treatment plan was successfully implemented within 21 sessions.

Treatment Plan for Suicidal Behavior (outpatient treatment)

Treatment Targeted Impairments:
1. Suicidal thoughts and plan (o.d. Valium/alcohol).

Goals of Treatment — to be met by (discharge date):
1. Assess lethality on 10-point scale.
2. Assess need for brief hospitalization to protect pt.'s life.
3. Assess need for intensive medication management if outpt. care is indicated.
4. Help pt. identify the precipitating triggers in self and others.
5. Assist pt. in clarifying options to handle hopeless feelings.
6. Enlist involvement of spouse/family/friends to support pt.
7. Homework: Bibliotherapy, *"Happiness Is A Choice"*; *"The Greatest Salesman In The World"*; *"Healing of Damage Emotions."*
8. Supervise involvement in self-help Emotional Health Anon. gp.
9. Homework: volunteer to help the needy in convalescent home (or other community service, helping those in great need).
10. Pt. will report at least 75% reduction in suicidal/hopeless thoughts/behaviors.
11. Pt.'s spouse will report at least 75% decrease in depressed mood & suicidal verbalizations by pt.
12. Pt. will willingly dispose of drugs in presence of wife.
13. Pt. will authorize therapist to consult with medical doctor to promote discontinuation of Valium prescriptions.

Let us again point out that these are only samples of actual treatment plans that we, or members of our staff, have developed and carried out successfully. Successfully, that is, from two perspectives: (1) the patient's presenting complaints and impairments were eliminated or reduced by the patient's own reports; and (2) the case managers who referred these patients to us were satisfied enough to continue referring other patients to us after receiving these reports. These are key criteria that measure how effective treatment and the treatment plans really are.

But keep in mind, dear colleague, that this sample of treatment plans represents our own clinical orientation and our own clinical and value-based comfort zone. Yours will doubtless be different, reflecting your unique style. It is our hope that what we've presented here will give you a model for preparing your plans in a simple, straightforward style that is entirely Managed Care friendly.

8. *"Patient Progress — Describe the* <u>*measurable*</u> *changes that have occurred or that you expect in patient's behavior or mood before treatment ends"*:

This section is important to you and the case manger in 3 important ways:

(1) **Predicts successful outcome:** Your responses on progress updates at regular intervals provides tangible evidence that treatment is meeting (or failing to meet) interim outcome objectives. Progress updates tell us, and the case rep, whether we are on target and on track, so that we can be "on time" accomplishing the final outcome objectives by the date expected.

(2) **Suggests treatment plan revisions:** Your responses to this item tell you and the case manager, in behavioral terms, where course-corrections are needed to increase the probability of achieving outcome goals. If outcome objectives are not being met, or if patient's

condition is getting worse, both therapist and case manager can re-evaluate the appropriateness of (a) the outcome objectives, (b) the treatment interventions being utilized, and (c) the diagnoses of the impairments or symptoms themselves.

(3) **Provides data to justify extensions:** The detail you provide under this section, and how you present it, can determine whether you are able to persuade (or fail to persuade) the case manager to authorize extensions of services for patients who need further care.

Many clinicians have told us during practice development consultations that they feel tense and uneasy in their dealings with case managers. In both written and telephone communication, they report sensing a kind of adversarial relationship with case reviewers. When asked for specifics as to how they complete the Patient Progress section of the treatment report, the reason becomes clear. Many of these clinicians simply have ineffectively defined patient change in *behavioral* terms. The case rep gets frustrated, pushes for more functional, observable data to measure progress, to do his/her job. The provider feels at a loss, that his or her clinical judgment is being challenged, gets defensive, or tries to "snow" the case manager with more fuzzy clinical abstractions. Therefore, an uncomfortable tension is created between rep and therapist that makes it harder for everybody to do their job, and can impede the patient from receiving the care they need.

Much of this can be avoided by simply knowing how to report patient change, or lack of it, in behavioral language from the point of view of the patient and her/his sphere of life. This kind of "hard" information helps both therapist and case manager corroborate treatment effectiveness, and provides the raw material for making the decisions to discharge the patient or to authorize continued care.

Behaviorally-focused data on treatment reports can also help save you a lot of telephone-tag and needless time on the phone justifying your work with patients to case reps. Ask any case reviewer and they will tell you that they are overwhelmed with paperwork with "holes" in it, and are backlogged with calls to providers to clarify information on treatment forms. If you give them concrete, objectifiable data that can save them this kind of follow-up with you, you will soon earn a reputation as one of their favorite providers (and, of course, that may very likely mean more referrals).

So what's the best way to describe changes in the patient in written documentation and during phone updates? There are 4 key ways to do this:

(1)   Specific behavioral statements from the patient describing how successfully outcome objectives are being reached — e.g., *"Patient reports 'I've been sober now 20 days and haven't missed a single day of work.'"*

(2)   Specific behavioral statements from significant others — e.g., *"Patient's wife reports 'John hasn't had a drink in almost 3 weeks and seems much less angry with the kids.'"*

(3)   Behavioral observations by therapist — e.g., *"Patient has chips for 10 AA meetings in past month, completed Steps 3 and 4 in workbook, & demonstrates less minimization and blaming (denial)."*

(4)   Objective reports by patient (or significant others) on psychometric instruments per pre- and post-tests data — e.g., *"Patient reports on post-test a 3-point reduction in stress on the job; and a 30% improvement on the Beck Depression Inventory."*

We'll briefly present here a few good examples of progress updates that make case manager's jobs easier, and stand you in good favor with them as you help them do their jobs more efficiently. Notice the objective, behavioral descriptions that support the conclusions we made about how the outcome objectives were, or were not, met.

Progress Toward Meeting Outcome Objectives
for Substance Abuse

(Estimated discharge date):

1. Patient now on supervised med. management for stress/depress., & daily Antabuse (W. Lee Burnes, M.D., Huntington Beach, reports good follow-thru).
2. Pt. verbalizes destructive effects of alcohol on self & family.
3. Pt. able to verbalize 12 Steps; has worked first 3 steps & now working on step 4 in workbook.
4. Pt. attending 4 AA meetings/wk.; has sponsor.
5. Pt.'s spouse attending 1 Al-Anon meeting/wk. and participating in pt's therapy; providing reality testing & confrontation.
6. Pt. able to verbalize & list triggers that cause stress to drink.
7. Pt. able to list options to prevent relapse.
8. Pt. attending Overcomers Outreach (Church support gp. for addicts) 1/wk.
9. Pt. shows decrease in depression demonstrated by 50% decrease in Beck Depression Inventory pre-post rating.

Progress Toward Meeting Outcome Objectives
for Dysphoric Mood

(Estimated discharge date):

1. Pt. on anti-depressant regime per referral to J. Nelson, M.D., Los Alamitos, who reports good response & follow-thru.
2. Improved self-image per pt.'s reports that "I find myself saying good things about me to me for a change."
3. Pt. able to release repressed anger per pt.'s statements, "I'm able to tell my parents how upset I am because they were not there for me when I was little." Pt. also writing letters to them.
4. Pt shows less depression demonstrated by ability to list 4 alternatives to prevent being overwhelmed by moods.
5. Pt. actively learning skills to handle rage; attended 2 anger workshops.
6. Pt. able to identify triggers of anger/depression and states, "I know who sets me off, and how to unhook from their tricks."

7. Pt.'s level of depression improved as demonstrated by 40% pre-post reduction in Beck Depression Inventory rating.
8. Pt attending weekly Emotional Health Anonymous gps. and reports, "I really get a lot off my chest in those groups."

Progress Toward Meeting Outcome Objectives for Panic Attacks

(Estimated discharge date):
1. Pt. refuses meds. for religious reasons, but reports feeling "better, less headaches, don't wake up in the middle of the night in cold sweats like I used to."
2. Pt. reports increased self-control over panic reactions per her reports "I know new ways to talk myself thru panic attacks."
3. Pt. better able to manage times of anxiety by controlling times of obsessional thinking per reports "I allow myself to let out my stress during evening vent sessions."
4. Pt. reading & writing daily affirmations, reports "I feel so much better now that I'm telling myself healthier things."
5. Pt. able to identify & unhook from anxiety triggers, "now I know how I let them cause me fear and guilt."
6. Pt. reports less helplessness, "Most of the time I seem to be able to ride the fears, rather than be buried by them."
7. Pt. reports increased support resources, "I call my sister-in-law when I feel like I might get overwhelmed, & she's a big help."
8. Pt. able to do graded approach exercises toward feared events.
9. Pt. demonstrates a 3-point reduction in anxiety per post-test anxiety scores; & reduction in anxiety from moderate to mild on Symptom Check List 90 (SCL-90).
10. Questionnaire to pt.'s husband reveals "she seems much more relaxed and easy to live with and our sex life is even better."
11. Pt. shows realistic attitude toward stress, "I used to try to get rid of all my anxieties, but now I just flow with it and accept it; I know World War III is not going to break out!"
12. Pt. is able to handle work responsibilities without leaving early.
13. Pt. is able to outline a course of action to handle future attacks.

When space does not permit listing all such evidences of progress, pick the best indicators and list them. You can mention some of the others during your phone updates with the case manager.

The important consideration is, as you have just noted, to use proof-statements and data to back up your assertions of improvement or reduction in impairments or symptoms. Instead of saying, "Improvement in level of depressed mood," it is far better to to say, "Decrease in level of depression as demonstrated by pt's reports "My appetite is better and I'm not thinking about how to kill myself any more." It is far better to say, "Pt. shows increased self-confidence per statements, 'I am able to make my own decisions now without always doubting myself,'" rather than, "Pt. shows increased self-esteem and ego strength."

Keep in mind that the key words are these: Observable, objectifiable, quantifiable, measurable, action-linked, impairment-specific, and behavioral representations of the patient's perception of things. We need to let the patient be the expert and listen carefully to their reports. We need to listen to their assessments and report them verbatim to case managers, rather than listening to our overstimulated clinical brains. They all too often crank out a load of vague psychological labels and ideas. Such high-flung abstractions may earn us praise from our professors in grad school, and can even help conceptualize some mental disorders. But they will get you into trouble with case reviewers.

To help the case manager make informed decisions about treatment success, discharge, or the need for extension of care, *keep it simple, keep it behavioral, keep it focused on statements of "how it is" from the patient or those closest to her or him.* To help the case manager make the decision to refer more patients to you, re-read this section carefully. Then practice writing summaries of your own in non-dynamic, non-fuzzy, behavioral, symptom/impairment-focused, language that emphasizes solutions rather than problems. This will be time well spent, as your appointment book will someday reflect.

9. *"Provider Information"*

No need to comment much on this section. We have found, though, that our administrative staff saves a lot of time using a rubber stamp or a sticker containing all the information required by certain Managed Care companies.

If you find yourself filling out a stack of treatment plans for specific firms, have a stationery outlet make a rubber stamp or sticker that will fit easily in the proper section of those forms. The items requested on the form determines the material to be printed. You'll need to tailor it to the requirements of each form. For a group practice, each provider should have her or his own stamp or sticker.

10. *"What is the anticipated discharge date?"*

"Whenever the patient's insurance benefits run out" or "When the patient feels he or she is ready to terminate" or "When the therapist has paid off the yacht" or "When the therapist is ready for retirement" — these responses will never do!

What the case reviewer is looking for, dear colleague, is simply a realistic time frame in which to certify treatment. By "realistic time frame" we mean a time-limited, brief period of treatment.

Our policy is to explicitly say to most patients that "We specialize in brief therapy, usually from 8 to 12 sessions." This is also presented in printed form in patient orientation materials from the time of intake. We also try to remind the patient throughout treatment that "we've had 6 sessions now and have about 2 remaining sessions in which to meet our original therapy goals..." This repetition helps both therapist and patient stay on target and conclude therapy on time.

Obviously, not all cases (like the incest survivor) can be discharged successfully within 8 to 12 session, but many can with effective brief therapy intervention. When it is possible, use the 8 to 12 session model to determine the discharge date. Remember that in the early stages the patient is typically seen more frequently, and latter sessions are spread out to every two weeks or once monthly.

Try, as much as it is professionally and ethically possible, to stick to that date. Try not to ask for extensions except in unusual cases. Many therapists make the mistake of asking for extensions as they would requesting extensions on books checked out at the library. The difference is profound. The librarian smiles happily as she renews books for bibliophiles. The case manager bristles when asked for extensions. Keep in mind that Managed Care exists to limit, not extend, quality mental healthcare. *Limit, not extend.* To be considered a team-player, try to limit your treatment and only ask for extensions in unusual circumstances.

We hope that you have found this material instructive and that your confidence in your ability to effectively communicate with case reviewers has been increased. And as we pointed out earlier in this text, remember that paperwork will seem a whole lot easier to tackle when you define it as *paper marketing* — Every treatment report or update gives you the opportunity to display your expertise as a valued provider to Managed Care. Do it properly and case reps become some of your best sources of new patients.

Paper WORK, no. Paper MARKETING, yes.

After all, in the final analysis, who benefits most? *It's the patient.* More of them will find their way via Managed Care reviewers into your office. It is our hope that the material we present in this text will enable you to treat more and more people because you position yourself as a key player in the healthcare of the future.

Chapter Nine

A Simple System for
Measuring Outcome in Brief Therapy

(Pre-treatment, Discharge, and
Aftercare Assessment)

A Simple System for
Measuring Outcome in Brief Therapy

(Pre-treatment, Discharge, and Aftercare Assessment)

Why bother adding another "chore" to our already heavy burden in private practice? Aren't we busy enough with the demands of doing active short-term therapy, handling all the telephone calls, keeping track of sessions and dates, doing the paperwork documentation required by Managed Care — aren't we busy enough? Why bother worrying about doing outcome studies on how effective our treatment is?

We do not intend to add "busy work" to your too-busy life. But we do intend to prepare you for the brave new world of Managed Care, and to warn you of those changes just up ahead on the horizon. One of those changes is the demands for evidence of treatment effectiveness.

Look at any list of Managed Care, HMO and EAP firms. You will see quite an array. But in the next few years, we believe that this list will shrink dramatically. These companies are fiercely competing with each other for the healthcare dollar. They must "sell" themselves to government and industry as effective and efficient means by which to cut healthcare expenditures. Those firms that can show "proof" of their ability to provide quality mental health services (as demonstrated by patient satisfaction), and reduction in monies spent for it (as demonstrated by fewer number of sessions and a less intense level of care), those firms will get the new contracts, while the others fall by the wayside.

And how do you suppose those companies who must justify their very survival plan to get that kind of data? That's right, from you, the provider!

We are at this writing witnessing the early stages of emphasis on outcome research. Right now Managed Care, and their "partner" providers are simply learning how to do what we do, at the same time trying to learn who we are and what this whole external review, cost-control business is all about. But once the dust has settled and Managed Care gets its identity straight and feet planted firmly on the ground of American healthcare, you can be sure that hard data for treatment success will be required.

The therapist who knows how to collect outcome data, and doesn't have to be told to do it, but who has already undertaken it, will be far ahead of other providers in partnering their work successfully with Managed Care. Providers who routinely do outcome studies demonstrate their value because they provide concrete data that Managed Care firms can use to justify their existence, hold on to their existing contracts, and win new ones.

As you can see then, outcome research represents much more than busy work to satisfy our curiosity about how we're doing. Those reports from the experts — the patients themselves — may come to represent the hard data of the survival or demise of our own practice. If that's true, we need to begin now to get comfortable with outcome research. We need to make it as much a part of our clinical work as formulating a definitive diagnosis of the patient's condition. *Outcome data becomes the definitive diagnosis of our own work as it impacts the lives of those we serve.*

Assessing all therapeutic goals accomplished

The best measure of treatment goal outcome is the report from the expert her/himself — *the patient.* The starting point for most counseling and psychotherapy is the complaint or presenting problem reported to the therapist by the patient. In most long-term therapy, however, the therapy process soon departs from that focus and a pursuit of related (and often unrelated) issues is undertaken. In brief therapy — the kind Managed Care reviewers prefer — therapy begins *continues, and ends* with the patient's complaints and problems.

Treatment success, then, or lack of it, is best judged by the same person or persons who came in evaluating the problem. They should go as they came — the expert on how the impairment affects their life. At intake we take their word about how the problem affects them as the definitive statement about its nature. Why not accept their word for it as treatment progresses and ends?

We have found that there are essentially 3 reliable ways to measure brief therapy outcome from the patient's reports: (1) The patient's definition/redefinition of the problem; (2) The patient's behavioral description of the problem; and (3) The patient's attempted solutions. Here are some key questions that can help formulate your own outcome measures under each category:

(1) The patient's *definition/redefinition of the problem:*

> How would you define the cause or causes of the problem?
> Who do you think is responsible for causing the problem?
> Who do you think is responsible for solving the problem?
> What or who do you feel causes the problem to increase?
> What or who do you feel helps reduce the problem?
> How does the problem control your life?
> How does the problem control the lives of others?
> What are you unable to do when the problem occurs?
> What is life like when the problem doesn't take place?

(2) The patient's *behavioral description of the problem:*

> How would you describe the problem?
> What people or events trigger the problem or make it happen?
> What specific things do you do that keep the problem going?
> What specific things do others do to contribute to the problem?
> What do you do that you don't want to do during the problem?
> What do you *not want to do* that you do during the problem?

How do others react when the problem takes place?
How do you respond to their reactions?
How do you feel about yourself when the problem takes place?

(3)   The patient's attempted *solutions:*

Do you believe that you can control the problem?
What have you tried to do to control the problem?
What has worked best? What has not worked?
When you can control the problem, how do you feel?
When it's over, how do you feel? What do you think about?
How can others help you control the problem?
What books, groups or other resources have helped you?
What are your concerns about the problem recurring?

Change in behavior, success of treatment, therapy goals accomplished are thus measured by *definitive shifts* in the responses from patient on pre- or intake-measures contrasted to post- or discharge-measures on the same questions.

In addition to how the patient reports change or alleviation of the problem, we also use other means to measure therapeutic success. As treatment strategies are brought to bear to attack the problem/complaint, we pinpoint certain *behavioral changes that are incompatible with continuation of the problem behavior.* When those incompatible behaviors or cognitive skills occur, we can safely predict improvement in the problem behavior. For example, a 29-year-old woman reported to us that she "actually completed my first 5K race on Saturday!" Her presenting complaint was intense depression and almost total isolation from all social contacts due to her "low self-esteem caused by my divorce." The homework, which she proposed herself, was quite incompatible with social isolation. And the glow of pride and satisfaction on her face reflected a deeper inner change.

Another reliable measure of behavioral changes in the patient are the reports from significant others. The brief therapist often obtains statements from spouse, children, parents, friends or others close to the patient and well aware of the problem, as to their view of the impact of the situation. This is always done, of course, with patient's written consent. In one case, for example, a father had "disowned" his son because he disapproved of his new wife. At intake he reported that his last conversation with his son ended with his evaluation of his son's wife as "a street-wise whore!" He then hung up. After 7 sessions the father had written two letters to the son, apologized for his attacks, the son wrote a letter of forgiveness to the father and a letter to us stating his willingness to reconcile with his dad. The son's report stated that "It's nice that my dad and I can finally start over."

The brief therapist can also rely on verbal and cognitive changes, behavioral changes, and non-verbal cues during clinical sessions, as well as psychological testing to measure successful progress.

Specific changes pre- and post-test should be reported to case manager, in addition to changes observed during the course of treatment. The important thing is this: *Be specific.* Don't say, "There is improvement noted in patient's level of depression." Do say, "The patient shows a reduction in depressive mood demonstrated by her report that 'I am sleeping better and I'm not missing any more work; even my concentration seems better.'" That's hard data case reviewers appreciate.

A simple system for measuring outcome: Pre-treatment intake questionnaire

One method which we have developed for obtaining a pre-treatment measure assesses (1) how patient rates *recent changes* in symptom severity and/or intensity, and (2) how patient describes the problem *prior to* treatment intervention. *The Browning Outcomes Survey Scale, BOSS-i* items are presented here with orienting and motivating instructions.

The *intake* questionnaire, the *BOSS-i,* is administered in a small, easy-to-handle booklet prior to his or her first intake session. This will provide baseline or pre-test data, as well as diagnostic details useful in developing a symptom-focused treatment plan for brief therapy interventions. What follows is a condensed version of this instrument.

HOW TO MAKE YOUR COUNSELING
MORE EFFECTIVE

Setting goals and finding solutions is the first step:

YOUR OPINIONS, thoughts and feelings are most important. How you describe what you want to change can help you and your therapist set specific therapy goals and find solutions more quickly. Each item has 2 parts, A. and B. In part A. simply circle the number that best represents how you feel the problem has changed recently. Then, in part B., briefly describe in your own words how the problem has bothered or distressed you within the last 7 days.

(1) A. How would you rate the problem today as compared to a few months ago?

1	2	3	4	5	6	7
Much Worse	Moderately Worse	Slightly Worse	About The Same	Slightly Improved	Moderately Improved	Much Improved

B. Please briefly describe the problem that brought you for counseling as it affects you today:

(2) A. How well do you understand the problem today as compared to a few months ago?

1	2	3	4	5	6	7
Much Less Aware	Moderately Less Aware	Slightly Less Aware	About The Same	Slightly More Aware	Moderately More Aware	Much More Aware

B. Briefly say what or who you think (a) causes the problem to occur, (b) increases the problem, and (c) helps reduce the problem.

Causes:

Increases:

Helps reduce:

(3) A. Compared to a few months ago, how would you rate any physical or medical symptoms caused by your problem?

1	2	3	4	5	6	7
Much Worse	Moderately Worse	Slightly Worse	About The Same	Slightly Improved	Moderately Improved	Much Improved

   B. Please briefly say how the problem affects you physically or medically? (For example, physical symptoms, doctors visits, medications, etc.):

(4) A. How is the problem affecting your work or school performance now as compared to a few months ago?

1	2	3	4	5	6	7
Much Worse	Moderately Worse	Slightly Worse	About The Same	Slightly Improved	Moderately Improved	Much Improved

   B. The problem causes me to *(check one or more)*: Be late for work ☐ Miss work completely ☐ Have conflicts with people at work ☐ Have trouble concentrating ☐ Have poor work performance ☐ In your own words, briefly describe these problems:

(5) A. How is the problem affecting your relationships with others today as compared to a few months ago?

1	2	3	4	5	6	7
Much Worse	Moderately Worse	Slightly Worse	About The Same	Slightly Improved	Moderately Improved	Much Improved

   B. At this time, please briefly comment on how the problem affects your relationships with others?

(6) A. How do you think others who know you would rate your problem today compared to a few months ago?

1	2	3	4	5	6	7
Much Worse	Moderately Worse	Slightly Worse	About The Same	Slightly Improved	Moderately Improved	Much Improved

B. Please briefly describe how you think others who know you would describe your problem?

---

(7) A. Compared to a few months ago, how does your problem affect your attitude and feelings about yourself?

1	2	3	4	5	6	7
Much Worse	Moderately Worse	Slightly Worse	About The Same	Slightly Improved	Moderately Improved	Much Improved

   B. Briefly say how you think the problem affects your attitudes and feelings about yourself?

---

(8) A. How much are you aware of sources of help for the problem now as compared to a few months ago?

1	2	3	4	5	6	7
Totally Unaware	Aware But Don't Use	Aware But Use Rarely	About The Same	Use Slightly More	Use Moderately More	Use Much More

   B. Aside from therapy, what resources are you aware of that can help you handle the problem?

---

(9) A. How effective are you today handling the problem as compared to a few months ago?

1	2	3	4	5	6	7
Much Less Effective	Moderately Less Effective	Slightly Less Effective	About The Same	Slightly More Effective	Moderately More Effective	Much More Effective

   B. Briefly describe what you've tried to do to handle the problem until now?

(10) A. When you think about the impact of the problem today, how would you describe your thoughts and feelings about the future compared to how you felt a few months ago?

1	2	3	4	5	6	7
Much Less Hopeful	Moderately Less Hopeful	Slightly Less Hopeful	About The Same	Slightly More Hopeful	Moderately More Hopeful	Much More Hopeful

B. When you think about the problem, describe your thoughts and feelings about the future?

Section 2

(11) Think about times when the problem is less intense, or is not occurring. Describe how things are different?

(12) On a scale of 1 to 10, rate the seriousness of the problem *right now:*

1	2	3	4	5	6	7	8	9	10

Unbearable,
Unable to cope,
Desperate for help

No problems,
Handling things great,
No need for help

(13) On a 10-point scale, what number would you realistically expect to be at when you've accomplished all your therapy goals? (enter # here) ____

(14) Suppose you reach all your goals in therapy. Briefly describe how you think things in your life would be different?

Thank you for taking the time to complete this questionnaire. Your responses can really help your therapist prepare a more effective treatment plan for you, which may help you get results much sooner. When it's complete, please give this questionnaire to your therapist, or to our secretary, at the time of your first session. We hope all that happens here will richly benefit your life!

Note that in Part 2 the patient encounters a shift in format. This is done to help orient the patient to expect something decidedly different from his or her counseling experience with us. We want to know what worked, and what didn't work in their previous therapy — implying that we are not reluctant to compare what's ahead with what they have encountered before.

Secondly, note the shift from the 7-point scales to the 1-to-10 scaling of their problem. Why this shift? Because this sets the stage for much of the solution-oriented, brief therapy that will follow. Throughout the course of therapy the patient is asked to rate and keep track of her or his progress on a 10-point scale. Most patients are quickly (and accurately) able to pinpoint their complaints along this scale. The 7-point scale, on the other hand, is a more precise device for statistical pre-post comparisons (especially as it has a definite "About the same" midpoint of 4). Our experience has shown that patients have a tougher time subjectively conceptualizing and placing their complaints on a 7-point scale, but seem to grasp the 10-point scale much more readily. So this helps orient the expectations of the patient even prior to their first session, setting the stage for a valuable clinical tool. With it we can actively enlist the patient in the solution process with questions like, "What do you suppose you will be doing when you reach 8?" or "What do you suppose you will need to do to get from 3 to 4?"

Post-test: discharge outcome questionnaire

The *Browning Outcomes Survey Scale, BOSS-d* is administered to the patient at the time of *discharge*. It is a good policy to give this to the patient at the time of the second-to-last session, and instruct her/him to bring it in at the time of their last session. Or, the patient can be asked to come in 15 minutes or so early for their final session to fill out this questionnaire. This will increase follow-through.

CAUTION: If the patient is asked to mail it in after their last session, you will have very few returned due to the ravages of procrastination (good intentions don't produce good outcome research!).

It is important to have the patient bring in the questionnaire in a sealed envelope. *The therapist does not read it in the patient's presence.*

Note in the discharge questionnaire a repetition of the items used in the pre-test, both Likert-scale ratings and patient personal assessments. Data from these ratings is highly valued input for most case managers. It tells both therapist and Managed Care company how successful therapy has been in resolving the problems brought to them in the first place.

The "Personal Comments" give us the subjective viewpoint of the patient as to how much positive change, wellness, and adequate functioning have actually occurred. These statements can be quoted verbatim in treatment documentations and contacts with case managers to support the achievement (or lack of achievement) of therapy goals.

Patient assessments also serve as a potent tool for diagnosing our own effectiveness, and give us specific clues to help sharpen brief therapy interventions. As we said earlier, what greater measure is there of the real value of our work than the reports of satisfied customers by the "experts" themselves?

On the following pages you'll find an abbreviated version of the discharge format of the *BOSS-d.* We believe it contains all the data necessary to measure outcomes of goal-focused, solution-based, time-sensitive brief therapy to assess how effectively you do what you do. The pre-post statistical reports offer the clinician hard-data to present to Managed Care organizations, employers, EAP programs, insurance companies and other third-party payers.

How effective was the counseling you received?

Solutions are the key to successful counseling:

YOUR OPINIONS, thoughts and feelings are most important. We would like to know how your counseling has affected the main problem you came in with, and how it's influenced your life. Please take just a few minutes to share your evaluation and comments with us. Each item has two parts, A and B. In part A. simply circle the number that best represents how you feel the problem has changed compared to how you felt when you first came in for therapy. Then, in part B., briefly describe in your own words how the problem has changed since receiving help in therapy.

(1) A. To what extent is there a change in your original problem?

1	2	3	4	5	6	7
Much Worse	Moderately Worse	Slightly Worse	About The Same	Slightly Improved	Moderately Improved	Much Improved

   B.   How is the original difficulty different or changed?

(2)   A.   As a result of your therapy, please rate how well you now understand what or who (a) causes, (b) increases, or (c) helps reduce the problem.

1	2	3	4	5	6	7
Much Less Aware	Moderately Less Aware	Slightly Less Aware	About The Same	Slightly More Aware	Moderately More Aware	Much More Aware

      B. What or who do you now believe —
Causes the problem?

Increases the problem?

Reduces the problem?

(3) A. To what extent is there a change in your physical symptoms, symptoms, doctors visits, etc.?

1	2	3	4	5	6	7
Much Worse	Moderately Worse	Slightly Worse	About The Same	Slightly Improved	Moderately Improved	Much Improved

     B. How has your therapy changed your physical symptoms?

(4) A. What changes has therapy made in your work or school perform-ance?

1	2	3	4	5	6	7
Much Worse	Moderately Worse	Slightly Worse	About The Same	Slightly Improved	Moderately Improved	Much Improved

     B. Since being in therapy, how are things different at work or school? The problem causes me to *(check one or more):* Be late for work ☐ Miss work completely ☐ Have conflicts with people at work ☐ Have trouble concentrating ☐ Have poor work performance ☐ Briefly describe how the problem is different now:

(5) A. How have your relationships with others changed?

1	2	3	4	5	6	7
Much Worse	Moderately Worse	Slightly Worse	About The Same	Slightly Improved	Moderately Improved	Much Improved

     B. What effect has your therapy had on your relationships, and how are they different?

(6) A. How would those who know and care about you, and who were most affected by how you were before therapy, describe you today?

1	2	3	4	5	6	7
Much Worse	Moderately Worse	Slightly Worse	About The Same	Slightly Improved	Moderately Improved	Much Improved

     B. What comments do you think people who know you best would make about you now since you've had therapy?

(7) A. How have your attitudes and feelings about yourself changed as a result of your therapy?

1	2	3	4	5	6	7
Much Worse	Moderately Worse	Slightly Worse	About The Same	Slightly Improved	Moderately Improved	Much Improved

B. How would you describe your feelings about *yourself* now?

(8) A. To what extent are you aware of and use resources other than therapy to help you handle the problem?

1	2	3	4	5	6	7
Totally Unaware	Aware But Don't Use	Aware But Use Rarely	About The Same	Use Slightly More	Use Moderately More	Use Much More

B. What resources did you learn about in your therapy that you can now use to help handle the original problem?

(9) A. How effectively are you handling your problem now as compared to how you dealt with it before you came for therapy?

1	2	3	4	5	6	7
Much Less Effective	Moderately Less Effective	Slightly Less Effective	About The Same	Slightly More Effective	Moderately More Effective	Much More Effective

B. What do you do now in responding to the problem that is different from what you did before your therapy?

(10) A. What are your thoughts and feelings about the future with respect to the problem that brought you to therapy?

1	2	3	4	5	6	7
Much Less Hopeful	Moderately Less Hopeful	Slightly Less Hopeful	About The Same	Slightly More Hopeful	Moderately More Hopeful	Much More Hopeful

B. How has your therapy influenced your thoughts and feelings about the future?

Section 2

(11) In your therapy, what do you feel was most helpful to you?

(12) In your therapy, what do you feel was least helpful to you?

(13) If you've had counseling before, how did the help you received here differ from previous counseling you received for this problem?

(14) On a scale of 1 to 10, rate the seriousness of the problem *right now:*

1	2	3	4	5	6	7	8	9	10

Unbearable,   No problems,
Unable to cope,   Handling things great,
Desperate for help   No need for help

Thank you for taking the time to complete this questionnaire. Your responses can really help your therapist evaluate how effective your therapy was, and may suggest ways to improve our services. When it's complete, please give this questionnaire to your therapist, or to our secretary, at the time of your next session. We hope all that happened here will richly benefit your life!

What about direct outcome interviews vs. written questionnaires?

Some therapists report the use of direct interviews with patients to evaluate outcome. James Gustafson, for example, in his insightful book, *The Complex Secret of Brief Psychotherapy* (1986), interviews patients at termination asking three questions:

1. Would you say your chief complaint is now about the same, improved, or worse?
2. What did you learn in therapy that stands out in your mind now, about how your complaint or difficulty is brought about, increased, or reduced?

3. How would your behavior be viewed by those who know you best, who are most affected by how you were before/during/after therapy? What would they comment?

Good questions. They provide, as Gustafson says, "minimal data on all patients...concerning relief of symptoms." But the data obtained is derived from face-to-face interviews with the patient. In our opinion, this may bias the patient's responses, because she or he may want to please the therapist, thus giving answers that please. For instance, is a patient likely to respond honestly to the question, "In your therapy, what do you feel was least helpful to you?", if that question is posed by the therapist who provided that therapy? You may get reliable responses from those with iron-solid ego strength, those who are well-schooled in assertive training, or perhaps from a sociopath! In our opinion, this method can cause seriously biased results.

Yes, it is true that you are more likely to get a greater number of responses completed using direct interviews. But the unreliability factor diminishes the usefulness of the method. We believe that the better approach is to administer whatever tool you decide to use (a) prior to the first session, and (b) prior to the final discharge session. Motivation seems higher at these points to prompt patient compliance. And, most importantly, the patient is free to "tell it like it is" from their heart without direct apprehensions about how their therapist will react to certain answers.

And if you must do direct interviews, have someone other than the attending therapist perform it. Preferably, someone on your staff the patient has never met. The reliability and validity are still suspect, but somewhat improved.

But in our opinion, *the best source of outcome data*

*is obtained via a personal questionnaire, filled out in the
confidence of privacy by the patient.*

Follow-up   outcome   questionnaire

The post-test questionnaire tells us, and our case-
manager colleagues, what life changes therapeutic intervention has brought about, and how successful or unsuccessful
we have been in meeting the patient's needs. But we are
not called upon by the patient or the case manager to do
"Band Aid" therapy. Both parties expect us to render services which will have lasting and meaningful impact for
good in the patient's life.

A patient who reports high levels of satisfaction and
wellness at discharge, and then is right back where they
were at intake with respect to their complaints and problems is no better off. In fact, they may even be more
discouraged and feel hopeless. We want a patient who not
only gives their therapy high marks of success at discharge,
but who also continues building on those gains and utilizes
the skills we have taught them in brief therapy. Brief
therapy done correctly should result in long-term emotional
health in which the patient attains *and maintains*
maximum growth and adaptive functioning on many levels.

Therefore, we believe that the true test of how well we
are doing cannot be accurately measured by the discharge
post-test alone. We recommend that a follow-up survey be
designed and sent to the patient 6 months and again at 1
year following discharge.

On the following pages is an abbreviated version of the
Browning Outcomes Survey Scale, BOSS-f, with items keyed
to the same important criteria measured on the intake and
discharge instruments. This can be sent to the patient 6
months and/or 1 year following discharge. It is presented
in the same small, easy-to-use booklet format.

SPECIAL   RESEARCH   PROJECT:
Evaluating   Progress   After   Counseling

You can contribute to a special counseling research project:

IT'S BEEN 6 MONTHS NOW since your last counseling session, and we'd like to know how things are going in your life? We'd like you to compare yourself *now* to how you were feeling, thinking and acting *at the time of your last session.* It should only take a few minutes. Each question has two parts, A and B. In part A, simply circle the number that best represent how you feel now. In Part B briefly describe your thoughts and feelings about how you are doing now. Then please return this to us in the enclosed stamped return envelope. This will really help. Thank you!

(1) A. Compared to how I felt at the end of counseling, I now
        believe my original problem is:

1	2	3	4	5	6	7
Much Worse	Moderately Worse	Slightly Worse	About The Same	Slightly Improved	Moderately Improved	Much Improved

    B. Comments?

(2) A. As a result of your therapy, please rate how well you now
        understand what or who (a) causes, (b) increases, or (c) helps
        reduce the problem.

1	2	3	4	5	6	7
Much Less Aware	Moderately Less Aware	Slightly Less Aware	About The Same	Slightly More Aware	Moderately More Aware	Much More Aware

    B. Comments?

(3) A. At this time, to what extent is there a change in your physical
        symptoms, doctors visits, medications, etc.?

1	2	3	4	5	6	7
Much Worse	Moderately Worse	Slightly Worse	About The Same	Slightly Improved	Moderately Improved	Much Improved

B. Comments?

---

(4) A. Now that time has passed, what changes has therapy made in your work or school performance?

1	2	3	4	5	6	7
Much Worse	Moderately Worse	Slightly Worse	About The Same	Slightly Improved	Moderately Improved	Much Improved

B. Late for work? Miss work? Conflicts with people at work? Concentration? Work performance? — Your comments:

---

(5) A. How have your relationships with others changed?

1	2	3	4	5	6	7
Much Worse	Moderately Worse	Slightly Worse	About The Same	Slightly Improved	Moderately Improved	Much Improved

B. Comments?

---

(6) A. How would those who know and care about you, and who were most affected by how you were before therapy, describe you today?

1	2	3	4	5	6	7
Much Worse	Moderately Worse	Slightly Worse	About The Same	Slightly Improved	Moderately Improved	Much Improved

B. Comments?

---

(7) A. In what ways have your feelings and attitudes about yourself changed since coming for therapy?

1	2	3	4	5	6	7
Much Worse	Moderately Worse	Slightly Worse	About The Same	Slightly Improved	Moderately Improved	Much Improved

B. Comments?

(8) A. To what extent are you aware of and use resources other
        than therapy to help you handle the problem?

1	2	3	4	5	6	7
Totally Unaware More	Aware But Don't Use	Aware But Use Rarely	About The Same	Use Slightly More	Use Moderately More	Use Much

  B. Comments?

(9) A. To what extent have you tried to handle the problem now
        differently from the way you responded before?

1	2	3	4	5	6	7
Much Less Effective	Moderately Less Effective	Slightly Less Effective	About The Same	Slightly More Effective	Moderately More Effective	Much More Effective

  B. Comments?

(10) A. What are your thoughts and feelings about the future
         with respect to the problem that brought you to therapy?

1	2	3	4	5	6	7
Much Less Hopeful	Moderately Less Hopeful	Slightly Less Hopeful	About The Same	Slightly More Hopeful	Moderately More Hopeful	Much More Hopeful

  B. Comments?

Section 2

IN LOOKING OVER YOUR OWN ANSWERS to the above questions,
to what extent would you say that the changes that have taken
place between the end of counseling and now are due to:

(Please check one for each item as to
HOW MUCH INFLUENCE it has had):

NONE   SLIGHT   MODERATE   STRONG

(a) The counseling I received
     at (name of your practice) ____   ____   ____   ____
(b) Counseling I received
     elsewhere at a later time   ____   ____   ____   ____

	NONE	*SLIGHT*	*MODERATE*	*STRONG*
(c) Help from family	___	___	___	___
(d) Help from friends	___	___	___	___
(e) Change in circumstances	___	___	___	___
(f) The passage of time	___	___	___	___
(g) Help from religious sources	___	___	___	___
(h) Self-help resources or groups I learned about in therapy	___	___	___	___
(i) Self-help resources or groups I learned about elsewhere	___	___	___	___
(j) Other _____	___	___	___	___

Thank you for taking the time to help by giving us your opinions, thoughts and feelings. It's gratifying to hear from you and to know how you are doing.

If you would like to share any additional comments, please write them on the reverse side.

Use the stamped return envelope to send back this questionnaire to us. Thank you again for your help.

Because motivation to take the time to do the survey and return it may be limited, here are 10 things you can do to increase the probability of response.

1. The questionnaire is sent with a stamped, self-addressed (back to you) envelope in which to return the completed survey.
2. Keep the questionnaire as short as possible.
3. Make it easy to respond.
4. Use colored paper and a colored return envelope.
5. Address the envelope to patient in handwriting; do not use a label (you don't want it to look like "junk mail").
6. Mail it on Wednesday or Thursday so the patient receives it near the weekend when they have more time to do it.
7. Add a Post-It note to the questionnaire indicating that when their response is returned, you will send them a special article, or something else you believe will interest them.

8. Add a brief personal note showing sincere concern for how they are doing now, mentioning a specific concern or person in their life that you are interested in.
9. Send a personal note and a photocopy of some article directly related to their problem/solution.
10. After no response in 2 weeks, have one of your support staff call the patient and in a friendly manner, gently ask if he or she could look over the questionnaire and send it back.

Using any or all of these methods should result in a much higher rate of returns to enable you to accurately assess how your work endures over time.

We trust that these instruments give you some practical ideas and techniques for preparing your own outcome studies. Copies may also be ordered directly from us for use in outcome research. Give pre-tests to all incoming patients, both Managed Care and full-fee patients, and give the post-tests to all patients at discharge. And send follow-up questionnaires 6 months and 1 year after discharge to measure how the patient is maintaining progress.

Be sure to share your findings with case managers, asking each how he or she would like to receive the data. Some reps appreciate a complete photocopy of the questionnaires. Others want a quick summary of the quantitative evaluations. But all of them welcome outcome research, because most of them never get any, since few providers know how (or take the time) to gather it. Now you know how. If you take the time to gather the data and communicate it succinctly to case managers, they will take the time to refer new patients to you.. You'll probably find that outcome studies produce incoming patients.

Your partnering relationship with Managed Care thrives on taking the time to ask outcome questions.

Making case managers happy is only one benefit you will derive from doing outcome studies. One positive aspect of administering outcome instruments to patients is their motivational value. From the earliest contact the patient has with you, he or she is indirectly influenced to think in solution, goal-directed ways. They also perceive their therapist as someone who is organized and methodical. They, in turn, approach therapy with a methodical expectation. And there is the sense that the most important aspects of their life are cared about.

We believe you will find that the most rewarding aspect of this work is the wonderful, tangible things your patients will tell you about *you* — about how what you have done to touch their lives has helped make those lives more liveable, and in some cases, worth living.

The feedback from less-than-satisfied "customers" also helps us examine ourselves and take stock. What are we doing that we shouldn't be doing? What are we not doing that we should be doing? Are we drifting, or are we on target, helping our patients meet goals? Are we spending too much time "exploring," or are we helping to reduce the pain of human symptoms? Our outcome research from those expert "customers" provides the raw material for refining and improving the services we provide.

Outcome research, then, has 3 important outcomes: (1) Managed Care companies get hard data to demonstrate the value and necessity of their external review and supervision; (2) the patient feels that his or her opinions matter and are respected; (3) and the therapist gets a written report card on strengths and weaknesses — only in this case, the student helps to develop a more skillful "teacher". About the future of outcome studies, an APA Practice Directorate states, "Outcomes data will become a competitive necessity...in a remodeled health care system...In order to compete, mental health providers will have to demonstrate results..." (*APA Monitor,* Oct.,1993).

Chapter Ten

Question & Answer Clinic:

Concrete, Detailed Responses
to Questions Therapists Ask

Personal Notes

Chapter Ten

Question & Answer Clinic:

Concrete, Detailed Responses
to Questions Therapists Ask

About 7 months ago we did a telephone consultation with a psychologist in New England. He said that he was about to leave the security of his agency job and launch out into his own full-time private practice. He was filled with excitement, visions of a busy waiting room and full appointment book, and dreams of the automomous life in private practice.

After we helped him determine an effective name for his new practice, the best location, design a strategic Yellow Pages ad, and begin the creative work on a new practice brochure, we asked him this important question:

> "How do you plan to develop a working partnership with the
> Managed Care companies in your area in order to build a
> balance into your practice in terms of referral flow?"

His answer was not surprising, because over the past 3 or 4 years we have heard this often (too often) when conducting face-to-face, written, or telephone consultations with therapists throughout the United States and abroad. He replied adamantly, "All that Managed Care stuff is just a lot of bother...I've talked to several of my colleagues here and they tell me how hard they have to work just to justify their work to people who are constantly looking over their shoulder; not to mention taking a lot less money for doing it." He concluded by saying, "No, I'm not going to have anything to do with Managed Care, HMO's, PPOs and all that... I'm going to work with only those who can pay cash, or who have indemnity insurance coverage."

Ah, the zeal of youth! And, oh, the rude awakening when the jaws of reality get hold of you!

We made some gentle efforts to dissuade him from this course of action, but he was not buying. So, we wished him well and had a feeling that we might be hearing from him again...

That's right, 4 months later we did another consultation with him. Prior to the phone session he faxed us a document to review. We were pleased to see a beautifully-done "Practice Profile" specifically designed to market his practice to Managed Care provider relations directors.

When we finally met on the phone to discuss this document, here is what took place:

> *BROWNING:* "We were really pleased to receive your fax! Can you tell us about your change of heart in deciding to get involved with Managed Care?"
>
> *THERAPIST:* "It wasn't fun...When I started out on my own I thought I had the world by the tail and that I would go after cash patients. But I've been out there for months now and I'm really worried... Even though my marketing is working, many of the people who call me can't afford to come in because they have to see someone under their Managed Care contract. I'm breaking even, but I finally realize that if I'm going to make it, I have no choice...So I want help learning how to play the game — *even though I don't want to.*"

This therapist is making a wise attitudinal shift. Even though he's not overjoyed about "having to" play the Managed Care game, he has come to understand that it's getting to be almost the only game in town; even in his small village in northern New England.

It's the same way all over the country. Therapists seem either stubbornly hostile toward making the adjustment, or they reluctantly relent. Those who do determine to bring their practice or facility into a Managed-Care-friendly position want practical answers to some good questions. They're ready to "join the team" but need some step-by-step advice on just how to go about it.

The information presented in this text provides more than enough concrete guidance for any practitioner, individual, group, or institution, to "court" Managed Care companies, and build rewarding working relationships with them.

But there still are a few loose ends that we'd like to go over with you. So what we'll do is respond to some of the most common questions we receive from therapists, and give you the same advice we'd offer at seminars, workshops or during consultations. Here are some tips, thoughts, and useful things we hope will be of help to you:

"Can my hospital staff membership help get me into Managed Care companies that have turned me down due to closed panels?"

It's possible, but it's "iffy". Hospitals where you hold staff positions may have provider status with many Managed Care companies. The person at the hospital may also have good relationships with provider relations and case managers. This certainly is worth pursuing, to see if he or she will represent you to the right people to open the gates.

If the hospital has a reputation for keeping patients in-patient as long as possible, and are clearly Managed-Care-unfriendly, you don't stand much of a chance to get through the gatekeepers. And, for that matter, if the hospital has this kind of reputation, you'd do better to keep your name and the reputation of your work as far as possible from being linked with them. Remember, you are known by the company you keep. So if you belong to a facility that is known to get patients discharged to day-care or outpatient care ASAP, let them promote you.

In general, most hospital programs hold little leverage when it comes to persuading gate keepers to open closed provider panels. The only exception to this might be CD programs with a strong track record for short-term, behaviorally-focused treatment. If you specialize in the same kind of substance abuse work, ask them to put in a good word for you. A CD specialization with a brief orientation, grounded in a 12-Step framework, may set you apart from 75% of other therapists who are also seeking entry.

"Are there any other ways to get the gate keepers to reconsider accepting you as a provider?"

One good idea is to get involved with a few medium or large-sized external EAP programs. These are profit-making companies that offer their services to industry and government agencies to coordinate mental health benefits. They structure provider panels made up of independent practitioners and group practices, negotiate lower contract fees for services, and supervise quality and time of treatment.

When you have knocked on the gates of Managed Care companies and have been told, "Sorry, our panel is full and we have no need for new providers in your location," the EAP company may be able to change that decision. Why? Because the EAP company represents the businesses or agencies who pay the bills. It's still true: "Money talks".

The EAP rep, if you've proven your value to them and they like your work, can promote you directly as a provider who is important to the companies they represent. They can get you approved as a full provider, or as an "ad hoc" provider. Ad hoc provider status means that you are approved on a case-by-case basis, but are not entitled to the privileges of full providers. But ad-hoc status is better than non-provider status. Once you have a toe in the door you can, by your good work, win the favor of case reviewers who can, in turn, persuade provider relations to bring you in under full-provider status. Either way, your chances are enhanced by forming good working relationships with EAP programs.

You can contact the Employee Assistance Professional Association at 4601 North Fairfax Drive, Suite 1001, Arlington, VA 22203; phone (703) 522-6272.

"Once you're a preferred provider, can you ever get an increase in the rate paid?"

Many therapists sign contracts with Managed Care companies and never think to renegotiate the contracted amount paid for services at the end of the contracted term. There's a truth that goes like this, "You have not because you ask not." And this can be the case when it comes to increasing what you are paid for your services.

One Managed Care firm we dealt with represented a large Southern California utility company. Several patients were referred to us during the first year of service, and in each case the patients were discharged successfully within an average 8-12 sessions. The company paid $60 per session, which is typical of many firms.

Inasmuch as we had done a good job in all cases referred to us, had asked for no extensions, and practiced in a strategic location to families living in the utility company area, we felt an increase was in order.

We summarized the first-year's track record with the company and indicated that many of the other companies that we dealt with paid more than $60. We accordingly requested $85, a $25 increase. Why not? — All they could do was to deny it. But they didn't. Instead, we got a call from the director of provider relations who authorized a $15 increase to $75. That was just fine with us. They sent us an updated contract for the new fee scale. That was 2 years ago. Had we failed to ask for that increase, we would have been earning $15 per hour less for over 2 years working with their patients.

If your reputation, and your track record, shine brightly, negotiate for an increase. But be mindful of the fact that many Managed Care firms have fixed and firm payment policies and will increase for no one. The best way to find out is (1) ask case reps you deal with what the policy is, or (2) write a letter of request demonstrating your value as a preferred provider, giving them your average number of sessions to successful discharge, and any outcome data you may have gathered in the past.

"Can you get paid a higher rate for certain specialty services?"

The answer is yes. The only way to know what the rates for different services are is to check your contract carefully. Many Managed Care companies pay different rates for different professional qualifications. For example, psychiatrists are paid at a higher rate, and licensed psychologists are sometimes paid at a higher level than MFCCs and clinical social workers. This obviously makes little sense, but it's foolhardy to argue with the "system".

Psychological testing, biofeedback, and group therapy are paid at differing rates by most companies. Check your contract or talk to provider relations about their specific coverage of these services before investing the time and energy providing them to patients.

*"What about psych testing? How do most
Managed Care reps look on testing requests?"*

As you know, many practices and facilities make it
standard policy to test all patients upon intake, using such
instruments as the MMPI, 16PF, sentence completion, and
even intelligence scales. If your bias is in this direction,
don't let case managers get wind of it! Using testing for all
intakes is about as popular as increased taxes or toothaches.

Most case reviewers are trained to look with a jaun-
diced eye on requests for psych testing. And should they
receive numerous requests for such services from you, or
those on your staff, you'll earn that dreaded *provider non
grata* status.

Most experienced brief therapists use psych testing
only in certain extreme situations; i.e., possible neurological
impairments, developmental disorders, or possible
psychotic conditions. Most brief therapists regard routine
testing as unnecessary in meeting outcome objectives. In
some cases, however, testing can enhance diagnostic
accuracy, and thus help pinpoint treatment targeted
impairments. But these instances must be carefully cleared
and documented to be acceptable to case managers.

Many case reps have official guidelines for approving or
denying the medical necessity of testing. For example, one
company instructs its case reviewers as follows:

> "Determination of the medical necessity of psychological
> tests always requires consideration of the clinical facts of
> the specific case to assure that tests given are a cost-effective
> means of determining the appropriate treatment for the
> individual patient."

After this disclaimer appears a list of several instruments
with the company's attitude clearly evident. For example:

ADHD Rating Scale .... "Allow 1 hr. to interpret checklists."
SUICIDAL IDEATION QUESTIONNAIRE .... "Questionable utility."
FIRO-B .... "Info derivable from interview; little
         clinician time."
SCL-90-R .... "Limited clinical value beyond interview."
BECK DEPRESSION INVENTORY .... "Questionable utility beyond
         interview."

We could go on. The list is long (and dull). But this should give you a feel for how case reviewers are oriented and how they view your use of testing.

No, they don't mind if you use these devices. But they do get uneasy when your use of such instruments is billed for. For instance, we find the Beck scales and the SCL-90-R excellent tools for outcome research purposes as pre- and post-tests. But notice that they are not given high marks by the Managed Care company "beyond interview." Translate this into English and you get, "DO NOT AUTHORIZE BILLABLE TIME FOR THIS INSTRUMENT." But if you use one of these instruments *and do not charge for administering or scoring them,* you are on safe ground.

We administer and score all pre- and post outcome research on our own time and do not bill for it. The data from the Symptom Check List (SCL-90-R) and the Beck Depression (and Anxiety) Scales are excellent measures for outcome purposes. The scales presented in this text are also good tools for this purpose. But we recommend that you avoid including these in billable time.

The bottom line, then, on using psych testing is this: Do it on your own time, or avoid using it altogether.

"When services or extensions are denied, should we pursue an appeal process?"

You can appeal decisions you disagree with. Most Managed Healthcare firms have several levels of appeals.

But remember this: You want to preserve a good working relationship with case reviewers. If you appeal, and if you win or lose, in the final analysis, you *lose.*

Why? Because the case manager made a decision. She or he said "NO" to the request for services. They felt that they had good reason to make that decision, right? Then they learn that you are challenging their professional judgment. If your appeal is denied or approved, you position yourself in an adversarial relationship no matter how you cut it. Even though many reps would deny this, they are not machines and there is some measure of ego at work in all of us. *A case rep offended is harder to be re-won over than a bear robbed of her cubs.* Well, that is an exaggeration perhaps, but it makes the point.

If you feel that undue harm will befall the patient if services are denied, then, by all means, do it. After all, the needs of our patients are our first commitment. But if your appeal has anything to do with pride or a competitive spirit — drop it and accept the case reviewer's decision.

"Is there anything I can do to enhance my practice reputation other than doing a good job on treatment plans and progress updates?"

Keep in mind that these professionals are overworked and overwhelmed by more paperwork and voice mail pressures than you can even imagine. So keep all your forms and calls succinct and easy to read or understand.

But, yes, you can help them do their job, and at the same time establish your name as an "elite" provider. How? Send them a *brief* quarterly outcome summary.

In this summary, include patient's name, Social Security #, number of sessions during that time period, and the discharge data. Show clearly the charge/use ratio for each patient; i.e., the total charges per total number of sessions from intake to discharge per patient. You'll make any case rep happy with this figure. You can also present data in very brief form reporting pre/post test evidence of positive outcome and treatment goals reached.

A safe estimate is that about 1 in 40 providers will provide this kind of data to help the case manager measure outcome success. If *you* are that one who distinguishes herself or himself by providing this kind of hard information — without even being asked to do so — how do you think you are perceived by the case manager? Positive perceptions and steady referrals are synonyms in the Dictionary of Managed Care. Have you incorporated outcome research into your practice? The one-in-forty therapist will receive more new patient referrals than the other 39 combined. Think about it.

You can also send case reps several laminated support resources cards (described earlier in the text). These are useful tools for him or her to use in communication with clients and other providers. And, of course, your own practice is featured on each card, in addition to recovery groups, self-help groups, shelters, emergency services, and other resources. This distinguishes you, too, as uniquely committed to excellence in short-term, quality care.

Some providers and consultants recommend taking case managers to lunch in their marketing efforts. This is risky business and we discourage our clients from doing so. We did this ourselves when interviewing Managed Care professionals for inclusion in this book, but we do not practice this to influence their referrals. Buying lunch can cross the line and be interpreted as "buying" referrals. It's like the purchase of friendship; you don't have to buy it, but simply show yourself friendly to win friends. Similarly, the best way to win the confidence of case reviewers who refer, is to demonstrate clinical excellence in brief therapy, and, follow the rules of external review healthcare. If they invite you to lunch, fine. Otherwise, keep it professional and let your work promote you.

What about letting them know about workshops, seminars, other presentations and support groups offered by your practice or facility? Good idea. Do it. Send them an announcement or flyer. They may attend themselves, refer clients, or simply take note that you are proactive in providing community services. In whichever case, your image and/or reputation increases in value.

Finally, try to find out what employers the Managed Care company represent. Then submit self-help-type articles to the company newsletters. If they are published, be sure case reps get copies. It's not hard to see that this positions you and your work as something special.

"Does the case manager represent the client, the Managed Care firm, the insurance company, or the employer?"

If you ask the wrong question, you are likely to get the wrong answer. Let's rephrase it like this: The patient is your most important client, but not your only client. Who is your other client? The case manager. Define the case manager and the Managed Care firm as your client and you will resist perceiving them as adversaries.

And yes, they do represent the insurance company and the bill-paying employers. But most of all, they exist, and enlist our help on behalf of the patient.

"How should I handle complaints from dissatisfied patients?"

You can please some of the people some of the time, and all of the people some of the time, but try to please all of the people all of the time and you will need help more than your patient. Yes, patients will complain to the case manager about your work, or about you personally. Here are some tips that should help nip these sticky problems in the bud:

1. Obvious or not, *do all you do with excellence* — the best way to avoid complaints.
2. When you know that a patient plans to complain, contact the case rep yourself, ASAP. Call them and send a note of explanation (without sounding defensive, and without blaming the patient).
3. Document this in the patient's case file.
4. When discussing the complaint with case rep, talk to them as a colleague, a fellow professional; not as an stern auditor.
5. Try to support the patient, as much as possible, in understanding their dissatisfaction. Point the finger at yourself.
6. Recommend other clinicians or services that might meet patient's needs if your services did not.
7. Don't be too serious. Lighten up. Keep a smile in your voice and project an easy acceptance of the patient attitude.
8. After putting the complaint to rest, change the subject. Give the rep an update on another patient — a happy one!
9. End the call with something up-beat or just plain fun. The case manager does not enjoy dealing with complaints any more than you do. Make it easier on both of you. Smile.
10. Send the dissatisfied patient a note of understanding with something helpful included (perhaps an article pertaining to the patient's impairment(s). Send a copy of this letter to the case manager "for your information."

Here's an example of a recent complaint brought against us to the referring case manager. The patients were a married couple, both experiencing moderate depression secondary to severe marital conflicts. The wife had found "my own therapist" but was angry that "that insurance person would not allow me to continue with him because he was not a provider." So they had to settle for us. She was not a happy lady. The husband was a "burnt-out" therapist, who appeared to respond well to interventions used. But the wife was determined to sabotage whatever we did to help them. Finally, she concluded, "I don't like the fact that you won't deal with my deeper feelings and the hurts from my childhood like my other therapist did."

We gently and patiently tried to explain that "it would be good if we could spend time dealing with the deeper issues, but her benefits required brief intervention to help handle here-and-now problems of their depression and the marital conflicts." She didn't appreciate this, stood up and walked out. The husband, to avoid further marital strife, dutifully followed her, apologizing as he went.

Following the good advice we just gave you, we called the case manager and in a easy-going manner went through the scenario. She laughed and said, "We all knew that she would put you to the test and wouldn't let you help them; she wants long-term therapy and just can't accept what her benefits allow." Relieved at the case rep's response, we then tried to suggest interventions that might work with this angry lady, including a trial with a female therapist who might better meet her needs. Later I sent the case manager a note summarizing the case, and sent the patient a letter of encouragement and sorrow that we couldn't help them. I also gave her information of several support groups that might help her. All's well that ended even better: Our reputation became even more strongly established as a result of handling this complaint.

It's also important to explain to your support staff (secretaries, receptionists) that a particular patient is displeased and may need special TLC with patience and understanding in the future. To protect the patient's confidentiality, you need not go into detail; simply coach them in the art of being compassionate and kind so they do not take anything personally in the future. This helps care for our support staff as well as for the patient.

The head of the Complaint Department is ... *you.* Do not delegate complaints to others on your staff. Handle them promptly and proactively yourself.

"What's the best way to handle a referral from a case manager that's outside my expertise?"

We've talked to some clinicians who are so grateful to get a referral from a case rep that they accept the referral even when they know that they have little experience or training handling this condition. When this happens discharge objectives are seldom reached, and several extensions are requested — damaging your reputation as an effective brief therapist.

There is a better approach. Simply admit your limitations (we all have our gifts and should know and admit areas in which we are weak or deficient). An example used earlier might help illustrate this point. We are preferred providers for one EAP group in which only one member of our staff is designated to see their clients. The case manager called one day with an urgent need. He had a parent in his office who had a suicidal teenager who needed care right away and asked our therapist if he could take the case today. The therapist told him that, yes, he had an opening in his schedule, but that he felt ill-equipped to handle adolescents.

At that time we were trying to cultivate a positive working relationship with this company. It was risky to turn down this new referral. But ethically we believed we had to take that risk.

The therapist recommended several therapists whom he knew were skilled with teens and attempted to assist in helping the rep find the right person. The rep was frustrated that he couldn't make the referral to our therapist, but accepted his integrity.

Since that time we have received several new referrals from this rep. It it always wise to deal honestly and candidly with case managers.

"I have a case in which the patient needs more care but the case manager refused to extend treatment. What can I do to help my patient?"

Although our emphasis leans heavily on knowing the Managed Care rules of the road and playing by them as a cooperative team member, there are other "rules" that take priority over these. Your first responsibility is to the patient.

We are licensed to provide professional services by whatever state board authorizes us, to assure the highest quality of service to the patient. We place ourselves under the guidelines of the professional associations which exist to assure ethical standards of those services so that our patients receive the best care possible.

The regulations of the board issuing your license, and the ethical standards of the professional associations to which you belong, set the "rules" that take precedence over any expectations imposed on you from any external review organization.

In the case of a patient who requests and requires more care but whose benefits have run out, here are some important considerations:

1. You cannot insist on continuing care even if you believe that discontinuing services is contra-indicated.
2. Try to assist the patient to accept the reality of limited benefits; to think in terms of "the next step" in their progress.
3. Research, on the patient's behalf, several alternative sources of outside help, including professional and self-help.
4. Offer to continue to remain available to consult with anyone the patient works with to help provide a smooth transition.
5. Research support groups available in patient's community.
6. With the patient's consent, enlist the cooperation of family, friends, work associates, EAPs, and clergy to give the patient encouragement and assistance.

7. Give the patient continuing homework to build on what you have done together in the sessions.
8. Maintain letter and phone contact with the patient, if he or she approves, to show your sincere concern for their well-being and progress.
9. Give the patient the phone numbers of local hotlines, help-lines, shelters, or other emergency services if this is appropriate.
10. Work with the patient's case manager to see if they are aware of any other resources to support the patient.
11. Encourage patient to tape record their sessions. The patient can then re-listen to sessions after termination, as well as during therapy to reinforce progress.
12. The patient should also be encouraged to re-read notes and journal entries taken during therapy sessions.
13. Work with patient's physician to supervise continuing medications, if appropriate.

The discharge date, or the case reviewer's decision to deny certification for continuing care, does not spell the end of care for the patient. It simply means that that form of benefits is withdrawn. But your compassion and concern for the patient is not withdrawn.

When you take the kind of steps we have just described (whether paid to do so or not), you demonstrate the highest level of ethical, professional and moral behavior. And when you come right down to it, what is the primary need every person we see in therapy brings with them? We believe it is the desire to be loved, to feel special, important and worthy. Many times we can communicate this even more powerfully by providing service to the patient for which we are not paid. Yes, we must be careful about crossing ethical boundaries, but we must be even more careful to go the extra mile in doing more than we are paid to do. If we are in this profession at all it is for more than financial reward, isn't it?

"What advice do you have for introducing my new practice to Managed Care?"

First of all, review carefully the material in this book and "do" what you learn.

Secondly, consider the name of your new practice. Our advice to mental health practitioners who are about to open a new office is this: Consider giving your practice a name which welcomes a broad spectrum of new clientele. It should communicate without confusion, without exclusion. It should screen *IN* as many patients as possible without discouraging patients from coming in. For example, calling your practice "Center for Impotence Therapy" or "The Women's Center for Counseling" will end up costing these therapists lost business. They may communicate well what you do, but may *discourage* many patients from coming to your office. The name "Westlake Counseling & Recovery Center" allows both impotence sufferers, their loved ones, and women to feel comfortable opening the door to the waiting room.

Next, name your practice to sell your practice. The work we do is hard work. If you don't plan to work till you drop, and may want to sell your practice someday, then keep this in mind when naming your practice. We were in our early 30s when we named our practice, "Browning Therapy Group, Inc." If we had it to do over again, we would not use our own name in naming the practice. Why? Because it is much easier selling a practice with a more generic title, like "Western Counseling & Recovery Center," "Long Beach Therapy Group," "Center for Family Therapy," or "Portland Brief Therapy Center." It's much easier for Dr. Jackson to buy a practice with a name like these than a name with "Browning" attached to its reputation. But that was about 20 years ago — *live and learn.* We're glad that you can learn from our mistakes.

Did you notice the "Portland Brief Therapy Center" name? That makes a good point. If you have not decided as yet on a practice name, consider adding the word *"Brief"* to it. Why? Because it quickly tells people like Managed Care screeners and gate keepers that your practice is not afraid of accountability for doing time-limited work.

"Does a group practice have any advantage over someone in their own solo practice?"

Another issue we commonly encounter in consultations: The answer is yes. As we pointed out earlier, the trend seems to indicate that Managed Care companies will lean more and more on the "one stop shop" — a group practice where the case manager can find all the clinical services he or she needs for a client saves work and time. If the rep has to call several providers to obtain medication, individual therapy, and family therapy, they will be more likely to turn to the practice with a wide menu of services in one place. This is sometimes called an "anchor group." Caution: It is most important to assure the Managed Care company that each therapist in the group is individually accountable and easily accessible to case managers.

The solo practitioner can work effectively with Managed Care. But the group practice specializing in time-sensitive, goal-focused therapy has a better chance of courting more new referrals. In the future this may be even more true than it is at this writing.

"How can a solo practitioner form an anchor group?"

Here are a few ideas that can help you put together a team of transdisciplinary professionals to position yourself as a group practice in high demand by Managed Care. These are 12 important fundamental considerations to help bring together a group of professionals who can work well together:

1. Determine to bring no one into your group whose orientation is analytical, dynamic, Rogerian, or "eclectic." They will probably be uncomfortable and ineffective providing time-limited brief therapy.
2. Enlist the services of therapists who feel competent doing therapy in an 8 to 20 session framework.
3. Do not consider interns, assistants, or trainees. Almost no Managed Care company will certify treatment with unlicensed providers. If interns show promise, consider them only after they become licensed. Train them in solution-focused brief therapy with full-fee, sliding scale, or clients with indemnity insurance that will pay interns.
4. Bring both male and female clinicians into your group.
5. All therapists must be willing to carry the maximum professional liability insurance, and must have no history of malpractice, lawsuits, or insurance denial.
6. They should be colleagues with whom you feel comfortable, those who are trustworthy, and those with whom you can feel confident linking your reputation with theirs. Keep in mind that each member's work reflects on the image and reputation of the group.
7. They should share values and beliefs in harmony with your own, and a psychotherapy orientation friendly to yours.
8. They should be willing to work out of your office. You don't want a group of "Lone Rangers" in separate settings.
9. They should be willing to commit to at least a two-year involvement with the group.
10. They should be willing to work for whatever the reduced fee scales paid by Managed Care, less administrative costs.
11. They should have no formal relationship with Managed Care, EAP firms or other groups to avoid conflict of interest.
12. They should have flexible hours; most should be willing to work some evenings or Saturdays.

We know colleagues who have bypassed these steps so that they could have a group practice to open the Managed Care gates. Yes, the gates opened easier. But the price paid was very high — internal jealousy, lack of a team spirit, too many people doing their own thing at the price of the group's reputation, internal bickering, etc., ad nauseum. So please take these 12 items seriously and *make haste slowly.*

What about the professional makeup of the staff? A well-balanced anchor group should have the following as a minimum:

(1) A consulting psychiatrist; preferably someone capable of handling disability and workman's comp evaluations.

(2) Therapists having the following overlapping specialties:
    (a) substance abuse and CD recovery.
    (b) crisis intervention.
    (c) adolescent and child therapy.
    (d) adult and geriatric therapy.
    (e) marriage, family, couple, and single parent therapy.
    (f) a psychological testing specialist.
    (g) codependency and ACA therapy.
    (h) women's issues counseling.
    (i) survivors and victimization recovery.

(3) Offer bilingual, multicultural, and/or hearing-impaired therapy.

(4) Have more than one office location in key demographic locations served by Managed Care firms.

(5) Have phone numbers convenient to diverse locations.

(6) Specify brief therapy orientation (from 8 to 20 sessions).

(7) Train support staff to work efficiently with case reps.

Other specialties that may be helpful, but that are not required include: Biofeedback, group brief therapy, play therapy, and rehabilitation counseling.

And be sure, when forming your group, that all who participate understand how Managed Care works, get them to commit to doing paperwork accurately and on time, and *insist that all read this book.*

A good way to find out what a specific Managed Care company considers an "elite" anchor group would be to ask them. They should be happy to give you their criteria.

*"I'm still an intern and want to
learn all I can about Managed Care.
What's the best course of action?"*

You are probably coming out of a recent graduate program in counseling in which you were taught almost nothing about Managed Care (unless this book was one of your texts). Since you are not ready to start your own practice, you are in a good position to gain some invaluable expertise from the inside.

We recommend that you seek employment as a case reviewer in a Managed Care organization. Most of them hire interns. Work with them for a year or so, and then try to find work with another Managed Care firm. The larger companies will give you the best experience. They've already been through the mine fields, have solid provider panels, and will provide good training for their staff.

After a few years of this kind of inside experience, you will be in an enviable position when the doors open in your new office. You'll have first-hand knowledge, know what pleases case managers, know what providers do to shoot themselves in the foot, and what the best providers do to get steady referrals. Enjoy paying your dues. They will pay big dividends when you become a preferred provider for the top companies.

And then please contact us. We would love to talk to you to integrate your expertise into upcoming updates of this text!

*"What about networking and promoting
solo practices to Managed Care?"*

Group practices may have some decided advantages, but those in independent practices can develop profitable working relations with many external reviewers. Consider forming therapist networks or consortiums or focus groups. Set a time each week, bi-weekly, or monthly in which you meet together over lunch or breakfast to brain-storm ideas for promoting your practices to Managed Care, EAPs, HMOs and other groups.

Share strategies on what's working to get closed gates open. What's making case reps happy. What's making them mad. What changes are emerging. What works with specific companies and not with others. Secrets of handling paperwork ("papermarketing"). Tips on handling phone contacts.

And you can plan a time for everyone to vent, dump, purge and cathart all those Managed Care frustrations and aggravations!

"I am reluctant to start my clients on meds. Is it necessary to refer my clients for medication consultation?"

Case reviewers are trained to look for certain indicators of cost-*ineffective* service. One of those red-flags is a provider who does not utilize medication to reduce symptoms in cases where medication obviously can help the patient function better.

Like you, we are trained and predisposed to working through patient symptoms in a drug-free approach. However, since the advent of Managed Care, we have had (been forced to) change that bias. When you see a patient, for example, diagnosed as "Major Depression" or "Generalized Anxiety Disorder," not to refer for medication eval is a definite red flag. And red flags signal possible provider incompetence, or unfriendly Managed Care team spirit. You don't want either of these assumptions linked to your name.

So, find (through the case manager) panel psychiatrists who are conservative in their use of medications — or hire one on your own staff — and make the referral for med evals and med trials. Then work closely with the psychiatrist and the patient to reduce the use of medication as impairments are reduced or minimized.

"I do sand tray and other non-traditional methods. How should I handle this with case managers?"

All case managers are not created equal. One rep may understand and believe in the value of sand tray therapy, or psychodrama, or biofeedback, or inner-child work, or Christian biblical therapy; while another rep may turn up his or her nose and raise both eyebrows and blood pressure when they hear of such methods.

The only safe advice here is this. Before embarking on a course of non-traditional methodology, *clear it with the case manager.* Call them and explain how you believe a particular method will work to quickly reduce impairments and lead to wellness. Send or fax them descriptive articles on the approach, validating research, and other information on how the method works. The key is demonstrating short-term effectiveness in symptom reduction.

If approved, keep the case manager updated via voice mail as to progress. Send them patient progress reports showing measurable change. And don't forget to send the case manager a Thank You note for their willingness to allow you to use innovative approaches with the clients they refer to you. You may even want to send them a copy of a good text outlining the method for their library. They will appreciate your thoughtfulness.

One word of caution, dear colleague. Recently we had calls from several patients whom we had referred to a therapist in a nearby city. We made these referrals because we have long held this psychologist in high esteem and had received good reports over the years. But the feedback this time was anything but positive. All three patients were calling for another referral. They reported feeling very uncomfortable with the interventions used by this therapist; methods involving a kind of accupressure on various parts of the body. We referred them to other therapists whom we knew and trusted.

We also called this psychologist and shared with him the concerns of these patients. He had some excellent theoretical data supporting what he now practiced. He believed that his work was more effective than before using the pressure-point methods. But one thing he did not have. He did not have the favor and goodwill of the people we referred to him. He also caused us to reevaluate his continued status on our referral list. His choice of using unorthodox techniques had resulted in the loss of 3 new referrals.

We do not mean to be judgmental here. We are not judging him. We are merely trying to caution you about using methods that could raise questions about your professional competence. If you do elect to use unusual or non-traditional strategies, try not venturing too far from the accepted path of approved clinical practice, and make sure that these methods can produce observable, behavioral change and symptom reduction.

"How often should I see a Managed Care patient?"

Except in more severe conditions, it is best to see a patient referred to you by a case rep no more than once weekly. After the initial phase of treatment, it is a good idea to spread out the sessions to every 2 weeks, every 3 weeks, and then to once monthly. Case managers appreciate the prudent spacing of sessions.

The exception to this is when seeing a patient 2 or 3 times a week as an outpatient will make it possible to keep the patient out of inpatient care. But *be certain to clear this with the case manager first.* It's also wise to ask the case manager if she or he has any opinion or preference about the best frequency for a given condition.

"What's the best way to handle requests for extensions?"

First, let us re-emphasize one important thing. Try to avoid requests for extensions. Attempt to set realistic discharge dates, specify treatment interventions that move the patient toward meeting outcome goals, and then discharge the patient on the expected date. This is what case reviewers most appreciate.

But if you must request extensions, do this:

1. Never continue seeing the patient without approval.
2. Postpone further sessions until certification is received (give patient homework to maintain therapeutic bond during this hiatus).
3. Find out the policy of the organization for requesting extensions and follow it carefully (some want direct calls to case reps, others want documentation only).
4. Never write "see prior treatment plan" on extension requests. Do a new treatment plan for the next phase of care as detailed as your initial plan.
5. Give, in behavioral terms, those treatment objectives which were reached and support each with patient statements and post-test data.
6. Give, in behavioral terms, treatment goals which were not met, reasons or hypotheses as to why they were unrealized, and any unforeseen events contributing to unmet goals.
7. Tell them why you believe specific techniques will result in meeting goals, why, and how this will be measured.
8. Set a new expected discharge date.

9. Be sure you are documenting the use of outside resources (homework, bibliotherapy, workbooks, support groups, medications) to reinforce change and therapeutic gain. Emphasize additional resources used during extension that will increase the probability of success during next phase.
10. Be certain that you are selecting treatment targeted impairments that are realistically susceptible to brief intervention, and using intervention strategies appropriate to the condition. Ask yourself if consultation with respected colleagues is in order?

These suggestions should help you justify and merit extensions when they are clearly indicated. But for the future successful relationship of your practice with Managed Care, we hope that you will use this method infrequently.

"What is Managed Care's attitude toward marital and family therapy?"

The primary concern here is how the patient's insurance coverage deals with these problems. Most case managers are skilled therapists themselves and understand the importance of marriage and family therapy to a patient's mental well being. But most insurance plans do *not* cover either. Therefore, if you use the DSM V codes as your primary diagnoses and request marital or family therapy, you will not receive certification.

What to do? Have you ever met a couple or a member of a family going through conflict that did not also manifest a clear-cut mental disorder? We have not. Therefore, the V code becomes a secondary Axis I diagnosis to a primary mental disorder; e.g., "Dysthymia", "Generalized Anxiety Disorder", "Post-Traumatic Stress Disorder". A diagnosis will have to be given to the designated patient, of course. In cases of family therapy, a specific family member, such as a child, must be defined as the designated patient.

With this approach the patient can be certified for care. The case manager will have no trouble then authorizing marital or family therapy.

Suppose a couple has been certed for "Conjoint Therapy" and only one spouse comes in; can you see them without the other being present? Our experience is that most reps will have no trouble allowing this. But be sure to verify this yourself with each rep just to be sure.

"What's the best location for my new office from a marketing-to-Managed-Care point of view?"

Before deciding on the location of your practice, or before setting up a satellite office, do your homework. Call several of the larger Managed Care companies in your area and ask them where they need new providers. The director of provider relations or a case rep should be able to give you this information.

Another rule of thumb is to locate your office in high-density population areas or areas close to large corporations or governmental agencies. Check with these companies and find out which Managed Care companies serve them to determine the direction of your research.

Try to locate your office in a larger, more well-known location. This will help case reps quickly locate your practice when they need a provider for a client. If your office is in a smaller city, you may get fewer referrals and have to educate case managers about your whereabouts. For example, our primary location is in a small city called Los Alamitos. Even though it is not too far from Disneyland, who ever heard of it? Even most case managers in Southern California don't know where it is! So we have to educate them, telling them we're between Long Beach and Anaheim. That takes work.

Freeway access is also very important in many cities. Therefore, if you can, locate in well-known areas. It will save you time and bring in more business.

"When a new therapist joins the practice, how can this be used to promote our services anew to case managers?"

The "one stop clinical shop" is highly appealing to case managers. In the high-pressure, too-much-work, too-little-time job of Managed Care reviewers, any practice that can offer a multi-faceted service menu with a single phone call finds itself high atop the preferred provider list.

Whenever you add a new staff member to your multidisciplinary team, send an announcement letter to case managers of all local Managed Care organizations — even those with whom you have not actively worked.

Don't just say that "Dr. Wonderworker has joined our staff." Say something like this: "We are pleased to announce the addition of a specialist in adolescent therapy to our staff. Dr. Wonderworker holds a Ph.D. in clinical psychology and offers solution-oriented therapy for..." Notice that we are not sending out announcements for their own sake, or simply to stroke Dr. Wonderworker's ego. With any new addition to the practice, we are marketing our value to Managed Care needs. Keep their needs in the foreground as you plan your staff announcements. And keep Managed Care concerns in mind whenever you hire new staff personnel. We recommend that you consider only those therapists who are Managed Care friendly as potential candidates to your staff.

"Is there any efficient way to handle all the detail required by Managed Care?"

Facing the stark reality of the situation, we must all

admit it: Managed Care = Complexity. Thoreau would doubtless have a tough go of it trying to find simplicity in the Managed Care world of today (it's no Walden Pond!).

We've tried to make the world of Managed Healthcare as simple as possible for you, and we know it isn't easy or simple! But when it comes to handling the details, we've found one way that does help put a handle on things.

The most common complaint from case reps is that therapists are not prepared when doing phone updates. Here is one good way to be on top of things when you are asked questions like, "What's the patient's Social Security Number?", "When was the first date of treatment?", "What is the expected date of discharge?", "The patient's diagnosis?", "Medications?", "Outside resources?". Put all this information on a rolodex card under the patient's name.

Add to this patient's address, phone numbers, family information and SS#s. Also list data on the case manager, including pager # and voice mail code #, and date of last contact.

This might seem like a lot of hassle doing this for each Managed Care patient, but it pays off. As we have pointed out before, case managers work under heavy pressure. They think fondly about — and refer more freely to — providers who are well-prepared with pertinent details. Try this system. It will help them, and you, do your job more efficiently with an increasing referral flow.

"If the patient requires additional therapy but the case manager refuses to certify more sessions, what can be done to give the patient the help they need?"

As we've said before, when you have a disagreement with a case manager, do all you can to avoid being disagreeable. An adversarial attitude is deadly to your "Managed Care friendly" reputation. We also recommend that you avoid appealing the case manager's decision, because this, too, can damage your favorable perception. Most case managers will not indiscriminately deny treatment. Thus, their denial is based on their clinical expertise. When you attack, argue, or appeal, you offend them on a professional level.

Many times we may have already accomplished most treatment objectives, found solutions to patient complaints, and realized symptom reduction, but other issues remain unmet. The case is nonetheless formally discharged (to the delight of the case manager) but treatment continues under a new agreement worked out with the patient, and put in writing and signed. Some ways we have found pleasing and rewarding to the patient include:

- The patient can be offered a significantly reduced fee to make continued out-of-pocket care possible and separate from his/her insurance coverage (but be sure this is permissible under your contract). The patient signs an agreement summarizing this plan.
- A specific number of sessions are agreed upon in which the patient receives our care at no charge in exchange for volunteer work with needy people of his/her choice (e.g., convalescent homes).
- We have offered supportive encouragement over the telephone at no charge to help the patient maintain therapeutic gains.
- We help the patient transition to a no-fee or sliding-scale clinic or agency convenient to their home.
- Some patients do well transitioning to low-cost group therapy, supported or not supported by their medical plan (in addition to outside support groups).

We feel morally and ethically responsible, as well as committed to our patients, to help assure continued care, whether their Managed Care coverage funds the care or not. We'll leave this to your own conscience.

"What's the best way to handle discharges to minimize any trauma to the patient?"

We do 5 things when discharging a patient to make the experience as painless as possible: (1) the therapist informs the patient how many sessions remain; (2) when the secretary greets the patient in the waiting room or on the phone, she reminds the patient gently how many sessions remain; (3) a letter is mailed informing the patient that they have one remaining session until discharge and discontinuance of benefits; (4) the case manager is advised of the discharge; and (5) we carefully assess follow-up care for the patient after termination of benefits; i.e., to arrange some other treatment arrangement with us, referral to another lower-fee treatment, and/or other outside resources. Follow-up phone calls and notes expressing concern for the patient's progress, as well as outcome research, reinforces our sincere interest in the patient over-and-above what we are paid to do. It helps to put follow-up activities on a tickler file system so that they don't end up in the realm of good intentions.

"What are some of the high-risk areas or things to avoid doing with case managers?"

We call these "red flags". Wave too many of them and you can wave good-bye to new referrals!

Here are a few of the words you should beware of using in any and all communications with case managers:

Intrapsychic • Growth • Psychoanalytic • Insight • Dynamic
Narcissistic • Process • Non-Directive • Gestalt • Transference
Projection • Ego • Id • Neurosis • Defense mechanisms • Symbolic
Working Through • Separation-Individuation • Intensive Psychotherapy
(and most terms you'll find in abnormal psych textbooks).

What are the things to avoid doing? Here is a list of the biggest offenders:

- Asking for too many extensions.
- Not returning case manager's phone calls quickly.
- Not getting paperwork in on time.
- Using abstract words in documentation (e.g.,supportive, exploratory, awareness, insight, prognosis guarded, etc.).
- Using no outside resources or homework in treatment plan.
- Too many inpatient admission requests.
- Poorly-documented inpatient admission requests.
- Too many patient complaints.
- Indefinite discharge date (e.g., "Discharge Date: ?").
- Allowing interns, assistants or trainees to see Managed Care patients.
- Untrained receptionists or secretaries who mishandle calls from case managers or patients.
- Sloppy, illegible, indecisive paperwork.
- Not being prepared, "fogging","B.S.'ing" or deceiving case managers in phone updates.
- Communicating a hostile, adversarial attitude toward the requirements of Managed Care.

We could go on with these ugly lists, but suffice it to say that they represent some of the most common offenders, according to case managers we've talked to (and according to our own unfortunate experience making some of these blunders ourselves — "blunders" are wonderful teachers!).

Carefully avoid such errors and there should be no red flags next to your name.

Linda Stern writes in the November, 1990 issue of *The Family Therapy Networker,*

> "The signs are that private practice will emerge as a great compromise between the total autonomy of the past and the bureaucratic management of the present."

She's right. Private practice and practitioners can grow and flourish if that compromise is made willingly, and if the clinician learns the new rules and becomes a team player.

In an incisive article in *The California Therapist,* Mary Riemersma, M.B.A., executive director of the California Association of Marriage & Family Therapy, says that mental health professionals

"...cannot stand on the sidelines of this new system and throw stones. The best way to cause change is to be involved from the inside and negotiate change as a respected player rather than a hostile outsider. Thus, don't throw in the towel—this new system is not that complicated or distasteful. Should you 'roll over and play dead,' you could find yourself excluded from the future of managed health care. Therefore, you are left with 'join 'em,'...learning a new way of thinking, developing methods of providing short-term, goal-oriented therapy, generating paperwork you never dreamed imaginable--(for which you will not likely be compensated), possibly aligning with a multi-disciplinary team, becoming accustomed to having a third party participate in your provision of treatment and even becoming dependent upon that third party as your future referral source."   (November, 1990)

Her last point merits repeating: "...and even becoming dependent upon that third party as your future referral source." Thank you, Mary, for such wise counsel.

We'll leave you with our sincere wish that something, or many things you found in this text will work to help you establish profitable working relationships with many case managers. And may these relationships result in a steadily increasing flow of new referrals to build a financially flourishing practice in the world of Managed Healthcare. And may God smile on all you do to touch the lives of others.

It's called many things: Managed health, managed healthcare, managed competition, and managed care. Some disgruntled therapists even call it "K-Mart Kare" or "Mismanaged Non-Care" or even "Less Time To Do More For Less." A recent APA workshop referred to the impact of Managed Care trends on a mental health provider's practice as: "Salvation or Armageddon?" And one influential member of Congress cynically called it "a Dr. Kevorkian prescription."

Whatever we choose to call it, this new budget-driven, clock-and-calendar-watching, quality-monitoring system is here to stay and will be a pivotal part of this country's healthcare reforms.

An era is drawing to an end, and the days are numbered for the patient who once said, "I'll give my therapist *one more year* to help me, then I'm going to Lourdes!" — She may have to head for Lourdes after 10 sessions by the looks of things (unless, of course, her therapist has studied and implemented the tools, tactics and techniques contained in this book!).

These are serious times as we accommodate ourselves and our work to today's healthcare reforms. Kenneth Linde, president of Principal Healthcare, Inc., paints a sobering picture for any mental healthcare professional:

> "In today's highly competitive healthcare environment, the weaker players are being forced out. Only the strong will remain in the long run. The 'shakeout' is already under way. The number of players in the competitive arena will be fewer, but those remaining will be strong..."

If you are to survive this "shakeout" and be found among the "strong players" in today's—and tomorrow's—healthcare reforms, you'll need a new working definition of Managed Care. May we offer you our own definition, conceived, of course, in the spirit of good brief therapy:

Managed Care is — ASAP/PDQ:

Affordable Services Applied Prudently
by Professionals Dedicated to Quality

APPENDIX A

ADVICE FROM THE INSIDERS:

Interviews with the Experts to Give You
Straight Answers to Tough Questions

ADVICE FROM THE INSIDERS:

Interviews with the Experts to Give You
Straight Answers to Tough Questions

W e've shared with you thus far what we have found effective from the clinical perspective. Now here is a look at the perspective of those on the "inside" of Managed Care.

We've shared with you a detailed look at what works, and what doesn't (learned the hard way) from the perspective of the provider.

Now we want to give you the opportunity to hear what the "insiders" have to say. Obviously, we believe that what we have said in this text is as complete and as accurate as possible. But, in case we might be biased, we decided to go behind those gates and let you hear from the real experts — those who work (or who have worked) inside the inner sanctum of Managed Care companies, EAP programs, and the insurance companies and employers who hire them.

We tried to think of the kind of questions that you might ask if you had the opportunity to sit down with these important and powerful people to "pick their brains." In that spirit, we tried to keep the questions non-theoretical, nuts-&-bolts practical, and down-to-earth so you would be able to translate their advice into action.

To help those we interviewed feel entirely free to share their opinions without hesitation, we use only their first names and do not mention the firm for which they work. You will see, we believe, a candid tone to their responses that represents their true feelings, not what they think their boss might want them to say, or not to say. We are grateful for their help in making this text even more valuable for you in building positive, cooperative working relationships with Managed Care professionals.

Advice from a Case Manager

His name is Phil. His educational background includes a B.A. in journalism-public relations; an M.A. in Marriage, Family & Child Counseling, and licensure as a Marriage and Family Therapist in California. He has worked in a private psychiatric hospital, and was a therapist at an HMO for 2 years. He is currently working for a large Managed Care firm and has his own part-time private practice.

He is responsible for case management and review of several large regions of the western United States. His firm manages the accounts of several large labor unions.

Here are his responses to some questions vital to any provider who wants to understand how case managers think, what they want, and how to cooperatively partner with these reviewers:

QUESTION: How is a provider's office location important to a case manager?

ANSWER: Location is very important. The case manager wants to refer to a provider who is within easy driving distance for the client. I recommend to providers who are trying to interest Managed Care in their work that they prepare a map.   Plan what communities are within a reasonable 20-minute driving distance of your office. Draw a circle covering that area on a map, with your office in the center. This will clearly demonstrate to the case manager the area that is serviced by your office. This is one good way to develop a new referral source; which is in effect the same way you would work to develop any other referral source. You let them know in the promotional materials you send them where you are and what you do.

QUESTION: What is a good way to interest a provider relations director in your practice, if you are not as yet part of the provider panel?

ANSWER: Find the specialty areas that Managed Care people are in need of, and which other therapists typically don't do, and inform Managed Care firms that you do them. In my experience, I don't see a lot of therapists working with children or adolescents. If you have these or other specialists in your practice, it would be to your advantage to make this known.

QUESTION: Does that include play therapy?

ANSWER: Well, I don't know if "play therapy" communicates well to Managed Care because it tends to suggest the picture of long-term care.   But if it is communicated to the case manager as "play therapy with a short-term focus," that would probably work. Also, try to link play therapy to facilitating diagnosis or assisting in your brief work with the parents.

QUESTION: Let's say a therapist is sending a Practice Profile to a new Managed Care company he or she is trying to join; would it help to actually define in this presentation of your practice what you specifically mean by "brief therapy"?

ANSWER: Absolutely, that would be excellent. In fact, there is a group which has contracted with us on a trial basis who says, "We'll do everything in 10 sessions." And it's worth seeing if, indeed, they can do this because most of the cases we refer are not significant levels of depression or anxiety (although you may not think so based on some of the referrals we've sent *you!*).

QUESTION: Do you think this will be a trend or a common expectation Managed Care has of providers in the future?

ANSWER: Oh yes, this is what I see coming — a group of clinicians coming together and offering that kind of a package to various Managed Care companies. They say, "We can cover a large geographical area for you and provide quality care within a time-limited framework convenient for your clients." If you think about it from the point of view of Managed Care, the fewer headaches that they have, the more that they can trust that this is done well, the more likely that they are going to be using that provider, instead of using someone else with whom they are having headaches or who has an attitude of resistance to the Managed Care programs.

QUESTION: In terms of the make up of the staff: Does it help a group practice to have a psychiatrist on staff?

ANSWER: Definitely, because Managed Care is based on the medical model. Many times you'll hear them talk about "symptom reduction." If a case manager sees that you have a medical person on staff, they know that you'll be likely to emphasize at least a look at what medication can do to help. We believe that for a psychotherapist to work alone to reduce all kinds of symptoms of anxiety or depression is, at best, grandiose. At worst, it's dangerous.

QUESTION: So the case manager, and all of Managed Care for that matter, believes that the use of medication can accelerate treatment outcome?

ANSWER: Or you could look at it another way: The use of medication simply *reduces symptoms.* And symptom reduction is at the top of Managed Care's priority list. You could see it as, "What benefits the client most?" And that would be reducing — not prolonging — a patient's suffering.

QUESTION: Would bilingual therapists on the staff be an advantage for a group practice trying to interest Managed Care firms in their work?

ANSWER: Yes, you've got a great concept there. In fact, we keep lists of specialty providers — bilingual providers, Christian providers, child and adolescent providers — these are hot items.

QUESTION: What are some of the "hot items" that Managed Care firms are seeking in terms of provider specialties?

ANSWER: The ones we just mentioned, for example, Christian therapy, bilingual therapy, child and adolescent therapy. Others include chemical dependency, ACA (as a consequence of chemical dependency), a tough item would be a "brief approach to sexual abuse." And if a provider has a reputation for being able to handle borderlines, and not letting the borderlines handle them — that would be something of high interest to case managers, because a lot of problematic cases involve borderline clients who try to control the whole process.

QUESTION: How does a case manager react to V code diagnoses on Axis I?

ANSWER: Most insurance companies will not pay on V codes. If a provider puts down a V code diagnosis on a treatment plan, he or she will not receive authorization for treatment. The V code is a pretty normal situation, and in life people will have various trials and crises that can be addressed or dealt with apart from therapy. This is the thinking of the people who are paying for the care. So if there is a V code, it had better be a secondary diagnosis along with a primary diagnosis of a definite mental disorder.

QUESTION: Aside from V codes, what are some of the other red-flags that case reviewers look for on treatment plans and other ongoing documentation?

ANSWER: One phrase that you do not want to have on any treatment plan is "supportive therapy." When Managed Care sees "supportive" this translates into "We don't need to pay for this." *Supportive means you don't get our support!* Therapy, in Managed Care, is for symptom reduction, not "maintenance" or "hand-holding".

QUESTION: What about support groups as part of the treatment menu for a provider?

ANSWER: Managed Care sees that there is a cost savings to them if a client can be seen up-front by a psychiatrist to get the crisis resolved, a course of therapy as needed, and then involvement in a weekly support group. But don't call it a "support group;" call it "weekly skills training" or something like that. The word "support" should be avoided when dealing with Managed Care people. Let's say someone's schizophrenic. It doesn't do them any good to have them in therapy after a period of time. But if they are on meds, they can be maintained in a weekly skills group as part of your practice. And if the same kind of care is available in support groups in the community, then you shouldn't offer it as part of your practice. But for some patients, perhaps a brief 6 or 8 week parenting skills group would be of interest to case managers. And in some of these cases, Managed Care will pay for this rather than have the patient in individual therapy.

QUESTION: Can you comment on what a case reviewer is looking for in a good treatment plan? What's the best approach to take in doing one correctly?

ANSWER: Think in terms of a beginning, a middle, and an end of treatment. It's not this open-ended thing that just keeps going until a person runs out of insurance coverage. Right away begin to ask yourself, "When is this person realistically going to be discharged, and what will it take to make that happen?" It's behavioral. It's symptom reduction, goal-focused treatment — so that if you're aiming at something you're going to hit it. If you're aiming at a potential discharge goal, you are more likely to realize it.

It's like I tell my private practice clients, "I'm in the business of working myself out of a job with you. If I really am doing a good job, you'll get better, you'll refer other people to me who need my help, and you won't continue to need my help." In fact, I try to define it as the client being a co-therapist with me. This works well because there is less resistance and homework tends to get done better. I try to give clients the expectation early on that we both desire that they would not be in therapy any longer than necessary, but would be learning to handle their problems on their own.

Specify to the case manager and to the client the goals for the beginning, the middle, and the end of therapy so they know what areas you are working on and how you are doing. Help clients maximize their ego strengths, by means of involvement in your treatment plan.

QUESTION: Should you list the specific beginning, middle, and end goals on the treatment plan?

ANSWER: A secret that takes a little bit of a "touch" is not to disclose everything up front that could cause your plan to be rejected. It's a little like going in for a job interview — you don't put in "de-selectors." And don't start out by putting in too much information, because you've got better things to do than just filling out paperwork.

One of the things that I would consider when trying to determine whether or not to pursue a Managed Care group is, "how complex is their paperwork?" The best groups have a one-page form. You want to be able to say it briefly, say it concisely, and that communicates that you know how to do the job. But if you fill out that form, rambling all over the place and using arrows and "see the back," this indicates to the case manager that you don't know what you are doing. And it's usually those people who complain that there's too much paperwork with Managed Care. They don't have a tight approach to managing their treatment plan, and don't have a tight approach to managing their time. Remember that all your contacts with case managers should be considered a form of marketing.

QUESTION: What's your philosophy of effective, efficient, Managed-Care-friendly treatment?

ANSWER: Let me share with you something our medical director says: You've got yourself a diagnosis. And you arrive at that diagnosis by having the symptoms that go with that diagnosis. So, what are you working on in your treatment plan? You're working on *reducing the presenting problem; you're not working on solving everything in the world for the client; you're working on the presenting problem.*

In most of your cases, you do not come up with a new presenting problem half-way through the treatment process. When you address the presenting problem, and outcome objectives are reached successfully, and in time, the case manager says, "Ah, Browning does great work! Let's give him another referral." That's how a provider needs to think — that if I do good, efficient therapy on most of my cases I will have a reputation that results in more referrals.

It's like the "holdouts" that we have in the hospital game. They think that, "If we can hold onto this patient for a long time, it's better for the hospital because it runs up the bill." But then they get the reputation for doing that, and they get no new referrals. That's the wrong way of thinking; that's the old way of thinking. And once you get this kind of reputation, it's hard to shake.

QUESTION: *Can you comment on the kind of providers you enjoy working with most, and those you like working with least? What do they do right to win your confidence and your referrals? And what do they do wrong to damage their relationship with you? In short, what causes you to choose to refer to one provider and not to another?*

ANSWER: It's very much like you wrote in your book, *Private Practice Handbook.* I like working with providers who think of themselves as a provider of service to the client and providing help to the case manager, as well as to the panel itself — an attitude of being partners in the treatment plan.

The therapist who takes a problem-solving approach instead of a whining approach will get a lot further with me. Therapists should take a look at their own issues when they whine and complain. I don't like working with those who are demanding or who are resentful toward Managed Care and those who are "resistant." If they would *work with me* they'd get a steady source of referrals. Those who have made that conversion, work cooperatively with us, and do quality work, they get a lot of referrals.

The ones I like are those who have made the mental adjustment. They call me up, and include me in the treatment team. They have said to themselves, "This is a steady source of referrals and I want to treat them right and I want to be cooperative with them. We are not adversaries." And that's what I frequently say to some providers who, because of their own issues, try to get me into an argument: "Listen, we are not adversaries." When therapists treat me as an adversary, is it any wonder that they get so few referrals?

QUESTION: *Are you looking for those who can provide time-limited brief therapy?*

ANSWER: The way we look at brief therapy is that it is not just 6 to 12 sessions. It could be more; it could be less.

Some cases can be resolved in just a handful of sessions, while others will go on because they are dealing with a life-long depression or something like this.

The therapist should not be thinking, "I'm going to get rid of all the client's depression." This is kind of grandiose. But to help the patient become more highly functioning, while the depression will be worked on outside of therapy over time — that's our preferred approach. We want the therapist to try to get the patient functioning well enough that they can maintain work and other kinds of responsibilities. And we want the therapist to help the patient get involved in other support groups in the community.

It's not wrong for a provider to think about the patient being discharged and then coming back for further care 6 months or a year from now. But it is wrong to have the attitude that, "I'll keep them coming forever." Some panels deserve all the hostility providers have for them because they are managed poorly. But good panels will want to keep their contract and they want to make sure that the service is provided well with high quality. These will not be restrictive if the patient needs to come back later for more care.

QUESTION: We have heard that some Managed Care companies have rating systems in which they rate various providers as to how well they are performing on the team. Can you comment on how this works?

ANSWER: Our company, and many Managed Care companies, use computers to rate providers. I don't want to feed anyone's paranoia, but there is a system that rates you by the average number of sessions you use per diagnostic category. So when a case manager pulls the provider's name up on the screen, his or her rating is right there. This is not commonly known, but we have to do this. Other rating categories for providers besides number of sessions per diagnosis include these: quality of paperwork, timely submission of paperwork, how many times has this provider requested extensions of treatment, and how many complaints from patients have been received on this provider. Providers who request many extensions are those, in my opinion, who are still hanging on to the old style of therapy — building a relationship, countertransference, working through and all of that stuff, and they just don't get the job done. But that's not what Managed Care is all about. It's about reducing symptoms, not building a relationship.

A highly rated provider is someone who is a team player who looks out first for the interests of the client. He or she decreases the length of treatment, addresses the problems in treatment, and is cooperative.

It's like the medical model: When you go to see a physician because you don't feel well, you don't expect to have an ongoing relationship; you're going there to get a problem solved. Your understanding is that when that is done, you won't be seeing the doctor thereafter. Many therapists are hostile to this model, and those who are tend to be hostile to Managed Care. And those who continue to be hostile to Managed Care will have a tough time surviving in the future.

QUESTION: What advice could you give to a therapist in private practice who wants to become a provider, but is told that the "panel is closed"? What can he or she do to become a new provider? And is it helpful to be part of a group practice rather than a solo practice?

ANSWER: Many panels will be closed when you approach them. But just like anything else, if there's a need for certain specialties, and you call them periodically, you'll build a human relationship with them. I suggest you put them on a rotation basis; contacting them every 2 to 3 months. Keep contacting them by phone and by sending your CV (vitae) or practice profile to them in the mail.

But there is one disadvantage because Managed Care is

going through so many changes that it may not be the same person you dealt with before. This is part of the game. It can actually work to your benefit because when you call at one time and get nowhere with someone, the next time you may get a more friendly reception. The key is to persist in contacting them at regular intervals.

But one of the ways "in" would be to visit the office with someone who is already a provider with that company and have them introduce you. This way you become a "real person" and at the same time you can give them some well-made brochures or some type of handout that they can use to identify you with after you leave. It should be something done with excellence that sets you apart from other providers. Introduce yourself, "I'm Joe Wonderworker and I work a lot with children ages 3 through 8 and I have an association with a child psychiatrist." Now they may be more interested in the child psychiatrist than in bringing you on the panel, but with this combination of benefits, it may get you on as a provider. So affiliation with a good psychiatrist, and having a specialty that is in high demand are good ways to get on a panel.

QUESTION: How do you set up this first meeting with the case manager?

ANSWER: You should not try to set it up with a case manager. Ask for a meeting with someone in provider relations. They then can introduce you to their case managers who happen to be there.

But keep in mind that most case managers are overloaded with work. I find myself that I have maybe 5 minutes at the most to talk with providers who come in. So you've got to be able to make a real good impression in 5 minutes. And it helps to know the clientele that the Managed Care company is working with. We have predominately labor contracts, so a provider has to quickly let me know that he or she knows how to do brief therapy with blue-collar people.

QUESTION: What about offering a workshop or seminar to case managers and provider relations staffs?

ANSWER: You could offer these to see what happens, and they do sometimes work to increase your visibility. But many people who deal a lot with providers say to themselves, "They're just using this seminar or workshop to get at us." So you've got to be creative.

QUESTION: What's the mental process that you go through when you are considering referring a client to a provider?

ANSWER: Basically, I'm looking for someone who is convenient to the plan in terms of distance the client must travel. Someone who works that kind of specialty, and has a track record for doing good, quality work in that area. And because they're rated that way, it's easy for me to look them up in the computer. And that's who I'm going with for the referral.

But I find that when I've had a recent conversation with a provider who's been helpful and supportive, I'm more likely to want to refer to that person. They've been in my office. They've shown me that they are competent just by their manner. So I am more likely to refer to that person over someone else.

QUESTION: What are some of the specific things you are looking for in a good treatment report?

ANSWER: The basics include the DSM-III-R diagnoses with the accompanying symptoms. A treatment plan to address the primary problem (and not "all the problems in the world"). A discharge plan with a beginning, a middle, and an end of treatment. And the treatment plan should have a good probability for success. Is a medication evaluation included for major depression, ADHD, panic disorder, or other such diagnoses?

QUESTION: Could you say more about the importance of the medication evaluation in your review of the treatment plan?

ANSWER: If we do not see that medication evaluation is part of the plan, we may say that we cannot authorize further care. Many times. I hear from providers, "Well, my patients do not like to be on medication." But I believe that many times the patient may have picked up that attitude from the therapist. Is it an economic issue that causes them not to refer for medications — so that they can keep the patient in therapy that much longer as the symptoms stay unresolved? Or, are you really wanting to help the person get well faster?

QUESTION: How do you react and what issues are raised when a provider requests more sessions or asks for extensions of time? What criteria would justify your granting extensions to a provider?

ANSWER: I don't think it's wrong simply to ask for more sessions as long as you can prove the need for it by medical necessity. One thing that could justify extensions is that there's been a sudden change in the patient's life, like an acute and major family crisis. Or if the patient has an adverse reaction to medication, this could justify more sessions. But if this happens in every case you are working on, you will not meet with much approval. Or if you wait until the end of treatment to get a medication evaluation, that doesn't look good.

Think in terms of medical necessity; that's how case managers come at it. They do not authorize on the basis of feeling good about you.

And sometimes patients will call and demand extensions of care because they think they are entitled. So what I'll say is, "Well, on your dental plan you're entitled to a root canal, but you don't get a root canal unless you need it. So, you're not entitled to unlimited care or counseling every day of the week or even once a week just because you want it. It has to be *because you need it."*

QUESTION: *What criteria would you say justifies psych hospitalization?*

ANSWER: Psych hospitalization is certified when there is a clear medical necessity of danger to self or others. Sometimes hospitalization is needed because it's real tricky managing the meds and the patient could become suicidal or unstable while the meds are being adjusted. But overall, hospitalization is only for stabilization and may not include the therapist in the inpatient treatment. And this can be acceptable and justified from the Managed Care's point of view by saying that the therapist is there for the patient once they are out, to help them adjust to life outside the hospital. Their brief stay in the hospital is for the psychiatrist to get them stable. The danger is that if we do all kinds of supportive work while they're in the hospital, we teach them to become well-adjusted to the hospital environment. Later, on the outside, when things get tough they may want to go back into the hospital. More and more, insurance will not pay for that.

A good case management firm is going to have different levels of CD or detox treatment; anything from simple recommendation for 12-Step groups, sober living houses, day-treatment, outpatient therapy, and all the way up to inpatient stays.

QUESTION: *What is Managed Care's attitude to the use of and request for psych testing?*

ANSWER: I think a case manager typically reacts unfavorably to the abuse of psych testing. This is true especially when it's done by rote — "Oh, I do this panel of tests for everybody at intake." This is not looked upon favorably, especially if you expect to be reimbursed!

However, there is one therapist who distinguishes himself by giving the Millon Multiaxial Clinical Inventory to every patient he sees. This gives him the focus of treatment that he can work with successfully in brief therapy. And he wisely does not charge the time or testing procedures to the patient's account. So the case managers have no trouble with this, or the use of other symptom-focused instruments to enhance brief therapy outcome or outcome research.

An occasional use of psych testing to tease out a psychotic diagnosis would be quite appropriate. And it would be particularly indicated as an adjunct to the prescription of psych meds. Most of the time MFCCs or social workers are not authorized to do the psych testing. Psychologists are the ones who are trained in testing methods.

QUESTION: What are the best "rules of the road" for providers to follow in their interactions with case managers over the telephone? What can a clinician do to work more effectively with you over the telephone?

ANSWER: Always use voice mail whenever possible. Keeping a case manager on the phone for any extended period of time is not a good idea. A brief update on the voice mail would be considered helpful. But don't deny yourself an occasional personal contact with the case manager on the phone. An example would be, "Phil, I need a psych med eval, would you please get back to me and let me know who to refer the patient to?" And always give the case manager what they need to do their job: Patient name, Social Security Number, diagnosis, meds, current symptoms, goals, number of sessions requested — this shows that you're in touch with what's going on.

And try to use paperwork more than the phone. We are *always* on the phone!

And chat just enough to be friendly, but don't overdo it. Remember that case managers are probably therapists themselves and occasionally enjoy talking "shop" with you briefly. Don't forget that they are persons with needs and feelings. You can "include the case manager as part of the treatment team" without sacrificing quality care.

QUESTION: What kind of input would you like to get from providers other than the formal forms and reports? Are there any that would really help you?

ANSWER: Basically, think in terms of trying to problem-solve things for this case manager, who is an important source of future referrals to your practice. If you make things easier for them by giving them certain kinds of information, you'll be more likely to receive more referrals in return.

The case manager's job is so complex that anything you can do to simplify it will be greatly appreciated!

QUESTION: How do satisfied clients or clients with complaints help determine your continued use of a particular provider?

ANSWER: Numerous complaints by clients about a particular provider lead to a check by provider relations on that therapist. If I've got a file filled with complaints by clients about a provider, that therapist is taken off the panel. Certainly, though, when clients "rave" about a therapist, there should be referrals that follow. Managed Care companies keep contracts by having satisfied clients.

QUESTION: Should a provider, upon successful termination of a client, encourage her or him to give a quick update to the case manager?

ANSWER: If the patient expresses to you that they are really thankful that they saw you, then you might say, "You know, the group that referred you to me would really like to hear this kind of report from you. Could you put that down on paper and send it to the person managing your case? They'd really appreciate it." Case managers are impressed by this kind of feedback from clients.

And many of the more ethical Managed Care companies survey clients to see how satisfied they are with the care they received from providers. But with the incredible amount of work, some don't do it. So it's best to encourage your patients to update the case managers themselves.

QUESTION: *What factors would cause you to lose confidence in and discontinue using a particular provider? What are some of the "red flags" that cause you concern about a provider's usefulness to you?*

ANSWER: A therapist who "explores" in therapy. For example, "I'm going to do some exploratory work to uncover sexual abuse trauma with this patient." That's a real red flag to us. If a patient comes in with weak ego strength and you tear them apart therapeutically by doing exploratory therapy, what are you really doing? You're tearing the car apart when maybe all it really needs is a tune-up to keep it going. Not to mention that it takes a long period of time to put it back together again. This kind of long-term, opening-up kind of stuff does not resolve the presenting problem, and it keeps most clients in therapy longer than necessary. Long-term therapy may be appropriate. But "opening up the wounds" in a client may not be in that person's best interests.

QUESTION: *How do you feel about providers who utilize outside support groups and other resources, as opposed to those who don't?*

ANSWER: We *do* want and expect outside resources to be an integral part of the treatment plan. Managed Care sees psychotherapy as *part* of the client's life solution, but not the end-all. The more the therapist helps the patient rely on outside supports, the less the patient will rely on the therapist and the sooner they will take charge of their own lives. "Broadening the base of support" makes healing more likely to occur.

QUESTION: Do any providers come to mind who are really outstanding and who have distinguished themselves with excellence in their service to you, or who have done some special things? If there are, can you tell me what specific things they have done.

ANSWER: Those who have done the best job with us are the providers who have a friendly, helpful staff. They do a quality job on the phone and with the paperwork.   And they build a trusting relationship with us — it's almost like seeing your case manager as a client, a business client. Work diligently to include the case manager as part of the treatment team. Communicate, communicate, communicate!

Answering services are less "friendly" than voice mail, actually, because information takes more than one phone call to pass on. If you don't have good office staff, use voice mail and a beeper.

QUESTION: What is your concept of "brief therapy"? And are there any criteria that you like to see in treatment reports to indicate that this provider practices short-term therapy?

ANSWER: In good brief therapy, I like to focus on what's going on *now*. The therapist does not attempt to rebuild the personality in treatment!   There are reasonable goals set that utilize the client's ego strengths in therapy. So instead of seeing a person as "sick," see treatment as "we're getting them well."

I look at it this way: We live in a kind of "entitled age." Our society seems to encourage a feeling of being entitled, or "it's my right to have this or that." The opposite of that is to be responsible. We can communicate the idea to our patients that "I will get better faster as I accept more responsibility for my life."

Homework is vitally important to successful brief therapy. It's very clear that clients are only in session with you once a week or once every two weeks, but they're in life all the time. Homework and other adjuncts to therapy help clients transfer their dependence onto themselves and take responsibility, rather than depending on the therapist for their wellness. "Being healthy" becomes a practice, a way of life, for the client.

And if you do good work, other people will hear about you. What's to keep you from using brief therapy techniques to get patients well so that they can recommend somebody else to you for therapy?

QUESTION: Let's say you have a close friend who is just about to complete her intern hours and become licensed as an MFCC. Her dream is to have her own practice, but she knows that the only way she can succeed is to become a trusted preferred provider with many Managed Care companies. She comes to you for the best "inside" advice she can get. What specific steps and advice would you give her to help her succeed and make her a valued managed care provider?

ANSWER: How well someone operates independently in private practice depends in large measure on how good the supervision has been. But assuming that a therapist has had excellent supervision, including good training in brief therapy and the mechanics of Managed Care, here are a few thoughts:

1. Learn to use treatment plans, outcome objectives and goals, and time-limited therapy in all therapy used, not just in those cases referred by Managed Care. So you are not doing two different kinds of therapy for two different kinds of reimbursement. Become proficient and highly skilled and comfortable doing brief, solution-oriented ther-

apy with all your clients.

2. Don't join too many panels, but serve several panels well with thoroughness and excellence.

3. Locate in a geographic area that's easily identifiable to case managers. You don't want your offices in an obscure, unknown area.

4. Attend workshops and seminars in brief therapy, behavioral therapy, and cognitive therapy, and list this on your vitae and practice profile. Learn the methodology and the language of these therapies.

5. Learn the language of Managed Care and case management.

6. Associate with, link up with, or form your own group of therapists having diverse specializations, and if at all possible, include one or more psychiatrists.

The concept of the anchor group is very important. An anchor group anchors down a particular geographical region. If I make one phone call to one group who has all the therapy services I need, including a psychiatrist, it's a lot simpler for me than making many phone calls.

7. Learn to work effectively with a multidisciplinary approach. This is especially important for someone who is trying to break into Managed Care in a new practice.

8. Develop 2 to 4 specialties that are needed by Managed Care: for example, CD, ACA, sexual abuse, child and adolescent issues, parenting issues. Work all of that into your curriculum vitae or practice profile. Provider relations is interested more in what you do than who you've worked for.

9. Find a way to do outcome research and report the findings to the case manager.

10. Read good articles and books (like this one) on Managed Care to get comfortable being a team player with us. We are working together, serving the needs of the client.

Advice from a Former Manager of a
Corporate EAP and Managed Care Program

Case managers take their lead from those who train them. They deal with providers according to that training. And the services they authorize are determined in large measure by those who supervise their work.

In this section you will have the opportunity to get some concrete answers to questions about how this training and supervisory process works. With this kind of information you should be more effective in dealing with Managed Care as a cooperative "insider", not an outsider struggling to prove yourself.

Let us introduce you to Dorothy. She offers first-hand advice from a background of training and supervising case managers:

For 13 years she was corporate manager for a large aerospace firm's Employee Assistance Program. During the last few years in this position she was responsible for the supervision and training of 28 case managers in both the U.S. and in Canada.

Prior to that she was the director of the Alcoholism Information Center in Los Angeles, sponsored by the National Council on Alcoholism.

Before Managed Care found its way into her company, Dorothy supervised the EAP assessment and referral functions for a company representing some 125,000 employees and 250,000 dependents and retirees. When the company changed to a Managed Care arrangement, she trained and supervised case managers in the "how to's" of cost-effective quality case management, as well as serving as a case rep herself.

During this time she also conducted her own part-time private therapy practice. Dorothy is now in full-time practice, serves as a consultant to many hospital and EAP programs, and is a popular lecturer and seminar speaker. Her comments are practical and to-the-point.

QUESTION: When did you begin to foresee the changes that Managed Care would have on mental health services?

ANSWER: We knew that something had to be done about the increased costs of healthcare in 1989, but we didn't know exactly what this would mean. The calls from clients kept escalating for mental health and chemical dependency services. We started preparing for its impact in 1991 when the handwriting was clearly on the wall.

QUESTION: How did the company you worked for go about bringing in Managed Care controls?

ANSWER: It was the consensus of opinion by going outside our EAP group per se to make the changeover. So the company hired an outside firm to work with EAP in setting up a Managed Care program. It was the EAPs job to be sure that this outside firm was an extension of EAP, to serve as an advocate of the employee. We wanted them to be a client-advocate firm rather than one that would try to simply restrict services. As you know, quite a few of the HMOs and other Managed Care companies make their money by taking so many clients at risk, and then they limit care by trying to make it so difficult for people to get into the system that they don't bother. We wanted to be sure that that didn't happen.

We then had to monitor inside the company how services were being provided, and listening to complaints by employees and providers. This told us that the client-advocate system was working. But to get a proactive organization like that is pretty difficult.

Even with the client advocacy system you still have to show the company that you will still be saving a lot of money, but that you don't save it at the employee's/client's detriment, and you hope that they'll get the right kind of treatment for the kind of problems that they have. That way the company is using the benefit wisely. And, of course, the reason for managing the care is to be sure the benefits are spent wisely.

QUESTION: What changes did you initiate in your EAP program to make the changeover from assessment and referral to a Managed Care system?

ANSWER: Prior to Managed Care our case managers were instructed, and it was clearly stated on the computers, that we are not to diagnose. This was to be left to the providers. When we made the shift to Managed Care, we started gearing up and trained the case managers to diagnose mental disorders. Many of the staff had clinical backgrounds, had a license, but hadn't done a lot of clinical practice. We had to help them understand what kind of treatment would be reasonable for a particular diagnosis.

The way we went about this was to take a consensus of opinion in the office as to what modality or intervention fit best with which diagnoses. We used reference books. We got key providers to come in an give us an in-service on what kinds of treatment or testing was appropriate with what kind of problems. We then assembled these clinicians' opinions, as well as getting instruction on what was effective short-term therapy.

QUESTION: What specific diagnostic categories did you determine to be not certifiable, those that would receive no authorization?

ANSWER: One of the things that we learned, with the kind of benefit package that we had, was that it would be better not to address or certify multiple personality disorders at all. Most of the Axis II personality disorders were similarly not covered. This is the case because we wanted to be able to *treat the current problem, and to get the client functioning again; not to go into any kind of long-term psychotherapy.*

QUESTION: Obviously you had certain providers that you used in your EAP role. How did you help them accept and adjust to the Managed Care, short-term, goal-focused perspective?

ANSWER: We did a 6-month transition period when the changeover was made.   During this time our staff, the providers, and the employees/clients were given the time to get used to the changes.   This was essentially a 6-month grace period wherein we could work with the providers to try to find out how we could provide effective care in a shorter interval.

At the end of this 6-month period we had a pretty good idea of who would be able to do short-term therapy, and who would not.

QUESTION: How did you know that a provider was an effective brief therapist and therefore "Managed Care friendly?"

ANSWER: We knew the particular diagnoses of the clients, and we knew pretty much how long these clients had been in therapy with a given provider. We also knew how cooperative the clinician had been with our case managers. We knew if their treatment plans made sense, whether the provider used homework, and there was a definite treatment plan established for each client. We looked at how the therapist might use contracts with a client: For example, chemically dependent people would contract to attend 3 AA meetings a week, and if they didn't, the provider might call back the case manager to say that the client is not going, and request a postponement of treatment until they do, and so on.   That kind of cooperation is very important.

We also looked at how the therapist brought in to the therapy significant others, treated the entire family, used outside resources, and carefully planned for aftercare.

QUESTION: What are the most common mistakes made by clinicians in their dealings with case managers?

ANSWER: I'm glad you asked, and I just made a mistake myself the other night that I'll share here. Last Friday night I had a client come in who was obviously psychotic. He is functioning, but he hears his dead mother's voice and hallucinates. Mother's Day was coming and I was really worried about him. So I asked him how he felt about hospitalization, to get through this brief period of pain until he began feeling better. He said, "No, I don't want to go."

Well, when I called the case manager at the client's company he got very upset that *I should suggest hospitalization without talking to them first.* And that's one of the things that we clinicians have to learn — that we do not make any independent decisions, and always check it out with the case manager first.

If I had to do it over, I think I would do exactly what I did in terms of talking to the patient. But when I called the case manager I would ask, "How should we go about getting him in-patient help if he needs hospitalization?"

Another mistake many providers make is to send in sloppy paperwork. Make it neat. Go over it 2 or 3 times; make sure you've got all of the sections filled in properly and accurately. In all that you do with Managed Care, have the attitude that *"I want to do all I can to cause these people the least amount of trouble possible,"* because they're really busy and just don't have a lot of time to fix mistakes. If you keep a cooperative, low-profile (not giving them any trouble and receiving no complaints) they will be much more likely to use you.

Also, give case managers good feedback. Call in the diagnosis; let them know if a client is not keeping appointments; when the client is completing treatment; being prompt with the paperwork you turn in. Avoid making mistakes in these areas.

One complaint that some case managers have is difficulty getting in touch with the provider. It is helpful for the provider to have a good secretary. If an answering service is used, be sure to check it often, and get back in touch with the case manager quickly. Don't wait to check messages till the end of the day.

Some of the Managed Care companies now are asking if your billing is computerized. This indicates to them that your practice is efficiently run and able to handle a large volume of work.

QUESTION: What is your advice to a therapist who obviously blows it, puts his or her foot in their mouth, and breaks one of those cardinal Managed Care rules? What's the best way to handle it?

ANSWER: What I did was just say, "Oh, I'm sorry, I was trying to prepare the client and I was so concerned for their well-being; I just didn't realize and I'll definitely call you first next time." It's simply a matter of being cooperative, non-defensive, and avoiding an adversarial attitude. An adversarial or hostile attitude is really death when you are seen as an adversary.

QUESTION: How do case managers react to providers who come across with a hostile or adversarial attitude?

ANSWER: Everybody's afraid of getting sued. So many times if a provider comes across too strong, pushy, or really fights for a specific treatment intervention, the case manager may bow down to that, saying, "OK, we'll let you do whatever you want to do with the client." But if this happens a few times the case manager will probably not use you as a provider any longer. It's unlikely that this provider would get any referrals from that case manager in the future because of this uncooperative attitude.

QUESTION: When should a clinician use voice mail as opposed to calling the case manager personally?

ANSWER: The voice mail is very helpful to case managers. Give succinct information, but you can go into detail if you must. This can save the case manger time.

I think it's good to talk to the case manager personally any time there may be a difference of opinion, or if you are requesting a higher level of care; for instance, if you need to hospitalize somebody, or get a medication evaluation — you need to get back to the case manager personally to be sure there's certification for that.

QUESTION: What typically goes on at staff meetings in a Managed Care organization? Are specific providers discussed in terms of their cooperativeness or lack of cooperativeness?

ANSWER: Oh yes. At weekly meetings those providers who are very cooperative are talked about. They talk about those who use excessive hospitalization, those who hospitalize when it's not necessary, those who over-prescribe drugs, those who use up all the client's sessions and do not leave any sessions for clients who may need them later in the year. And we're really concerned about the excessive use of drugs — we've worked with some psychiatrists who will put the entire family on drugs or in the hospital. These are some definite red flags. When these things come up, one case manager will say, "I've had this problem with this provider; how do you feel about them?"

The provider needs to remember that his or her interaction with one case manager can influence their reputation with many others.

In a good Managed Care company, the staff meetings are essentially a client advocate meeting.

Many times in a meeting things will come up that clinicians request that are really outrageous! One therapist, for example, wanted to hospitalize an infant. Or, hospitalizing a 2-year-old because he says "no." Or, in another case a psychiatrist was treating a married couple; the husband was depressed because his wife didn't want sex — but in his treatment of the wife, he had her so drugged that she didn't know what time of day it was! Some therapists do some truly outrageous things that are hard to believe.

QUESTION: What advice would you have for a provider who has been told, "I'm sorry, our panel is closed and we don't need anybody in your location".

ANSWER: Yes, I know that that is really tough. But one of the things some of the newer providers do is they will ask a Managed Care firm, "Are there any areas or locations where you are not represented by providers?" Then they make it a point to put an office there to help the Managed Care firm. This would then in turn help that provider to be seen favorably by those in the firm who make referrals. This could open the way for you to join the panel, and may help you get referrals to your other office locations, if you have them.

QUESTION: If a newly-licensed therapist came to you and asked how she should go about partnering with the Managed Care firms in her area? What steps would you tell her to consider?

ANSWER: First of all, she should read this book! I think that an individual just starting out should become actively involved with a more experienced group practice. I think they will need the help, encouragement, and the expertise of that group. The supervision and consultation they could receive within the group practice would be invaluable.

Advice from a Hospital-Based
Specialist in Managed Care Contracts

The words "Managed Care authorized hospitalization" fit together about as well as "joyful sorrow" or "make haste slowly" or "fragrant odor." In-patient treatment is the highest level of care, and the costliest, for mental health disorders, and case managers are reluctant to certify it.

But hospitalization is not optional for some patients. Those who are of high suicidal risk, those who are a danger to others in the community, or those who are severely impaired and unable to care for themselves — for these patients in-patient care is not optional.

If you have such a patient, how should you go about persuading case managers to authorize hospitalization to provide the help the patient needs most? Then, how can you do so without harming your own reputation with the Managed Care organizations?

To give you practical answers to these questions, we interviewed Dierdre. Her diverse background gives her a rich understanding of Managed Care. Prior to her present hospital position, Dierdre worked in an HMO setting, and for a third-party administration of self-funded employee benefit plans; a company that put together and managed self-funded insurance programs. In this role she helped oversee the expenditure of trust fund accounts for large companies, buying cost-effective professional services for member employees.

Currently Dierdre handles all hospital liaison activities between her hospital, a 146-bed, free-standing psychiatric hospital in southern California, and PPOs, HMOs, and the 28 Managed Care panels she's helped develop. Dierdre also works closely with medical, psychiatric, nursing and other staff helping them understand how to work effectively with Managed Care concepts and expectations.

Her answers to the following questions provide the same kind of help she offers to her own hospital staff.

QUESTION: We'd like to pose a very real example to begin: A therapist has a patient whom they believe is in need of in-patient care. This therapist understands all too well that the Managed Care firm representing this patient does not look too kindly on hospitalization. How would you coach this therapist to approach the case manager so that the therapist can get the patient the help that they need?

ANSWER: The first thing that I would suggest is for the provider to have already talked at length with the Managed Care organization on a number of different issues. You first of all want to know what is *the average length of stay,* or what is *the expectation of the length of stay* for that particular Managed Care firm. And that way, going in, the provider would know what the expectation is; rather than having a patient in the hospital, treating the patient, and then in retrospect, getting the unpleasant feedback that you exceeded the average, expected length of stay.

Most Managed Care organizations do not have their average length of stay broken out on a diagnosis-specific basis (at least not yet). At this time, most Managed Care firms express their statistics in 2 ways: (1) They express that they have a certain number of admissions per 1,000 members. This is called *the number of admissions per thousand.* We are talking here about in-patient admissions.

QUESTION: Aren't the case managers trained to keep the number of in-patient admissions and the length of stay to a bare minimum to make care cost-effective?

ANSWER: Absolutely. The Managed Care companies and the third party insurance companies closely monitor how well the doctor and the admitting psychologist, as well as the case managers, are doing by the number of admissions per thousand. And that's just admissions. They also monitor the number of days per thousand.

And when you are asking these kind of questions of a Managed Care firm, you need to identify whether the statistics being given are monthly or annual averages. This information is easily obtainable from the provider relations department of most Managed Care companies.

QUESTION: How important do you think outcome research is for a provider? Can it enhance his or her relationship with Managed Care companies?

ANSWER: You will see that more and more Managed Care organizations are asking providers for outcome research. I would strongly suggest that any clinician, if they have the ability, should start collecting and accumulating data. The Managed Care firms will come to the institution, the facility or the private practitioner and will want to be able to compare us one against another. Provider competition for the healthcare dollar is becoming more a reality now than ever.

QUESTION: What do you foresee as the direction of healthcare in the United States in the near future?

ANSWER: One thing is for sure: It will not be a free-choice-of-provider system as we have always known it. Those days are over. I believe that healthcare will take one of two forms. It will either be a government networked, contracted, and developed program, or it will be a government sub-contract to private enterprise — one or the other.

QUESTION: What other advice would you have for providers to help them relate well with case managers, so that they can successfully get their patients the in-patient help they need?

ANSWER: One of the most important things they should do is this: When they are calling for a pre-authorization, they should give the case manager very precise descriptions of the patient's problems. They should document tangible characteristics. They should demonstrate that out-patient care has already been pursued to its fullest as an option. They should then show why outpatient treatment can no longer be used effectively to help the patient. They should demonstrate that medication trials have been tried on an outpatient basis. And they must answer the question: *"Why is the admission necessary now?"*

QUESTION: What is the best way to document the answer to the question, "Why is the admission necessary now?"

ANSWER: At our hospital we circulate to our staff what we call "Clinical Justification for Admission". Whenever a 5150 or an emergency hold is able to be written on a patient, in which the patient is determined to be of danger to themselves, of danger to others, or gravely disabled — this is as strong and concrete a justification as you can possibly get, and almost always merits certification by case managers. This also would include those who are of danger to property — such as those who light fires.

Other justifications would include seriously disordered behavior accompanied by impaired reality testing. Those who require a planned medical evaluation, special drug therapy, special intense treatment requiring continued hospitalization, or need for skilled, intensive observation after failure of outpatient treatment.

As I just mentioned, stabilization of drug treatment is an important justification for hospitalization. On many psychotrophic drugs it commonly takes from 7 to 14 days for a patient to become stabilized on medications. The therapist must be able to show that this kind of stabilization cannot be achieved outside the hospital. It may be that with a given patient when the patient is at home and unsupervised, they become severely suicidal or homicidal. The psychosocial considerations must be documented here. Most Managed Care organizations consider this a reasonable justification to certify hospitalization.

QUESTION: In your treatment planning sessions in the hospital, what advice is most commonly given to the practitioners, nurses and other staff with respect to effectively working with Managed Care?

ANSWER: Over and over in our staff treatment planning sessions I hear certain consistent themes: Be more concrete ... Give it a very specific period of time ... Set specific goals ... Make sure that everything that is put in that chart is precise and observable ... Use the patient's own words whenever possible ... Don't interject your own opinion whenever possible ... Use measurable and behavioral outcomes to document patient conditions ... Don't state anything in a way that would suggest that the same outcome could be achieved on an outpatient basis, because that would definitely create a chink in the armor of your argument, and increase the probability that an in-patient stay would be denied. Or I should say "non-authorization" as opposed to "denying in-patient care" — this is an important legal distinction that the Managed Care organizations are very sensitive to.

It's also important for a provider to know as much as possible about a particular Managed Care firm's admission patterns: (1) their admissions per thousand, and (2) their days per thousand. Then when it comes time to make as strong a case as possible, they can do their very best to use short-term methods to get the patient discharged within that period of time. It is very easy for a Managed Care organization to have 1 or 2 admissions on an in-patient basis from a provider, and then say, "Well, I don't like their length of stay, and therefore I'm not going to refer to this individual in the future." The pattern of admissions per thousand or days per thousand varies between the different Managed Care companies as to how many admissions are acceptable, as well as how many days are acceptable.

QUESTION: Are there any specific considerations a provider should observe when presenting the initial treatment plan to the case manager in order to increase the likelihood of hospitalization being authorized?

ANSWER: The treatment plan may carry more weight if a full treatment plan is presented right from the beginning. The provider wants to show the case manager that he or she is not only depending on in-patient care to reduce symptoms, but is also planning to help the client or patient get help in other ways. Any opportunity that the therapist can take to demonstrate that all the options have been considered, that an established and balanced treatment plan is in place with varying levels of care, this can create more credibility with the case manager. It's also important to have a clear plan for how the patient will be helped after discharge to maintain gains obtained while in the hospital. Especially important in this regard is the use of outside support groups and other community and family resources.

The therapist might also want to show a progression from an intensive in-patient care, to a partial hospitalization, and then to outpatient care, followed by some support group involvement. I have seen, for example, a couple of patients come in with a 7-day in-patient authorization, then another 7-14 days partial hospitalization in which the patient arrives at the hospital at 8:30 in the morning and goes home at 6 o'clock. Managed Care organizations like day treatment or partial hospitalization because it is approximately 50% less expensive as full in-patient care. Then, following partial hospitalization there might be once-a-week outpatient treatment, faded to once every 2-weeks, then to once a month, and so on.

QUESTION: What are the trends in Managed Care when it comes to psychiatric hospitalization?

ANSWER: What seems to be happening now is that more Managed Care companies (in order for a facility to be a member of their network) are requiring that the facility must accept an all-inclusive rate. This means that any and all services rendered to the patient while in the hospital must be included in the per diem (or the rate per day). This would include the fees for the attending physician or therapist, all group sessions, all recreational and occupational therapy sessions, all personal items, any and everything that would be billable while the patient is in the hospital. In the past it included only room and board. Now they want everything covered under the same flat fee.

This means that the hospitals have to begin negotiating with the providers. This is called incentivization. It also means that the hospital is now placed in the role as the gate keeper, as well as those manning the gates at the Managed Care company. This is the current trend in Managed Care, which is about as popular as toothaches and taxes.

Many of the Managed Care organizations are taking these kinds of measures, getting very tough and aggressive. This will undoubtedly be the wave of the future, in which both the hospital and the providers will have to absorb the cuts. What I see in all this is a delegation of the review authority and responsibility at the lowest possible level, at the closest level to patient care.

QUESTION: Can hospital staff membership be advantageous for a provider by helping him or her get accepted on various Managed Care panels?

ANSWER: Yes it can. I am often asked for our staff roster by Managed Care provider relations directors. They are comparing providers they contract with to those whom we have already granted privileges. They do this to see if they already use a therapist who already has admitting privileges. This can save time for case managers when it comes to referring to providers so that there is no need for juggling for temporary privileges and such tangles. From their point of view, it's a matter of efficiency. They want to be proactive rather than reactive.

With those therapists who become staff members, we want to add value to the relationship with them. Most hospitals these days feel this way. One of the things we do in this regard is to provide a list of contracts with the 28 Managed Care organizations we work with, along with the key contact persons names. We publish this for our staff members a couple of times a year. We suggest that these providers direct their requests for admission to the panels to these individuals, suggesting that they use the name of our hospital as part of their introduction.

We suggest, in addition, that they play up the geographical location of their practice, any bilingual services in their practice, areas of specialization that they provide — and anything that might set them apart. We suggest that when mentioning their membership on our staff that they point out that we are Managed Care savvy and specialize in short-term care. We want them to know that as a facility, we join in partnership with them, and we are not trying to be adversaries. We know that the minute we become adversarial, we've alienated them for good. Once you alienate them, it takes from 12, 18 or 24 months to get back around to a good, working relationship.

Another thing we do to get on closed panels is this. We try to find out which psychologists and psychiatrists on our staff are already providers with the Managed Care firm we have not as yet been able to join. I then ask that provider to write a letter to the Managed Care provider relations director, requesting that our facility be added. I submit their letter with a letter from us, saying that "we will bend over backwards to meet your every need!" Actually, this technique works very well. We opened the door of one of the largest Managed Care firms in California using this method.

Perseverance also pays off — refusing to take "no" for an answer. They also want to hear that you will *give them lower costs where you as the provider assumes more risk.*

QUESTION: *Many therapists struggle with accepting the realities of Managed Care, resenting the controls and the limitations over their work, as well as the reduced fees. What advice would you have for those clinicians in the midst of this struggle?*

ANSWER: We fully understand this struggle. We've gone through it ourselves, and continue to do so. But I would recommend that we accept that Managed Care means *change.* It means that each provider, each hospital, must change the fundamental way that we do business.

We must recognize that *our long-term survival as a practitioner is based on our ability to adapt.* I would recommend that you jump in with both feet. Get as much continuing education as possible — seminars in Managed Care, brief therapy, cognitive therapy, and other short-term modalities. We need to continue to demonstrate to the Managed Care organizations that we as providers or facilities are open and accepting of the changes in healthcare.

One thing your readers might want to do is to sponsor their own workshops or seminars in brief therapy, behavior therapy, cognitive therapy, or Managed Care cooperation and then invite case managers of the various firms to attend. *This would show them what you're doing, and that we are doing it in response to their needs.*

We've gone out and asked each Managed Care company specifically, "What do you need from us?" "What's going to make our relationship with you more beneficial, and therefore, your referrals to us more plentiful?" As a result, we've gathered a lot of information about what they want, and what they don't want.

One of the things most of them have told us is that they don't want us to, say, take somebody into the hospital for a 3-day detox and expose them to some of the really in-depth therapy groups. If the patient is going outpatient in 3 days, opening deep wounds will not give them time to patch it all up and cope on the outside. They are in the hospital simply to medically stabilize. Case managers don't want to have to authorize 60 to 90 days of therapy putting the patient back together and all the pieces back into place. No matter how needful or important the deeper forms of therapy would be for the patient in the hospital on a short stay, we no longer can afford to do that. We must, instead, continue to try to develop short-term programs. We must steer away from root-causes and aim at symptom reduction and symptom management.

QUESTION: What would you say to a provider who has contracts with HMOs or Managed Care organizations but receives no referrals?

ANSWER: We have found that it is important to ask each firm, "Who has the decision-making responsibility for making referrals?" Many of the companies have delegated the authority for referrals to other organizations. The provider should call whichever company they want new patients from and ask, "I am in this geographical region; who has referral authority or responsibility?"

They may say that is the patient themselves if it's a PPO arrangement. Or they may say the case manager right there at their organization or another Managed Care group. Or they may say it's a medical group that they have capitated to handle all members. This will tell you where to go to get the referrals flowing. Many providers have contracts but receive no referrals because they have never taken the time to cultivate a relationship with those who have the authority to refer, making them aware of who you are, where you are, what your specialties are, and why they should send you new referrals, versus some other provider down the street.

APPENDIX B

Help for Office Managers, Secretaries, & Other Support Staff

How To Make Your Work with Managed Care Easier & More Effective

---

Personal Notes

Advice from an Office Manager Who Has Managed to Manage the *Transition to Managed Care*

Some wise soul has said, "While clearly we are not able to direct the wind, we can, however, adjust our sails." And Teddy Roosevelt added, "Whenever you are asked if you can do a job, tell 'em, 'Certainly I can!' Then get busy and find out how to do it." If a practice or facility is to survive the "storms" and the many changes thrust upon us by Managed Care, both of these must happen.

When the Managed Care "storm" appeared menacingly on the horizon several years ago, we resisted the changes in wind direction, and dug in our heels — refusing to "learn how to do it." But as the waves got higher, and our "practice boat" began filling with water, we made a crucial decision: "Embrace Managed Care or perish."

One of the key people who helped us "adjust our sails" and "learn how to do it" is Marion Nixon, office manager for Browning Therapy Group, Inc. Marion has been with us before, during, and after the transition to Managed Care. As we continued seeing patients, supervising staff, and conducting other practice marketing, Marion stood courageously at the administrative helm, interfacing with insurance claims departments, EAP reps, provider relations personnel, and case managers. Step by step she helped instruct our staff in how to navigate the complex, tricky waters of Managed Healthcare.

Without Marion Nixon, and her able deckhand-assistants, Peggy Oquist, Stephanie Smith, Linda Wong, and Margie Gahan, our practice would certainly be in deep trouble — and this book would very likely never have been written.

We asked Marion to share her ideas, tips and practical suggestions with you in this section. Your office manager, secretary, receptionist, and other support staff should find her advice tremendously helpful.

QUESTION: *How do you answer the telephone at your therapy office?*

ANSWER: We answer with, "Good Morning" or "Good Afternoon", the name of our practice, "Browning Therapy Group", "This is _____ (our first name)", and "May I help you?"

QUESTION: *Do you use the same tone and manner we usually associate with business offices?*

ANSWER: Good question! We want to conduct the "business" part of the day in a competitive, effective business-like manner. This is true particularly with regard to record-keeping, tracking information on referrals, billing, etc. However, while accomplishing those tasks we also want each patient to hear genuine concern and compassion in our voice that lets potential new patients and ongoing patients know that they are an individual who is *special.*

We want them to hear comfort in the tone of our voice and reassurance that they will not have to face whatever is going on in their life at this time all by themselves. Patients who are currently seeing our therapists and many of those who have completed their counseling have called to let us know they felt cared for and that they value the help the therapist gave them. This gives us ever increasing confidence in our therapists. This feedback is always appreciated and is so gratifying.

QUESTION: *How do you obtain information from the new patient for your records during the initial telephone contact?*

ANSWER: Our procedure is to take information using the *New Patient Information Form* that we've designed for this purpose. Often the caller may seem to hesitate or may seem frightened. We take our time, often letting our new patient give us information in an informal, conversational manner which we organize appropriately as he or she speaks.

QUESTION: *What information do you ask the new patient to give you?*

ANSWER: Some of the important items on our *New Patient Information Form* include these: Name, address, day and evening phones, SS#, name of person referring them, insurance and Managed Care information, case manager's name and phone number, number of sessions authorized (if they know), days and times they would like to come in, and a brief description of their problem or what brings them to therapy.

Some patients give so much detail about what is troubling them that you have to encourage them to be brief. Others sometimes feel hesitant or uncomfortable giving us details about their problems. When this happens, it is best to accept this graciously, simply asking, "That's fine, I just need to know if therapy will be for you alone, for you and your spouse, or for your family?" This will help the clinical director know which therapist is best equipped to help him or her.

QUESTION: *Is the referral source important to you?*

ANSWER: The person referring them to us is particularly important and we track this very carefully. We know how busy the case managers are, however, we try to thank them personally as often as possible. We do this whenever they call us, and we also leave voice mail "Thank You" messages whenever they refer us someone, giving them details that the patient has called and is scheduled to see a specific therapist on a specific day.

We also acknowledge our appreciation for referrals from M.D.s, other professionals, current and former patients, pastors, and advertisements. It is a good idea to keep a *New Patient Tracking Sheet* close at hand to enter each new referral and the referral source at the time of each call. This is then used to send out "Thank You" letters or calls.

QUESTION: *Do you find that Managed Care is a "fact of life" with most new patients who have insurance?*

ANSWER: The greatest majority of our callers are part of Managed Care.

QUESTION: *When they do have Managed Care coverage, how do you reassure an apprehensive new patient who asks, "Does the case manager need to know everything about my situation? How will this affect my employment? Is the information kept confidential?" How do you handle this flurry of questions?*

ANSWER: We always admire a new patient for having the courage to make that first call to our office. After asking a few necessary questions, including insurance coverage, we guide the new patient back to the case manager for explanations about the optimum insurance benefits and explain that this is the procedure each new patient must follow. This is the normal procedure we use when assigning patients to our therapists. We have the telephone numbers of many of the insurance companies and give them to the caller. Many times we can direct them to a case manager, however, if we don't have a particular name, we ask them to call the Managed Care office.

The patient is reassured when we explain that they need to tell the case manager only enough to let him or her know of the need for therapy, not the details of their situation which they will share in depth with their therapist. We try to encourage them by letting them know that the case managers are careful to keep all of the patient's information strictly confidential. We also remind them that the case manager is there to help them get the help they need from providers who are carefully screened, to be able to meet their needs. In other words, we want to do all we can to help create a positive and accepting attitude in the patient before he or she calls the case manager. This makes the whole process more healing for the patient, and prepares them for their relationship with the case manager and with their therapist, once they receive authorization.

QUESTION: *How do you handle the new patient who refuses to go through the "system"?*

ANSWER: We give them the option of coming to our group as a private patient, paying the full fee at the time of each session, if they do not wish to go through the Managed Care process. When we explain that our usual fee is $110 per hour, and their Managed Care co-payment is $8, for example, most patients quickly appreciate the difference between the Managed Care coverage and the out-of-pocket costs. Some new patients, in fact, discover that they have no co-payment at all once they receive certification or authorization from Managed Care. We want to convey the confidence we have in Managed Care to the patient in order to help them avoid adding financial burdens to their other problems.

In some cases patients are fearful of having their mental health needs treated under their insurance plan and must pay the entire fee out-of-pocket. With the approval of the clinical director, we may offer these patients a discount from our usual fee, from $110 to say $85 or $65 per hour. This helps make services more affordable for such patients who cannot take advantage of their Managed Care benefits. In some cases we have seen the patient for "no charge" after his or her Managed Care benefits have run out. In our practice we offer this service to some patients if they will commit to volunteer their services to the needy at a local convalescent home of their choice. We believe that this plan helps the patient receive the continued help they need, and at the same time encourages them to give of themselves to those less fortunate. It's a wonderful plan!

QUESTION: *How do you work with the patient when they come in to the office to help them handle Managed Care procedures?*

ANSWER: Some Managed Care companies require that the patient sign various forms at the beginning of treatment. We give each patient these forms to fill out and keep copies in their files, in addition to mailing the original back to the Managed Care company. We also have the patient sign release of information forms, so that we can get authorization to talk with the case manager and others who may need to be involved in the patient's treatment. We use a release form that allows us to list several authorized names on one sheet; this saves time and paper.

In some cases we make a photocopy of the patient's insurance I.D. card; with others this is not necessary. We may also get insurance forms from those who have them. Be sure all of the forms are signed.

In the office, or over the telephone, we try to help remind the patient about their current status in terms of how many sessions they may have remaining. Our sessions/end-date tracking system helps with this. We also remind them when they call in or come in about any co-payments due or overdue.

When a patient nears the end of their treatment, it's a good idea to encourage them to call their case manager and let him or her know how they're doing. For example, you might say, "I'm really pleased that your therapy with Dr. B. has gone so well. I'm sure your case manager, Lisa Finestein, would appreciate knowing you're doing so well — you know, she usually hears a lot of 'bad news', and some good news like yours would really make her day ... Why not call and give her an update now that your therapy is completed?" This would probably make Lisa Finestein's day, and would also do good things to help gain more referrals for your therapists!

QUESTION: When a new patient calls and is "overwhelmed" with their situation or problems, how do you encourage him or her to call to verify their insurance coverage?

ANSWER: Each person who calls has the best opportunity to find out accurate information on insurance coverage because he or she has all the pertinent information, i.e., Social Security number, employer information, employee I.D. number, claim numbers, etc. We let them know that the call to their insurance carrier is in their own best interest. In addition, we point out that in many cases, the insurance company will not give us benefit information, and will discuss this only with the person insured.

If the patient feels particularly upset, we might encourage him or her to call their insurance company later; at a time when they are feeling better. We also ask them to write down certain things to ask their claims representative, giving them a list of the things to ask, and instruct them what not to say, in some cases.

For example, some patients need to come in for marital counseling. Most Managed Care and insurance companies will not authorize this kind of treatment. So we encourage them to tell their case manager about their marital problems, but to describe their specific complaints or symptoms; like depression, panic attacks, anxiety or stress, feelings of hopelessness, suicidal feelings, and so forth. We certainly don't want our new patients turned down when they call the case managers. This would only create a new problem for them.

It's very important with the overwhelmed person to give them plenty of structured information and get them to write it down, and then read it back to you. This helps make them feel more in control of their own life. Also, if you use initials and abbreviations in your office, be sure to explain to the patient what they mean; for example, MFCC, LCSW, Psy.D., Ph.D., M.A., etc.

QUESTION: What difference has Managed Care made in day-to-day office work in your practice?

ANSWER: We are handling a greater volume of paperwork than ever before. Adjusting to the increase in paperwork has been a concern. However, each piece of paper in some way facilitates the patient's care, and helps us build a positive reputation in order to serve other new patients in the future. Keeping that in mind makes the adjustment easier for us. We have carefully avoided paperwork for paperwork's sake; trying to run the office with the utmost efficiency.

QUESTION: In what way does increased paperwork help the patient?

ANSWER: Tracking the number of sessions, session dates, number of certified sessions remaining, expiration date of cert, etc. — all of this helps the patient receive the sessions the case manager has certified. We also need to know the name of the person who has the insurance coverage and his or her Social Security number. Is this person a parent, spouse, a guardian? We need this information.   If the patient is a union member, we need to know the employee or badge number. The paperwork is the documentation that keeps services active and authorized. Without it services may be disallowed or unauthorized, and no payment received for services rendered.

QUESTION: Is the paperwork standard for all Managed Care organizations?

ANSWER: No!   That's what keeps it "exciting" and "challenging." Each of the Managed Care companies has its own unique requirements. We would like to think that by supplying accurate information to the employee assistance program representative or case manager, we alleviate stress for the patient. Our goal is to help the patient feel confident that our office is taking care of the paperwork as an extension of the care and courtesy they receive from our therapists.

QUESTION: *Does your office really need to keep track of all that detail? Isn't that all in the computer at the Managed Care office?*

ANSWER: Their computers are a great help. However, many times we have found that the Managed Care office needs our information as backup. It is also possible that the information is not in the computer as yet and we can provide it quickly. We've also called case managers and found their computers to be "down." They really appreciate it when ours isn't, and we can briefly summarize all the information they need on a patient and his or her care.

QUESTION: *How or where do you keep all of this information so it is easily at hand to give to case managers?*

ANSWER: Our clinical director has a keen ability to create forms which concisely organize information. Our patients are given the opportunity to track their own sessions on a special form developed and provided by our office. We keep a duplicate of these forms in our files. When our patients track each session, they know what the co-payment is without calling us to find out.

We also keep a rolodex card on each Managed Care patient. This card contains not only name, address, phone numbers, but also Social Security number, date of first session, number of sessions authorized, end date, DSM diagnosis, and information we need for contacting the case manager. This method makes it possible to pull up information quickly when a case manager calls, or when calling them. The same data could also be kept in your computer, if each secretary has access to it.

QUESTION: *How often do the Managed Care case managers call your office?*

ANSWER: We receive calls daily. Our contact with these case managers is *another extension of patient care.* The telephone is usually the only way we "meet" the case managers. We want to cooperate. We believe they form their opinion of our services and therapy group partially on the basis of how the office staff handles their calls. *The most effective care for each patient is assured when the therapists, the therapists' office staff, and the case manager all work cooperatively together as a team.*

QUESTION: How does your office support your therapists in keeping current with Initial Treatment Summaries, Ongoing Treatment Reports (and their counterparts), certification dates, number of sessions used, expiration dates and other details?

ANSWER: Over the past few years our therapists have experienced a tremendous increase in time spent on paperwork to insure the best possible insurance benefits for our patients. Our Office Assistant, Peg Oquist, devotes a great number of hours each week preparing the OTRs and other forms for each therapist.

We have found that a custom-made rubber stamp simplifies this task. It includes the therapist's name, license number, tax I.D. number, our practice name, address, phone number, fax number, etc. This stamp also speeds up the paperwork process, resulting in faster payment.

One method that helps save the clinician time and effort is to fill out as much information as you can on documentation forms prior to giving them to the therapist to complete. You might fill out all identifying patient information, the DSM diagnoses (if found on previous forms), indication of (a) number of sessions certed, (b) number of sessions used to date, (c) whether the cert is for individual, conjoint, family or group therapy, and (d) the end or expiration date, if any. Provider information can also be filled out or rubber stamped. Staff therapists will applaud you for helping with these details!

Ongoing Treatment Report Forms are given to the individual therapists three weeks prior to the date the case manager needs them. This gives the therapist one week to complete the forms, so that we can send documentation in to the case managers *two weeks before the cert expiration date as requested.* Using this procedure assures that our therapists will not earn the reputation of being late with paperwork and are considered to be valuable providers to the case managers. On some occasions we will fax in treatment reports and updates, as well as mailing them in, if the case manager is in a hurry.

It's also a good idea to give Managed Care forms to the therapists in colored folders; red, green, etc. — clearly labeled, "Important Forms for Managed Care Patients" along with the therapist's name. Colored folders helps catch the therapist's eye to distinguish it from other folders or items on his or her desk. It also signals the importance of giving items inside high priority.

We have received many compliments from Managed Care representatives on the efficiency of our documenta- tion. We strongly recommend that you consider using this 3-week-early system in your office.

QUESTION: Do most of the Managed Care companies require the same amount of paperwork?

ANSWER: This is one of our greatest challenges. In some organizations the case manager wants hard copy. If we are working on a limited time basis, we will fax the information and then mail the originals. Some companies request that the therapists use their voice mail almost exclusively after the first telephone contact. Other organizations we deal with have required us to send in paperwork at every stage of the treatment process, and then later, changed their policy, eliminating most of the paperwork in favor of voice mail updates.

You will find that because of the constant changes in Managed Care, you will need to stay very flexible in giving them what they want. Our clinical director has asked us to keep index cards and files on each Managed Care company, and on each case manager, indicating the specific needs and requirements of each. These are updated when they change their requirements.

Our goal is to supply all the information each case manager wants and needs, in the form they want it, when they want it, and not too little, and certainly not too much in terms of quantity of information.

QUESTION: How do you handle telephone calls from case managers for the therapists?

ANSWER: Telephone calls from case managers are most important. Most communications between Managed Care and your office will be handled by phone. Calls should be handled with great care. Therapists should be encouraged to get back to case managers the same day the call comes in. Because most of our therapists see patients back-to-back and carry a heavy caseload, it is not always possible for the therapists to return calls the same day — especially if the case manager calls in the mid-afternoon. In cases like these, we will call the case manager's voice mail (which should be listed on her or his rolodex card) and let them know that the therapist appreciates their call, and a specific time they can expect a return call from the therapist. This let's the case manager know that his or her call has not been ignored and is being handled responsibly. Handling calls this way helps maintain a reputation for excellence for the practice as a whole, and for the particular therapist involved.

Because the therapists are so busy, it is a good policy to remind them at the appropriate time about returning the case manager's calls. This can be done by intercom, notes in their mail box, or by jotting down a reminder message in their appointment book (or using a "post-it" note). They will appreciate the reminder.

If a call comes in for a therapist who is not in the office, or does not come in when the call is to be returned, you can take the initiative to call the case manager's voice mail and say something like this: "Hello, this is Marion; I'm Dr. Browning's secretary. He's out of the office at present and unable to return your call as he had hoped. Please call me at (310) 596-2142 if there is any information I can provide. He should be in the office by 2 p.m. and plans to call you then. Again, our number is (310) 596-2142. Thank you, and have an especially good day! Good-by." Your tone should be friendly, professional, and courteous. The important point is to return calls promptly, even if the therapist is unable to do so personally.

QUESTION: What is the best way to handle complaints from patients, the patient's family, or from case managers?

ANSWER: Never allow yourself to get defensive or angry when complaints come in. Keep in mind that the people we are dealing with are patients because they are suffering. Many of the people who serve them, like case managers, are over-worked and have high-stress jobs. Try to be patient and understanding.

If someone calls with a complaint, *encourage them to tell you about it. Thank them for bringing this to your attention. Be interested in all they have to say. Tell them you are writing down all their comments because you know your clinical director will want to know how they feel and what has happened. After they tell you their story, ask them if you can repeat back to them what you have heard, to see if you are accurately understanding how they feel. Thank them for taking the time to share their thoughts and feelings with you, and reassure them that you will be sure to let the clinical director or therapist know all that they have said. End the call by telling them who will get back to them and what actions they should anticipate. This will* really help relieve their frustration or anger. It will also pave the way for your clinical director or supervisor when he or she follows up on the complaint. Then be very sure to give the person in charge at your office a written report of the complaint, as well as a verbal account of it.

Like a squeaky hinge, complaints should be seen as opportunities for course-corrections, and signal ways we can improve the way we provide service to others.

When you receive complaints (or any information for that matter) from the family of patients, you must remember one key word: *CONFIDENTIALITY!* By law and by ethical practice we are forbidden from even acknowledging that a person is a patient at our office, even if the person calling is a family member. So before even discussing a patient with anyone, be sure to (a) clear it with your clinical director or supervisor, and (b) check to see if you have a release of information on file that permits you to discuss anything regarding the patient with this specific individual. You should also have on file a release of confidential information in order to talk to case managers regarding the patient. Lawsuits are terrible things. Our job is also to protect our boss, and the entire practice reputation, from any and all lawsuits due to violation of patients' confidentiality.

QUESTION: *Do you have any advice on ways to conduct staff meetings to help therapists and support staff stay current with Managed Care procedures and changes, and to become more effective?*

ANSWER: It is important to start staff meetings on time. It's equally important to keep the information brought to the meeting by the office staff succinct. We have a staff of six in our office. We want each member of the support staff to have the opportunity to clarify any issues or concerns with each therapist. A brief "pre-meeting" helps clarify areas of concern and insures that each question is asked only once, since many areas of our office support work tend to overlap. This "pre-meeting" should take 30-minutes or less. It is helpful to organize issues so that each office staff member has something to bring to the Staff Meeting. Participation creates good communication between all staff.

QUESTION: Do you enjoy working with case managers?

ANSWER: I quickly respond with an unqualified "Yes!" They call when they need information on one of our patients. Our patients are needy, hurting, sometimes very desperate people who need all the loving care we can provide. We are happy to cooperate with case managers who are there to serve the patients. Many of our patients tell us how much they feel cared about by their case managers, as well as by us and our therapists. It is a privilege being part of a team that makes such differences in the lives of so many people.

QUESTION: How would you describe the transition and all the changes we are experiencing now in healthcare as it affects the everyday business and administration of a private practice or clinic?

ANSWER: The changes we encounter continue to confront us with the opportunity to grow and stay on our toes. We find it a real challenge to maintain all of the paperwork for our patients and for the Managed Care companies, while at the same time concentrating on making each patient feel individually cared for.

Managed Care? *It's the future* — and we're glad to be part of it!

Advice from an Accountant
Who Has Figured Out How To
"Manage the Numbers of Managed Care"

To most clinicians new to the Land of Managed Care, the greater emphasis (if not obsession) seems to be, "How do I get on all those panels that they tell me are 'closed'?" Once they manage to get their names on those panels and provider networks, their next less-than-magnificent-obsession seems to be, "Now that I'm on these provider lists, how can I increase utilization and get them to refer clients to me?" Once they manage to do this, happily, they are faced with an unexpected challenge, "Now that I'm on those lists, and now that I have the 'blessing' of all these case managers, and now that I have all these new clients — How in the world do I handle the bewildering accounting, tracking, and pressure-deadlines?"

The questions posed by these clinicians are the very same ones we asked ourselves as we became part of the Managed Care "team." We understood that this new form of external review meant a reduction in the overall length of sessions, and a corresponding reduction in level of fees for service. But what we didn't anticipate were the tremendous complexities of the Managed Care numbers game.

As we noted throughout this text, most of the Managed Care companies have quite different demands and expectations. Some certify a given number of sessions at a given rate of payment. Others add to this a specific deadline at which point all services, whether used or not, are no longer valid. Some have no patient co-payment. Others have on-going patient co-payments. And still others have a formula for increasing patient co-payments over time based on the number of sessions utilized.

If all this sounds confusing, that's because it is — at least to us "clinical types" who are not exactly numbers-friendly. To help you make some sense of the Managed Care numbers game, we asked Linda Wong, C.P.A. to share her skillful expertise with you.

Linda Wong is staff accountant and Patient Accounts Manager at Browning Therapy Group, Inc. She was also with us prior to the "giants entering the land" and as she puts it, "lived through the transition to Managed Care!" She has been experimenting with different methods, procedures, forms and strategies for the past 3 years now, attempting to fit the multi-faceted demands of Managed Care into some workable system.

Linda Wong helped us, and continues to help us, navigate our way successfully through the ever-changing seas of Managed Care. She discusses her methods here, in the hope that they may help you navigate your own way more smoothly and painlessly.

QUESTION: What kind of system did you use or develop to get through all the new tracking and record keeping requirements of Managed Care?

ANSWER: It was definitely a challenge to come up with a system that would let us know when a patient's authorization was nearing completion and to get that information to the therapist in a timely manner so they would have enough time to prepare for discharge, or to request additional treatment, if necessary.

Previously, the only concern we had was to make sure a patient had not exceeded his/her annual dollar limit under their insurance plan. With Managed Care we are faced with 3 important new guidelines: (1) the expiration dates, or (2) the total number of sessions authorized for the period, or (3) the maximum allowable number of sessions per calendar year. We needed something that could handle all 3 new parameters, and handle them efficiently.

Fortunately, our computer billing system (MediMac) has a feature called *Treatment Plans*. It let us enter the authorization data in the patient ledger: beginning and expiration date, number of sessions authorized by procedure code, and the therapist's initials. Then, whenever we had to enter a patient charge, we could open up the treatment plan data and reduce the number of sessions authorized by one.

This updated information then prints out on a Treatment Plan Report to show how many remaining sessions are left for each patient. Each week we review this report and if the report shows that a patient is down to 2 or fewer sessions, we give the therapist a special notice to advise them of the patient's status. This early warning notice will give the therapist time to complete a treatment report to request additional sessions if required. Most Managed Care organizations want this report at least 2 weeks prior to the expiration date.

One caution, however: This treatment plan procedure does have to be handled with care. Since we have to manually reduce the session count by 1 each time, we do cross check the sessions remaining for accuracy when 2 or less sessions are remaining. We make sure that *the number of sessions used plus the number remaining equal the total authorized.*

We found that we had to supplement our computerized treatment plan report with 2 other documents in order to meet all 3 of the above parameters.

First, we utilized a spreadsheet program to prepare a *Patient Authorization Listing.* This report lists all the patient authorizations by therapist along with data for beginning and ending dates, number of sessions authorized, case manager, social security number of the insured, and the DSM diagnosis code.   This report was very useful in showing upcoming expiration dates when a sort routine was used for the expiration date field. Then the patients who were approaching their expiration dates within the next 3 weeks were selected to have the data exported to a therapist notice. To this therapist notice, we also add information about the patient's last date of service and the number of the authorized sessions used. This notice again helps the therapist to prepare treatment reports in sufficient time to meet Managed Care requirements.

The Patient Authorization Listing has also been a very handy report for the therapist to refer to. We give them an updated report each week and include the number of sessions remaining when the count gets down to 2 or less sessions. The secretaries also receive this report each week and it lets them know *if the patient has authorized sessions before scheduling an appointment.* Scheduling patients beyond this date can result in non-payment.

Another form we created is called the *Session Tracking Sheet.* This shows, at a glance, all session dates, charges, and co-payments for the year. This helps us make sure that a patient does not come for more than the maximum allowable visits per year. You'll find an example of this invaluable form on page 64 of this text.

For example, one Managed Care organization allows a maximum of 30 visits per year and also requires the patient to pay a higher co-payment for every 10 sessions. So we designed this form in 3 columns with 10 boxes in each column to enter session dates. This device has been very useful not only in tracking annual visits, but also in billing the patient the correct amount of co-payments. We keep these forms in the patient files and update them at each billing cycle. We also offer these forms to the patients to assist them in keeping track of their own session authorizations and co-payments due. Some of our therapists also use them to track the same data.

QUESTION: What happens when a patient wants to come in before an actual authorization letter is received from the case manager?

ANSWER: The therapist wants to minimize any interruptions in the patient's treatment. Often they may call the case manager and receive a verbal authorization by phone. We've created a form to report the new authorization data that's been received over the telephone. We will put this form in an pending file to make sure we receive the confirming authorization letter.

Whenever we enter a charge and do not find an authorization, we will ask the therapist if they have received a verbal authorization. It is possible something has slipped through the cracks.

QUESTION: What other new procedures had to be designed or implemented because of Managed Care?

ANSWER: Because of changing co-payment levels, we created a form letter to the patients to let him or her know when their co-payments increased. We also give a copy of this letter to the therapist so they know when to collect a higher co-payment for future visits. This letter helps avoid any unpleasantness for the patient being confronted by higher co-payments at the time of their sessions.

We also had to create a procedure for rebilling insurance companies when we were underpaid on authorized sessions. Many times this occurs because of a timing lag between our insurance billing and the authorization not arriving prior to that billing. At other times we fail to receive payment because the therapist has failed to get certification prior to providing care.

When this occurs, we ask the therapist to attempt to get a retroactive certification from the case manager. We then make a copy of the Explanation of Benefits letter and type a note on it to "please reconsider our claim for additional payment" and attach a copy of the patient's authorization letter now received. A copy of this billing letter is kept in a pending file to make sure we receive our payment. If the payment is not received in about a month, we will make a copy of the letter and send it out again as a second request. In most cases, the insurance company will pay when we persist in this manner.

On some occasions, we learn that the insurance company has correctly paid us less than we billed because the patient had received treatment elsewhere, reducing their total benefit. This in turn affected the authorization count. In such a case we then bill the patient for the amount due. It is important to include a statement on your new patient information sheet, signed by the patient, that he or she agrees to be responsible for all fees not covered by their insurance company. This will facilitate collections, should this be necessary.

QUESTION: Do you have any other practical advice for handling the accounting complexities of Managed Care?

ANSWER: With all the increased paperwork, we found that having different colored forms and folders greatly helps in getting the information to the right place and to the right person.

We also put post-it notes on Ongoing Treatment Reports to remind the therapists: (1) how many sessions have been authorized, type of session (e.g., "indiv", "Conj/fam", "group"), expiration date, and the date the form is due in the case manager's office. We also assist the therapist by entering the diagnosis (obtained from the initial report), and patient identifying data. This allows the therapists to devote more time to writing treatment plans and updating progress.

It does take more time to work with Managed Care. And as the demands of Managed Care organizations change, you are required to be more creative and innovative, devising procedures to efficiently deal with these needs. Our future goal is to develop methods for having reports computerized and consolidated in our billing program.

(If you have developed accounting, tracking, or computer systems that you believe would be instructive and useful, send them to the publisher. If selected, they will be included in the next edition of this text with thanks and acknowledgements to you as contributor).

APPENDIX C

The Language of Managed Care:
Key Definitions

Personal Notes

The Language of Managed Care:
Key Definitions

PPO, EPO, HMO, PRSO, EAP, MAP, IPA, TPA — these are just a few of the terms you will not find in Webster's Dictionary. And for that matter, you will not find them in most of the professional literature even five to ten years ago. But you can be sure that you will encounter them with increasing frequency in the future.

Here are the most common terms and abbreviations with simple definitions to help you get comfortable getting a handle on them.

ADMISSION REVIEW — The evaluation of a patient's case by an external reviewer to determine medical necessity and appropriateness of admission to treatment, at the time of, or immediately following initiation of treatment.

ANCHOR GROUP — A multidisciplinary group practice, typically made up of psychiatrists, psychologists, MFCCs, clinical social workers, and testing specialists that receives preferred referral consideration because of their broad services "menu" and one-stop convenience.

ASAP/PDQ — "Affordable Services Applied Prudently by Professionals Dedicated to Quality."

BENEFITS ADMINISTRATORS (or UR) — see UTILIZATION REVIEW.

BRIEF THERAPY — Therapeutic intervention by a mental health practitioner to resolve a patient's complaint or problem to restore maximum functioning within a time-limited and goal-focused context. Emphasis is placed on solutions and symptom reduction.

CAPITATION (or CAPITATED) — A pre-set, fixed fee for which subscribers receive as much health care as needed from contracted healthcare sources. This is an alternative for a fee-for-service arrangement. This method is used by most HMO organizations.

CASE MANAGEMENT — The process by which a case manager identifies and then recommends appropriate and cost-effective healthcare for a given patient or family during the period of treatment.

333

CASE REVIEW — The process by which an external case reviewer assesses the medical necessity for treatment and cost-effective ways to render that treatment for the best interest of the patient and the employer.

CD — Chemical dependency, substance abuse.

CENTERS OF EXCELLENCE — A group practice or clinic that provides quality brief therapy, focuses on time-limited symptom reduction or symptom management, and is considered to be a "team player" and has the reputation of being Managed Care friendly. An anchor group is one example of a center of excellence.

CERTIFICATION (or CERT, or CERTED) — The authorization for treatment, number of sessions, or length of time in which treatment services are provided to a patient.

CLOSED PANEL — A healthcare program that requires participants to use only those approved providers or facilities who contract with the health plan; e.g., HMOs and PPOs. Closed Panels have also come to be thought of as Managed Care provider lists closed to a given therapist or group practice (perhaps better called a "full panel").

CONCURRENT REVIEW — The examination of cases to determine medical necessity and appropriateness of treatment during the time services are being provided.

DEPENDENT — A member (usually someone within the family) who is enrolled and eligible for benefits under the EPO, PPO, EAP, or HMO through the subscriber's plan.

DISINCENTIVIZATION (OF PROVIDERS) (or DISINCENTIVIZE) — The Managed Care firm withholds or refuses to refer patients to a provider, or to certify sessions, or to pay the entire fee to providers who practice unnecessary, long-term, higher levels of costly treatment.

DRGs / DIAGNOSIS-RELATED GROUPS — A system established to categorize Medicare patients into at least 475 conditions based on the diagnosis, procedure, and related impairments, for purposes of determining appropriateness of medical treatment and payment for that specific condition. Mental health disorders have been exempted from the DRG system, but the DSM-IV (to be released in 1994) may provide more precise links between diagnosis and treatment.

DSM-III-R (or DSM-IV) — *The Diagnostic and Statistical Manual, III, Revised,* American Psychiatric Association, is the primary source of determining diagnoses to justify medical necessity for treatment by Managed Care case managers. The DSM-IV is scheduled to be released in 1994.

EAP / EMPLOYEE ASSISTANCE PROGRAM — An in-house or external program of assessment, referral and brief counseling for employees of select companies, with emphasis on quality, cost-effective care.

EPO / EXCLUSIVE PROVIDER ORGANIZATION — A rigid type of PPO closely related to an HMO wherein the subscriber employee is required to use only designated providers or sacrifice reimbursement altogether.

HMO / HEALTH MAINTENANCE ORGANIZATION — An organization licensed by the state to administer a closed panel, flat fee, health plan of either full service, medical and mental health, or mental health and EAP services. There are 4 kinds of HMOs: (1) Staff Model: Services are provided at the HMO facility, by HMO clinicians; (2) Group Model: Services are contracted for with outside group practices on a flat or capitated fee basis, services provided at the group's private offices; (3) Network/Direct Contract Model: Services are provided to subscribers by individual or small group practitioners on a maximum fee or capitated basis, rendered in the provider's offices (sometimes referred to as an "open panel," even though it is not "open" to all practitioners who apply); (4) IPA / Independent Practice Association: Services provided by a large number of professional associations or individual providers, in their offices, at fixed capitated fees or fee-for-service which are sometimes paid only if target goals are met; also considered an "open panel," but must be strategically approached to break into that panel, often in association with colleagues for best results.

ICD-10 / *INTERNATIONAL CLASSIFICATION OF DISEASES, 10TH REVISION* — The medical counterpart of the DSM-III-R or DSM-IV, used to classify physiological disorders and conditions.

IMPAIRMENTS — see SYMPTOM DESCRIPTION.

INCENTIVIZATION (OF PROVIDERS) — The Managed Care firm offers patient referrals, certification of services, and payment of fees to an approved provider who successfully provides focused, time-limited, solution-oriented, cost-effective treatment for patients covered by the Managed Care plan. (see DISINCENTIVIZATION).

INDEMNITY COVERAGE — An insurance plan that pays a given percentage of healthcare to a licensed provider, with no controls on length or type of treatment; but an annual maximum may be set.

IPA / INDEPENDENT PRACTITIONERS ASSOCIATION — A large group of providers collectively associated to offer mental health services or other medical services to an HMO, providing services in each provider's own offices, on a fee-for-service or capitated fixed basis. The IPA is called an "open panel" but it is only "open" to those who know how to strategically win the trust of the gatekeepers.

LOCK-IN — Member subscribers are required to use only those providers on the approved PPO providers list for all treatment covered by their insurance.

MANAGED CARE (or MANAGED HEALTHCARE) — The authorized imposition of explicit and implicit controls and restraints upon the condition, amount, source, site, fee, modality or manner of services rendered. Managed Care firms are hired by insurance or employer organizations to cut healthcare costs and limit utilization, while providing quality care to subscriber-patients. Services are provided by practitioners selected by the Managed Care firm who are believed to be focused, brief, outcome oriented members of the Managed Care treatment "team."

MCO / MANAGED CARE ORGANIZATION — An organization that is hired by industry or an insurance company to administer Managed Care programs, for the purpose of limiting utilization and costs.

MAP / MEMBER ASSISTANCE PROGRAM — Much like an EAP, MAPs provide benefits, services, and referrals to subscribers or employees who are covered by a Managed Care plan.

NO LOCK-IN — A member or subscriber to a PPO can use any provider they choose, either preferred or one not on the list, providing they agree to follow the plan's policies; typically meaning that there is a co-payment required of the subscriber if a non-preferred provider is used. Subscriber premiums for such a plan are almost always higher under this approach.

OTR / ONGOING TREATMENT REPORT — A brief but thorough documentation of diagnosis on all 5 DSM-III-R axes, problem or symptom description in observable terms, outline of specific progress during treatment, and anticipated date of discharge with measurable criteria for determining discharge success. The OTR is mailed to the case manager at specified intervals by the provider.

OPEN PANEL — A healthcare program that permits participants to use the provider of their choice. In recent years this has also come to mean a Managed Care organization with easy access for any clinician who wishes to become a preferred provider. This is most commonly found in new Managed Care companies trying to get a foothold in the healthcare market.

PEER REVIEW — The examination of patient case data to determine medical necessity and appropriateness of treatment, usually for purposes of assuring cost-effective, quality treatment, and performed typically by an external clinician of the same specialty as the provider.

PEER REVIEW IMPROVEMENT ACT — Legislation passed in 1982 which required Medicare providers to turn over case records to private external reviewers to determine whether payment would be denied, reduced, or allowed. This opened the door to the many external peer reviewers, case management companies, and Managed Care organizations we see today.

PRO / PEER REVIEW ORGANIZATION — see PRSO.

PRSO / PEER REVIEW SERVICE ORGANIZATION — An organization hired by an insurance company or self-insured company or union trust to evaluate medical necessity and/or the appropriateness of cost-effective treatment, with special emphasis on quality care. This system of external review is commonly called PRO review.

PPO / PREFERRED PROVIDER ORGANIZATION — A healthcare provider arrangement whereby a third-party payor contracts with a group of independent healthcare providers who agree to furnish appropriate services at negotiated, reduced fees in return for prompt payment on claims, and a regular patient volume. PPOs keep healthcare costs down by stringent controls on fees and utilization. PPOs are usually intermediaries between the patient and an insurance company, companies that self-fund insurance coverage, or for union trusts handling insurance benefits.

PRE-CERT, PRE-CERTIFICATION, PRE-AUTHORIZATION — A requirement imposed by the payor of benefits, or the review organization for the examination of patient cases to determine the medical necessity and appropriateness for admission or treatment within a specified time frame prior to the actual admission or continuation of treatment. Pre-cert, pre-authorization may be waived in the event of emergency need for care. A provider may fail to be paid for services if pre-certification is not obtained, both verbally and in writing.

QUALITY ASSESSMENT - Activities intended to determine whether standards of healthcare are being adhered to in order to render maximum benefit to the patient.

QUALITY ASSURANCE — Activities intended to determine adherence to standards of professional conduct and care and to eliminate any deficiencies identified.

QUALITY CARE — Providing the patient-subscriber with the greatest achieveable health benefit with minimal unnecessary risk and use of resources, and in a manner that resolves patient problems and complaints.

RETROSPECTIVE DENIAL — The denial of payment to a facility or a clinician based on breach of contract or lack of satisfactory documentation of medical necessity, or because of proven unethical conduct.

RETROSPECTIVE REVIEW — The examination of patient cases for medical necessity and appropriateness of treatment after the termination of care, or in the midst of ongoing treatment.

RISK MANAGEMENT - The process whereby risk to the organization and all who are served by it and associated with it is evaluated and controlled in order to prevent or reduce further loss or threatened loss.

SHORT-TERM THERAPY — See BRIEF THERAPY.

SUBSCRIBER — An employee who has enrolled in a Managed Care plan, who, in doing so, agrees to abide by the conditions of that plan, usually resulting in a saving in premiums to the subscriber.

SYMPTOM DESCRIPTION — Observable, demonstrable complaints or problems of the patient in terms that clearly point to measurable treatment interventions. They should be in behavioral descriptions or verbal reports about behaviors, in terms of excesses or deficits.

TPA / THIRD-PARTY ADMINISTRATOR — An external organization hired to oversee and control healthcare benefits, with an emphasis on cost-effectiveness.

TREATMENT PLAN — A brief but detailed description of patient problems or complaints with specific treatment interventions, symptom by symptom, predicting the desired outcome in as few sessions as possible. The Treatment Plan is mailed to the case manager after assessment has been done by the provider, or if an extension is requested. The Treatment Plan should be focused, time-limited, and framed in measurable outcome terms.

TREATMENT TARGETED IMPAIRMENTS — The precise, observable behaviors or verbal reports that constitute the patient's complaints or problems, that are susceptible to brief therapeutic intervention to assure maximum patient satisfaction and adjustment in a cost-effective manner. TTIs make verbal and written documentation between provider and case manager succinct and goal directed. They help both parties determine the appropriateness of care and modalities needed. The concept encourages the clinician to link specific therapy method of choice to a given patient problem much more than "symptoms" or "symptom description" nomenclature tends to do.

UR / UTILIZATION REVIEW (or BENEFITS ADMINISTRATORS) — The fourth party in the services loop. The UR firm is hired by the insurance company, the self-insured organization, or the Managed Care firm. UR companies implement the pre-authorization or retrospective review process. Only the provider can negotiate with the UR firm on the patient's behalf; the patient cannot do so.

APPENDIX D

References For Further Research In
Managed Care, Brief Therapy,
Outcome Assessment &
Practice Development

Personal Notes

References

Aiello, T.J. (1979). Short-term group therapy of the hospitalized psychotic. In H. Grayson (Ed.), *Short-term approaches to psychotherapy,* (pp. 101-123). New York: Human Sciences Press.

Aldrich, C.K. (1968). Brief psychotherapy: A reappraisal of some theoretical assumptions. *American Journal of Psychiatry,* 125, 585-592.

Altman, L., & Goldstein, J.M. (1988). Impact of HMO model type on mental health service delivery: Variation in treatment and approaches. *Administration in Mental Health,* 15, 246-261.

American Psychiatric Association. (1994). *Diagnostic & statistical manual of mental disorders: DSM-IV.* Washington, DC: American Psychiatric Association.

American Psychiatric Association. (1987). *Diagnostic & statistical manual of mental disorders: DSM-III-R (3rd ed. revised).* Washington, DC: American Psychiatric Association.

Applebaum, S.A. (1975). Parkinson's law in psychotherapy. *International Journal of Psychoanalytic Psychotherapy,* 4, 426-436.

Avnet, H.H. (1965a). Short-term treatment under auspices of a medical insurance plan. *American Journal of Psychiatry,* 122, 147-151.

Avnet, H.H. (1965b). How effective is short-term therapy? In L.R. Wolberg (Ed.), *Short-term psychotherapy* (pp 7-22). New York: Grune & Stratton.

Barten, H.H. (1971). The expanding spectrum of the brief therapies. In H.H. Barten (Ed.), *Brief therapies* (pp. 3-23). New York: Behavioral Publications.

Bassett, D.L., & Pilowsky, I. (1985). A study of brief psychotherapy for chronic pain. *Journal of Psychosomatic Research,* 29, 259-264.

Beck, A.T. (1976). *Cognitive therapy and the emotional disorders.* New York: International Universities Press.

Beck, A.T., Rush, A.J., et al. (1979). *Cognitive therapy of depression.* New York: Guilford Press.

Beck, A.T., & Emery, G., et al. (1985). *Anxiety disorders and phobias.* New York: Basic Books.

Bellak, L. (1984). Intensive brief and emergency psychotherapy. In L. Grinspoon (Ed.), *Psychiatry update: The American Psychiatric Association Annual Review* Vol. III, (pp. 11-24). Washington, DC: American Psychiatric Press.

Bellak, L. & Siegel, H. (1983). *Handbook of intensive brief and emergency psychotherapy (B.E. P.).* Larchmont, N.Y.: C.P.S., Inc.

Bergman, J.S. (1985). *Fishing for barracuda: Pragmatics of brief systematic therapy.* New York: Norton.

Bloch, S., Bond, G., et al. (1977). Outcome in psychotherapy evaluated by independent judges. *British Journal of Psychiatry,* 131, 410-414.

Bloom, B.L. (1981). Focused single-session therapy: Initial development and evaluation. In S. Budman, (Ed.), *Forms of brief therapy* (pp. 167-216). New York: Guilford Press.

Bloom, B.L. (1990). Managing mental health services: Some comments for the overdue debate in psychology. *Community Mental Health Journal,* 26, 107-124.

Boettcher, L.L., & Dowd, E.T. (1988). Comparison of rationales in symptom prescription. *Journal of Cognitive Psychotherapy,* 2, 179-195.

Boland, P. (1991). *Making Managed Care Work:: A Practical Guide To Strategies & Solutions.* New York: McGraw-Hill.

Bonstedt, T., & Baird, S.H. (1979). Providing cost-effective psychotherapy in a health maintenance organization. *Hospital & Community Psychiatry*, 30, 129-132.

Brabender, V.M. (1985). Time-limited in-patient group therapy: A developmental model. *International Journal of Group Psychotherapy*, 35, 373-390.

Brabender, V.M. (1988) A closed model of short-term inpatient group psychotherapy. *Hospital & Community Psychiatry*, 39, 542-545.

Brodaty, H., & Andrews, G. (1983). Brief psychotherapy in family practice: A controlled prospective intervention trial. *British Journal of Psychiatry*, 143, 11-19.

Browning, C.H., & Browning, B.J. (1993). *Private Practice Handbook: The Tools, Tactics & Techniques for Successful Practice Development*, (4th Ed.). Los Alamitos, CA: Duncliff's International.

Budman, S.H. (1981). Looking toward the future. In S.H. Budman, (Ed.), *Forms of brief therapy* (pp. 461-467). New York: Guilford Press.

Budman, S.H., & Clifford, M. (1979). Short-term group therapy for couples in a health maintenance organization. *Professional Psychology: Research & Practice*, 10, 419-429.

Budman, S., Demby, A., et al. (1980). Short-term group psychotherapy: Who succeeds, who fails? *Group*, 4, 3-16.

Budman, S.H., Demby, A., et al. (1988). Comparative outcome in time-limited individual and group psychotherapy. *International Journal of Group Psychotherapy*, 38, 63-86.

Budman, S.H., & Gurman, A. (1983). The practice of brief therapy. *Professional Psychology: Research & Practice*, 14, 277-292.

Budman, S.H., & Gurman, A.S. (1988). *Theory and practice of brief therapy*. New York: Guilford Press.

Budman, S.H., & Springer, T. (1987). Treatment delay, outcome, and satisfaction in time-limited group and individual psychotherapy. *Professional Psychology: Research & Practice*, 18, 647-649.

Budman, S.H., & Stone, J. (1983). Advances in brief psychotherapy: A review of recent literature. *Hospital & Community Psychiatry*, 34, 939-946.

Burke, J.D., White, H.S., et al. (1979). Which short-term therapy? *Archives of General Psychiatry*, 36, 177-186.

Burlingame, G.M., & Behrman, J.A. (1987). Clinician attitudes toward time-limited and time-unlimited therapy. *Professional Psychology: Research & Practice*, 18, 61-65.

Burlingame, G.M., & Fuhriman, A. (1987). Conceptualizing short-term treatment: A comparative review. *The Counseling Psychologist*, 15, 557-595.

Canter, A. (1984). Contemporary short-term psychotherapies. In R. Munoz (ed.), *New directions for mental health services*, No. 23 (pp. 13-31). San Francisco: Jossey-Bass.

Chapman, P.L.H., & Huygens, I. (1988). An evaluation of three treatment programmes for alcoholism: An experimental study with 6- and 18-month follow-ups. *British Journal of Addiction*, 83, 67-81.

Chick, J., Ritson, D., et al. (1988). Advice versus extended treatment for alcoholism: A controlled study. *British Journal of Addiction*, 83, 159-170.

Ciarlo, J.A., Brown, T.R., et al. (1986). *Assessing mental health treatment outcome measurement techniques.* DHHS Publishing. No. (ADM) 86-1301. Washington, DC: U.S. Government Printing Office.

Connors, M.E., Johnson, C.L., et al. (1984). Treatment of bulimia with brief psychoeducational group therapy. *American Journal of Psychiatry,* 141, 1512-1516.

Cross, D.G., Sheehan, P.W., et al. (1982). Short- and long-term follow-up of clients receiving insight-oriented therapy and behavior therapy. *Journal of Consulting & Clinical Psychology,* 50, 103-112.

Cummings, N.A. (1977). Prolonged (ideal) versus short-term (realistic) psychotherapy. *Professional Psychology,* 8, 491-501.

Cummings, N.A. (1986). The dismantling of our health system: Strategies for the survival of psychological practice. *American Psychologist,* 41, 426-431.

Cummings, N.A., & Duhl, L.J. (1987). The new delivery system. In L.J. Duhl & N.A. Cummings (Eds.), *The future of mental health services: Coping with crisis* (pp. 85-98). New York: Springer.

Cummings, N.A., & Follette, W.T. (1968). Psychiatric services and medical utilization in a prepaid health plan setting: Part II. *Medical Care,* 6, 31-41.

Cummings, N.A., & Follette, W.T. (1976). Brief psychotherapy and medical utilization. In H. Dorken & Associates, (Eds.), *The professional psychologist today: New developments in law, health insurance, and health practice* (pp. 165-174). San Francisco: Jossey-Bass.

Daley, B.S., & Koppenaal, G.S. (1981). The treatment of women in short-term women's groups. In S.H. Budman (Ed.), *Forms of brief therapy* (pp. 343-357). New York: Guilford Press.

Davanloo, H. (Ed.). (1978). *Basic principles and techniques in short-term dynamic psychotherapy.* New York: Spectrum.

Davanloo, H. (1979). Techniques of short-term dynamic psychotherapy. *Psychiatric Clinics of North America,* 2, 11-22.

Davanloo, H. (Ed.) (1980). *Short-term dynamic psychotherapy.* Northvale, NJ: Aronson.

deShazer, S. (1985). *Keys to solution in brief therapy.* New York: Norton.

deShazer, S. (1979). On transforming symptoms: An approach to an Erickson procedure. *American Journal of Clinical Hypnosis,* 22, 17-28.

deShazer, S. (1982). *Patterns of brief family therapy: An ecosystemic approach.* New York: Guildord Press.

deShazer, S. (1988). *Clues: Investigating solutions in brief therapy.* New York: Norton.

deShazer, S., & Molnar, A. (1984). Four useful interventions in brief family therapy. *Journal of Marital & Family Therapy,* 10, 297-304.

Diehm, Phillip, *Marketing to Managed Care,* Fountain Valley, CA: Diehm.

Diehm, Phillip, *Managed Care Strategies: A Training Group for Professionals.* (Tape series). Fountain Valley, CA: Diehm.

Dorosin, D., Gibbs, J., et al. (1976). Very brief interventions: A pilot evaluation. *Journal of the American College Health Assoc.,* 24, 191-194.

Drob, S., & Bernard, H. (1985). Two models of brief group psychotherapy for herpes sufferers. *Group,* 9 (3), 14-20.

Duhl, L.J., & Cummings, N.A. (Eds.) (1987). *The future of mental health services: Coping with crisis.* New York: Springer.

Dulcan, M.K. (1984). Brief psychotherapy with children and their families: The state of the art. *Journal of the American Academy of Child Psychiatry,* 23, 544-551.

Fine, S., Gilbert, M., et al. (1989). Short-term group therapy with depressed adolescent outpatients. *Canadian Journal of Psychiatry,* 34, 97-102.

Fisch, R. (1982). Erickson's impact on brief psychotherapy. In J.K. Zeig (Ed.). *Ericksonian approaches to hypnosis and psychotherapy* (pp. 155-162). New York: Brunner/Mazel.

Fisher, S.G. (1984). Time-limited brief therapy with families: A one-year follow-up study. *Family Process,* 23, 101-106.

Flegenheimer, W.V. (1982). *Techniques of brief psychotherapy.* New York: Aronson.

Fox, R. (1987). Short-term, goal-oriented family therapy. *Social Casework,* 68, 494-499.

Frank, J.D. (1968). Methods of assessing the results of psychotherapy. In R. Porter (Ed.), *The role of learning in psychotherapy* (pp. 38-60). Boston: Little, Brown.

Franks, C.M. (Ed.) (1969). *Behavior therapy: Appraisal and status.* New York: McGraw-Hill.

Garfield, S.L., & Bergin, A.E. (eds.) (1978). *Handbook of Psychotherapy & Behavior Change: An Empirical Analysis* (2nd ed.) (pp. 725-767). New York: Wiley.

Gelso, C.J., & Johnson, D.H. (1983). *Explorations in time-limited counseling and psychotherapy.* New York: Teachers College Press.

Goldman, W. (1988). Mental health and substance abuse services in HMOs. *Administration in Mental Health,* 15, 189-200.

Good, P.R. (1987). Brief therapy in the age of regapeutics. *American Journal of Orthopsychiatry,* 57, 6-11.

Goodman, M., & Brown, J., et al. (1992). *Managing managed care: A mental health practitioner's survival guide.* Washington, DC: American Psychiatric Press.

Greenwald, H., (Ed.) (1974). *Active Psychotherapy.* New York: Aronson.

Greenwald, H. (1973). *Decision Therapy.* New York: Wyden.

Gustafson, J.P. (1986). *The complex secret of brief psychotherapy.* New York: Norton.

Haley, J. (1976). *Problem-solving therapy.* San Francisco: Jossey-Bass.

Haley, J. (1972). *Strategies of psychotherapy.* New York: Grune & Stratton.

Haley, J. (1967). *Advanced techniques of hypnosis and therapy: Selected papers of Milton H. Erickson.* New York: Grune & Stratton.

Haley, J. (1973). *Uncommon therapy: The psychiatric techniques of Milton H. Erickson, M.D.* New York: Norton.

Haley, J. (1984). *Ordeal therapy.* San Francisco: Jossey-Bass.

Hall, A., & Crisp, A.H. (1987). Brief psychotherapy in the treatment of anorexia nervosa: outcome at one year. *British Journal of Psychiatry,* 151, 185-191.

Horowitz, M., Marmar, C., et al. (1984). *Personality styles and brief psychotherapy.* New York: Basic Books.

Horowitz, M., Marmar, C., et al. (1986). Comprehensive analysis of change after brief dynamic psychotherapy. *American Journal of Psychiatry,* 143, 582-589.

Horowitz, M.J., Marmar, C., et al. (1984). Brief psychotherapy of bereavement reactions: The relationships of process to outcome. *Archives of General Psychiatry*, 41, 438-448.

Hoyt, M.F. (1985). Therapist resistances to short-term dynamic psychotherapy. *Journal of the American Academy of Psychoanalysis*, 13, 93-112.

Jones, K.R., & Vischi, T.R. (1979). Impact of alcohol, drug abuse and mental health treatment on medical care utilization: A review of the research literature. *Medical Care*, 17, (Supp.), 1-82.

Kinston, W., & Bentovim, A. (1981). Creating a focus for brief marital or family therapy. In S. Budman (Ed.), *Forms of brief therapy* (pp. 361-386). New York: Guilford Press.

Klein, R.H. (1985). Some principles of short-term group therapy. *International Journal of Group Psychotherapy*, 35, 309-330.

Koss, M.P., Butcher, J.N., et al. (1986). Brief psychotherapy methods in clin clinical research. *Journal of Clinical & Consulting Psychology*, 54, 60-67.

Kreilkamp, T. (1989). *Time-limited, intermittent therapy with children and families*. New York: Brunner/Mazal.

Krupnick, J.L., & Horowitz, M.J. (1985). Brief psychotherapy with vulnerable patients: An outcome assessment. *Psychiatry*, 48, 223-233.

La Court, M. (1988). The HMO crisis: Danger/opportunity. *Family Systems Medicine*. 6, 80-93.

Lazarus, A. (1972). *Clinical behavior therapy*. New York: Brunner/Mazel.

Leibenluft, E., & Goldberg, R.L. (1987). Guidelines for short-term inpatient psychotherapy. *Hospital & Community Psychiatry*, 38, 38-43.

Lewin, K.K. (1970). *Brief psychotherapy: Brief encounters*. St. Louis, MO: Green.

Lipchik, E., & deShazer, S. (1988). Purposeful sequences for beginning the solution-focused interview. In E. Lipchik, *Interviewing*. (pp. 105-117). Rockville, MD: Aspen.

MacKenzie, K.R. (1988). Recent developments in brief psychotherapy. *Hospital & Community Psychiatry*, 39, 742-752.

MacKenzie, K.R., & Livesley, W.J. (1986). Outcome and process measures in brief group psychotherapy. *Psychiatric Annals*, 16, 715-720.

Malan, D.H. (1976). *The frontier of brief psychotherapy: An example of the convergence of research and clinical practice*. New York: Plenum.

Manaster, G.J. (1989). Clinical issues in brief psychotherapy: A summary and conclusion. *Individual Psychology*, 45, 243-247.

Mann, J., & Goldman, R. (1982). *A casebook in time-limited psychotherapy*. New York: McGraw-Hill.

Marmar, C.R., & Freeman, M. (1988). Brief dynamic psychotherapy of post-traumatic stress disorders: Management of narcissistic regression. *Journal of Traumatic Stress*, 1, 323-337.

Mathews, B. (1988). Planned short-term therapy utilizing the techniques of Jay Haley and Milton Erickson: A guide for the practitioner. *Psychotherapy in Private Practice*, 6, 103-118.

McDowell, J. (1989). *Evidence that demands a verdict*. San Bernardino: Here's Life. *(Note: A reference essential for lasting & ultimate success)*

Mumford, E., Schlesinger, H.J., et al. (1984). A new look at evidence about reduced cost of medical utilization following mental health treatment. *American Journal of Psychiatry*, 141, 1145-1158.

O'Hanlon, B., & Wilk, J. (1987). *Shifting contexts: The generation of effective psychotherapy.* New York: Guilford.

O'Hanlon, W.H., & Weiner-Davis, M. (1989). *In search of solutions: A new direction in psychotherapy.* New York: Norton.

Parloff, M.B. (1982). Psychotherapy research evidence and reimbursement decisions: Bambi meets Godzilla. *American Journal of Psychiatry,* 139, 718-727.

Peake, T.H., & Ball, J.D. (1987). Brief psychotherapy: Planned therapeutic change for changing times. *Psychotherapy in Private Practice,* 5(4), 53-63.

Peake, T.H., Borduin, C.M., et al. (1988). *Brief psychotherapies: Changing frames of mind.* Beverly Hills, CA: Sage.

Phillips, E.L. (1985). *A guide for therapists and patients to short-term psychotherapy.* Springfield, IL: Thomas.

Phillips, E.L., Gershenson, J., et al. (1977). On time-limited writing therapy. *Psychological Reports,* 41, 707-712.

Reich, J., & Neenan, P. (1986). Principles common to different short-term psychotherapies. *American Journal of Psychiatry,* 40, 62-69.

Reid, W.H. (1989). *DSM-III-R training guide: For use with the American Psychiatric Association's Diagnostic & Statistical Manual of Mental Disorders.* New York: Brunner-Mazel.

Rush, A.J. (Ed.) (1982). *Short-term psychotherapies for depression.* New York: Guilford.

Ryder, D. (1988). Minimal intervention: A little quality for a lot of quantity? *Behaviour Change,* 5, 100-107.

Shulman, M.E. (1988). Cost-containment in clinical psychology: Critique of Biodyne and the HMOs. *Professional Psychology: Research & Practice,* 19, 298-307.

Small, L. (1971). *The briefer psychotherapies.* New York: Brunner/Mazel.

Spitzer, R.L., et al. (1989). *DSM-III-R: Diagnostic & Statistical Manual of Mental Disorders.* Washington, DC: American Psychiatric Press.

Strupp, H.H., & Binder, J.L. (1984). *Psychotherapy in a new key: A guide to time-limited dynamic psychotherapy.* New York: Basic Books.

VandenBos, G.R., & Pino, C.D. (1980). Research on the outcome of psychotherapy. In G.R. VandenBoss (Ed.), *Psychotherapy: Practice, research, policy* (pp. 23-69). Beverly Hills, CA: Sage.

Watzlawick, P., Weakland, J., et al. (1974). *Change: Principles of problem formation and problem resolution.* New York: Norton.

Weakland, J., Fisch, R., et al. (1974). Brief therapy: Focused problem resolution. *Family Process,* 13(2), 141-168.

Weiner-Davis, M., deShazer, S., et al. (1987). Building on pre-treatment change to construct the therapeutic solution: An exploratory study. *Journal of Marital & Family Therapy,* 13(4), 359-363.

Wolberg, L.W. (Ed.) (1965). *Short-term psychotherapy.* New York: Grune & Stratton.

Wolpe, J. (1973). *The practice of behavior therapy.* New York: Pergamon.

Yoken, C., & Berman, J.S. (1987). Third-party payment and the outcome of psychotherapy. *Journal of Consulting & Clinical Psychology,* 55, 571-576.

Zeig, J.K. (Ed.) (1982). *Ericksonian approaches to hypnosis and psychotherapy.* New York: Brunner/Mazel.

APPENDIX E

Practice Development Resources

Practice   Development   Consultation   Worksheet

To arrange a personal, private practice development consultation with the Brownings, simply complete the following preliminary worksheet and fax or mail it to the address on the reverse side. You will be contacted to set up a convenient time for either a face-to-face or telephone meeting.

(please print plainly)

Name _____ Degree _____ Date _____

Address_____ City _____State _____

Zip _____ Daytime Phone (___)_____ Beeper _____

Fax (___)_____ Practice Name _____

How long in private practice? _____ Full-time ☐ Part-time ☐

How many therapists in practice _____ # clients seen/week _____

Describe clinical orientation _____

Describe office location(s) _____

_____

Average # of sessions per patient from intake to discharge _____

Are you skilled in: Brief therapy techniques ☐ Cognitive therapy ☐
   Behavior therapy ☐   Directive therapy ☐   Use of homework ☐

Do you typically use outside resources, support groups, homework,
   workbooks, workshops & other resources in your work _____

How do you advertise your services? _____

_____

What is your primary source of new referrals? _____

_____

What % of your practice is made up of Managed Care clients? _____%

Frankly describe your feelings and attitude toward Managed Care:

Describe your positive and negative experiences working with
Managed Care provider relations and case managers:

Positive Experiences	Negative Experiences

Continued on other side →

Describe the goals/objectives for your practice _____

_____

_____

What are the specific issues and/or questions you would like addressed during your consultation (rank-order according to importance to you):

What materials would you like reviewed for recommendations?

Are you requesting a personal, face-to-face consultation? ◻

Or would you prefer a telephone consultation? ◻

How to prepare for the consultation:
1. Carefully complete both sides of this worksheet. Then mail to the address below, or fax to the fax line.
2. If you would like comments and recommendations on brochures, advertisements, letters, profiles, flyers, or other materials, mail or fax them, along with this worksheet, prior to the time of your consultation (time spent reviewing materials is billable time).
3. It is recommended that your consultation be audio-tape recorded so you can review it for later implementation.
4. All consults are scheduled on a half-hour or one-hour basis.

For **information on scheduling, call:**   (310) 596-5465

To **fax worksheet and other materials:**   (310) 799-6657

Mail worksheet and other materials to: **Duncliff's International**

| (For more writing space, simply enlarge this form) | **3662 Katella Ave., Dept. 226/C**
Los Alamitos, CA 90720 |

Attracting Fee-For-Service and Other
Non-Managed-Care Clients To
Your Practice or Facility

In a well-managed practice, Managed Care referrals should represent from 40% to 60% of the total practice business and income. Because of the changing status of some Managed Care organizations, it is wise for the mental health practitioner to focus on marketing activities that will generate fee-for-service, sliding-scale, and other non-Managed-Care clients. This assures the stability and security of the practice or facility.

To assist the clinician in establishing a balanced client base, the Brownings have developed a marketing program for enhancing the visibility and reputation of the private mental health practice to private-pay clients. This strategic marketing plan is presented in *Private Practice Handbook: The Tools, Tactics & Techniques for Successful Practice Development,* now in its revised and expanded 4th edition.

Some of the topics covered in this valuable text include: Getting more referrals from Yellow Pages listings. How to create a compelling brochure for your practice. Establishing regular word-of-mouth referrals. Getting referrals from physicians, community organizations and other professionals. Methods for increasing practice income. Also included are case studies showing how many of the most successful therapists established their practices using strategic marketing tactics.

To order *Private Practice Handbook (softbound, 4th Edition),* write on your letterhead, or attach your business card, and request your copy, indicating the address to which you would like the book shipped. Enclose a check for $29.95, plus $4 postage and handling (California residents add $2.32 sales tax).

For faster ordering, you can call in your order, charging it to your VISA or MasterCard. Have your card handy and call the number below, giving name, address, card number, and expiration date. Your copy will be shipped within 48 hours.

All Duncliff's publications are offered with an unconditional, unlimited satisfaction guarantee.

Duncliff's International
3662 Katella Avenue, Dept. 226/P
Los Alamitos, CA 90720
Fax   (310) 799-6657
Phone   (800) 410-7766

351

What Sponsors & Participants
are Saying about the New "Therapist Survival Workshop"
How To Partner With Managed Care

Iowa Chapter of the National Assn. of Social Workers:

"I want to say once again how much I appreciated having you as speaker for our managed care conference. The event was a huge success. Conference participants were unanimous in their praise of your delivery style and the content of your message. They also appreciated your handouts, which will be adaptable to their agencies' use. The comments on evaluation forms ranged from: 'excellent' to 'The best conference I have ever attended!' One social worker told me that he had attended three or four managed care workshops this year, but this was 'far and away the best.' I enthusiastically recommend your presentation to any conference planner who is charged with providing a concrete educational experience for mental health professionals. They couldn't go wrong in inviting you!"

— Leila R. Carlson, A.C.S.W., L.S.W.
Executive Director

California Family Study Center:

"Dr. Beverley Browning recently presented a one-day workshop at the California Family Study Center on <u>How To Partner With Managed Care</u>. This was presented to a sophisticated, post-graduate audience and received wonderful evaluations and rave reviews. Our scale runs from 1 to 5 for satisfaction, with 5 high. Her reviews were generally in the 4.5 to 5 range, with unanimous agreement that it was an excellent program . . . Dr. Browning's style of presenting was engaging, warm and totally comprehensible. The audience felt her as approachable and 'on their side.' The day was valuable for all who attended, and I have no hesitation in giving the highest recommendation for this workshop."

— Jennifer Andrews, Ph.D.
Director, PACE Program

How Participants Described The Experience:

"Highly useful, well paced, {a} clear-headed and pragmatic approach."
"Useful, excellent. Very well organized, good samples and illustrations."
"{Dr. Browning} knew the information well, {was} . . . passionate about the subject."
"Excellent clarity, very well done, presented in a very interesting fashion."
"Excellent dissemination of information, materials and resources."
"A very beautiful presentation. Humorous and understandable."
"{Dr. Browning was} very well prepared, engaging, warm, intelligent and current."

Some of the Practical Workshop Content They Were Referring to:

- How to present a desirable application package to a managed care group.
- How to break into closed panels.
- How to get more referrals once on the panel.
- How to develop positive working relationships with case managers to become a busy preferred provider.
- How to avoid making costly mistakes and to recognize the "red flags" to maintain a team-player reputation.
- How to write effective treatment reports that get approval.
- How to easily handle telephone contacts with case managers.
- The use of effective Brief Therapy in a managed care context.
- Legal and ethical issues and guidelines in dealing with managed care.

To arrange an intensive workshop for your group or staff, call for information and date availability:

1-800-410-7766

Index

Index

Personal Notes